THE
New Yugoslav Woman

THE
New Yugoslav Woman

REPRODUCTIVE REGULATION IN SOCIALIST YUGOSLAVIA

Branka Bogdan

INDIANA UNIVERSITY PRESS

This book is a publication of

Indiana University Press
Office of Scholarly Publishing
Herman B Wells Library 350
1320 East 10th Street
Bloomington, Indiana 47405 USA

iupress.org

© 2025 by Branka Bogdan

All rights reserved
No part of this book may be reproduced or utilized in any form or by any means, electronic or mechanical, including photocopying and recording, or by any information storage and retrieval system, without permission in writing from the publisher.

First Printing 2025

Cataloging information is available from the Library of Congress.

ISBN 978-0-253-07417-1 (hardback)
ISBN 978-0-253-07418-8 (paperback)
ISBN 978-0-253-07420-1 (ebook)
ISBN 978-0-253-07419-5 (web PDF)

This book is dedicated to my wonderful children,
Eva and Tommy,
from your loving Mama.

*In one way or another, you have been part of the
writing of this book from its inception.
Every day, you continue to show me
what's really important in life.*

CONTENTS

Acknowledgments ix
Abbreviations and Acronyms xi

Introduction 1

1. Establishing a Legal Landscape of Reproductive Regulation, 1945–1953 29

2. An Infrastructure to Medicalize Reproduction, 1945–1965 67

3. Yugoslavia and Fertility Control Technology, 1960–1974 107

4. Yugoslav Sex Education and Family Planning, 1960s and 1970s 135

5. Deconstructing Yugoslav Women's Recollections of Reproductive Regulation 165

Conclusion: Regulating Reproduction in Yugoslavia during Socialism and Beyond 191

Glossary 197
Bibliography 201
Index 229

ACKNOWLEDGMENTS

I am deeply grateful to the many generous people who have supported me since the project's first inception in 2014, through the completion of my PhD in 2019, and finally to its publication. Firstly, I would like to acknowledge Paula Michaels and thank her for her support while I completed my doctoral research. She committed to this project from the very beginning, and I always felt like I was in safe hands. She, along with Michael Hau, guided me through the intellectual and creative aspects of this adventure and backed me as I dealt with life's ups and downs. Paula also mentored me as I sought the ideal publisher and provided sage advice along the way. I also want to thank the three anonymous reviewers from Indiana University Press who helped me cement the purpose and direction of the finished book.

In the past decade, I confided in many peers and colleagues who read and commented on my work. Thank you, Ivan Simić, Genevieve de Pont, Charlotte Greenhalgh, Kershia Singh, Cheryl Ware, Jess Parr, and Emma Sadera, for your wise words and thoughtful feedback throughout the entire breadth of this experience. I especially want to thank Ivan for helping me expand my academic network, sharing sources, and for his intellectual generosity. I greatly benefited from the endless support and mentorship provided by Charlotte and Tatjana Buklijas as I progressed through the book proposal stage and finalized the manuscript, and I thank them both for their mindful guidance. I have also been fortunate enough to be part of several research groups, one of which is the Wāhine Research Collective at the University of Auckland. The group, populated by wonderful women historians, bolstered and nurtured me throughout the various stages of this project. Barry Reay's supervision of my master's thesis, particularly in exposing me to oral history and histories of sexuality, helped establish the foundation from which this project grew.

Several people were instrumental in making it possible to study the history of a country in which I did not reside. I received help from archivists and librarians from US, Serbian, Croatian, and Slovenian repositories, who corresponded with me regularly, sent me catalogs and collection inventories, and digitized copies of archival sources.

Thankfully, I've been rich in support from my family and close friends. Thank you to Chris, who always believed in me, and who gave me the courage to throw everything I had at researching, writing, presenting, and finishing the work and who held my hand as I navigated the postdoctoral abyss.

My parents, Branka and Tomislav, were excited about this project from the beginning. They chauffeured me around Slovenia, Serbia, and Croatia during my big research trip in 2016, connected me to relevant locals, flicked through women's magazines and medical journals with me, and treated me to weekends away on the Croatian and Slovenian coasts to rejuvenate my strength and spirits. I thank them for giving me the resilience and self-belief necessary to complete this feat.

Halfway through my doctoral candidature, I was delighted to find out that I was pregnant with my first child. Though Eva wasn't in the picture when I embarked on a five year journey into researching women's health in socialist Yugoslavia, she was the driving force for me to finish the work. My parents and my mother-in-law, Karen, helped me immensely by caring for Eva so that I could write and prepare for submission. I am eternally grateful to them all for their help. My son was born in 2020 as I entered postdoctoral life and started to prepare for publication. My two children, who believe in me so much, kept me going despite significant obstacles.

Finally, I want to thank the many women and men who invited me into their homes and family lives, spoke to me about their personal experiences both in formal interviews and informal conversations, and entrusted their intimate memories to me.

This research was supported by an Australian Government Research Training Program (RTP) Scholarship. This book is part of a LEVIATHAN project that has received funding from the European Research Council (ERC) under the European Union's Horizon 2020 research and innovation programme. (Grant agreement No. 854503.)

ABBREVIATIONS AND ACRONYMS

AFŽ	Antifascist Women's Front (Antifašistički Front Žena)
CPY	Komunistička Partija Jugoslavije (Communist Party of Yugoslavia)
D&C	dilation and curettage
EU	European Union
FNRJ	Federativna Narodna Republika Jugoslavija (Socialist Federal Republic of Yugoslavia)
IPPF	International Planned Parenthood Federation
IUD	intrauterine device
KDAŽ	Konferencija za Društvenu Aktivnost Žena (Conference of the Social Activity of Women)
Kosmet	Kosovo and Metohija
LARC	long-acting reversible contraceptives
NICHD	National Institute of Child Health and Human Development
NGO	nongovernmental organization
OCP	oral contraceptive pill
STI	sexually transmissible infection
SŽD	Savez Ženskih Društava (Union of Women's Societies)
UN	United Nations

UNESCO	United Nations Educational, Scientific, and Cultural Organization
UNFPA	United Nations Population Fund
UNICEF	United Nations Children's Fund
USAID	United States Agency for International Development
WHO	World Health Organization

THE
New Yugoslav Woman

Introduction

In a 1958 advice column, in the popular Croatian women's fashion magazine *Svijet* (World), a woman asks for more information about contraception, a topic that interests her because of her personal situation: "I already have four children and I simply do not want to have any more. My current personal circumstances, my work and my health, will not allow it. I have to confess that I have had a few abortions already and that the fear of them has influenced intimate relations between myself and my husband. I also do not hold much faith in all these modern means of birth control. I am afraid of their side-effects and I don't really know who I can go to for help and to answer my questions."[1] The resident gynecologist, Davor Rogić, responds with concision, stating that "the protection of women's health by our socialist homeland has become the responsibility of our highest health authorities, who will help women avoid unwanted pregnancies, protecting their health and that of future generations."[2]

Having been published in a state periodical, this exchange and the characterization of the medical expert and the private citizen reveal at least as much, if not more, about the socialist state's view of these roles as it does about the anxieties and experiences of ordinary people. The woman posing the question, identified only by her initials, M. V., represents all that contemporary medical officials viewed as undesirable in women's fertility control practices: M. V. does not trust or apparently use modern contraceptives, has already had "a few" abortions, and does not know how to navigate the medical system in her search for appropriate fertility control measures. In her letter, however, there is a glimmer of hope, as she seeks to engage medical professionals to help her plan her future fertility. In seeking expert advice, M. V. enacts the state's aspiration for citizens to entrust their health to, as Rogić put it, the "highest medical authorities." Rogić speaks for the state: he gives M. V. a political answer, and not a particularly detailed or useful response, elevating the efforts of the current socialist government in ensuring the health of present and future generations. The relationship between questioner and respondent reflects a rift between state and society, a rift that the state sought to mend. The doctor underscores the state's commitment to improving the lot of this female reader and, by implication, the lot of all Yugoslav women. One of many exchanges published in similar state women's magazines, this dialogue, whether invented or real, underscores the complex and dynamic relationship between the party, the state and media, and the masses.

In this book, I address women's health, reproduction, contraception, and abortion in Yugoslavia during the period of 1945–1989—that is, from the establishment of Yugoslav socialism at the end of World War II (WWII) to the fall of communism in Europe. Throughout the socialist period, the state continually held that progressive laws, free health care, and investment into the domestic production of sex education materials and contraceptive technologies bolstered Yugoslav gender equality. The pervasive image of a state committed to equality of the sexes has seeped into the country's postsocialist legacy. Even though Yugoslavia was a highly fragmented federal state with a decentralized structure of political authority with relation to the republics and autonomous provinces, the central federal party vision and agenda remained pervasive. But to what extent were the state's domestic and international efforts to regulate reproductive matters an expression of its commitment to gender equality? Yugoslav communists were troubled by the state of the population's health, particularly that of infants and birthing women. They also worried about fertility rates, which were in constant and uneven decline, the dearth of medical services and specialists around the country, women's reliance on abortion in the absence of contraception, and how these cumulative factors held the potential to affect the future of the nation and its people. Motivated by the belief that abortions performed by unlicensed practitioners outside the medical establishment were detrimental to women's health, gynecologists dedicated their careers to improving fertility-control techniques and technologies and educating the masses about safer ways to space births. In addition to these health concerns, communist leaders had their own ambitions for the Yugoslav citizenry and wielded reproductive regulation as a tool of state formation and international geopolitical positioning.

Women and men in Yugoslavia internalized messages like the one conveyed in the exchange between M. V. and Rogić. The narrative of socialist Yugoslavia as a modern and progressive utopia found expression in recollections of the past as Yugoslavia began to crumble and then devolved into war. In the 1980s and 1990s, I was growing up in Vojvodina—a hotly contested autonomous province—in a principally female household that saw the state's gender equality agenda evidenced in my mother's career as a physician and scientist, a path my elder sister was set to follow. When friends and family reminisced with nostalgia and warmth about socialist Yugoslavia, women's health was a common topic. I was told that women could go to a clinic or hospital and access abortion services after their request for a termination was approved. Contraception was also readily available, and doctors educated patients on its use. Books on sexual health and sexual development had been available and used by parents to guide children through puberty. Popular perceptions held that women in Yugoslavia had accessible and affordable health care in comparison to elsewhere in postwar Europe or in the United States. These details buttressed the overarching contention that Yugoslav women were equal to Yugoslav men in all aspects of public and private life.

In my research, I found a far more complex picture, where matters of sexual health, including reproductive sex within marriage, were fraught for women, both during the socialist period and since. Women interviewed for this project have told me that feelings of guilt and shame were common in relation to matters of sex, sexuality, contraception, and reproduction. Medical professionals called women "whores" while in the delivery room, and women often received no support or pain relief when having an abortion, even though pain relief was available. The 1970s work of the sociologist Mirjana Morokvasić revealed that popular opinion held that if women were on the oral contraceptive pill, they would be more likely to cheat on their husbands; the public also primarily believed that the responsibility for birth control lay with the male partner, mostly through coitus interruptus.[3] These recollections left me confused. I tried to reconcile free access to reproductive and sexual health services, including contraception and pregnancy termination, coexisting with women's daily experience of their sexuality and reproduction as sites of stigma and abuse. I pondered how such discrepancies between policy and practice could exist. How could the warm remembrances of the not-so-distant past depart so much from everyday life experiences?

The figure of the New Yugoslav Woman helps to navigate the tensions of everyday socialist life in Yugoslavia. Gender was a tool of nation building for Yugoslav socialists, as it was for other socialist and nonsocialist states at different points throughout the twentieth century. Based on Soviet practices, Yugoslav communists joined other Eastern European countries in investing sustained effort imagining and then enacting a new world where groups that were previously the most disadvantaged—such as women, particularly ethnic or religious minority women—would benefit the most. Jill Massino and Shana Penn contend that "gender as a social construct and women as individuals were essential to the socialist project and that, as a result, both the term 'woman' and women's actual lives underwent transformation under state socialism."[4] To create a new socialist world, new imagined socialist identities were forged for both men and women. The story of the New Yugoslav Woman was pervasive across all forms of state media, especially so in the early socialist period (1945–1953). The Yugoslav women's press used the term "New Yugoslav Woman" starting immediately after WWII, following the Soviet example, and referenced it in titles ("Our Woman," "New Woman," "Woman Today"). The heavy patriotic rhetoric of the first two postwar decades eventually waned, yet the image as a vehicle for larger messaging remained.

The idealized female figure appeared as a nation-building tool across Europe from the early twentieth century, burdening women with multidimensional and changing expectations regarding work and domestic life. In 1981, Barbara Evans Clements argued that the "ideal Soviet woman of today grew out of the hybrid heroine of the thirties. The present ideal woman is dedicated, hardworking, and modest like her grandmother of the revolution, but she is also loving and maternal, the keeper of the family hearth."[5] Socialist publications served as vehicles for gendered expectations across socialist Europe.[6] Soviet women's publications were transposed across the Soviet Union, and their format, tone, and content were mirrored with local examples. Lynne Attwood published a study of two women's magazines, tracing the state's construction of the New Soviet Woman, between 1920 and 1955.[7] According to Attwood, the Soviet construction was an ambiguous character: "The magazines continued to celebrate women's achievements in the workplace, but held up motherhood as their most important function. They glorified the family but encouraged the single mother. They insisted that the era of self-sacrifice was over but demanded self-sacrifice on the part of wives of wounded veterans."[8] Julia Mead and Kristen Ghodsee argue that in the case of Bulgaria and Czechoslovakia, leaders of communist mass women's organizations and the editors of their affiliated women's magazines "actively acknowledged the constructed and performative nature of gender roles even as they operated within the political constraints of the state socialist system," and the Ceaușescu-era Romanian "worker-mother-wife model of womanhood [was] constructed in the media and disseminated among the public."[9] The media offered a powerful platform for disseminating gendered notions and expectations of citizens, who constituted their workforce in the wake of total war.

Chapter by chapter, this book explores the construction of the powerful image of the New Yugoslav Woman and how it was used as a vehicle for bigger political, social, and cultural messages. Except for Jelena Batinić's work on wartime partisan womanhood, literature on Yugoslavia generally eschews discussion of the New Yugoslav Woman and Man.[10] This book foregrounds the concepts' existence and explores its evolution, providing unique insight into the disjuncture between policy and practice across Yugoslavia's socialist history. The book's focus on reproduction is also novel, permitting a critical examination of the various aspects of daily life of Yugoslavs, including science and medicine, gender, and morality, as well as domestic and international politics.

Reproduction, contraception, abortion, and family planning sit at the intersections of global conversations on population control and human rights; public and private life; society, culture, and politics; and medicine and custom. These topics collectively reveal the collaborations and disjunctions between official party agendas, the interests of the state and its ministries, and the ordinary individuals that made up the Yugoslav population. Tangled within this narrative is the role of the women's press and how state actors and individuals navigated its potential. I redefine the periodization of the Yugoslav story by demonstrating the ways that Yugoslav communists built on the legacies of their predecessors and as the legacy of socialism bled into the postsocialist world. Changing this periodization offers a more expansive understanding of socialist modernity and acknowledges the complexity of nation building. Running through these central themes is my analysis of the gendered challenges and experiences that were particular to women living in socialist Yugoslavia. I examine the local, national, and transnational elements of this story to change the picture of state interventions into private reproductive behavior across Europe during the Cold War period. The book highlights the centrality of gender and women's reproductive rights and health to Yugoslav state formation. Furthermore, it situates Yugoslavia as a conduit not only between East and West but between the Global North and Global South. While the state's position was certainly not unique, the Yugoslav case offers insights into the idiosyncratic ways that nations navigated the mercurial Cold War world.

Socialist Yugoslavia: A Brief Glimpse

Yugoslavia did not exist as a country prior to the early twentieth century; however, Slavic tribes came to settle in the region that would later come to be known as Yugoslavia from the sixth century. In the eighth and ninth centuries, Croats, Slovenes, Bosnians, and Serbs converted in significant numbers to

Christianity, and over the course of several centuries thereafter, they experienced different rule, including the rise and fall of local dynasties, as well as foreign empires (for example, the experience of Slovene lands coming under the control of the Viennese Habsburg dynasty in 1460).[11] The Kingdom of Serbs, Croats, and Slovenes formed in 1918 after World War I, after the breakup of the Habsburg and Ottoman Empires. The political system in Yugoslavia favored Serbs in both governance and industry, and non-Serbs, who made up 60 percent of the total population, grew in discontent.[12] Ethnic tensions rose during the interwar period because of Serb hegemony, and fascist movements emerged in both Croatia and Serbia.[13] The kingdom was overwhelmingly Christian (almost 90 percent), almost evenly split between Eastern Orthodox and Roman Catholic Christians, with the remaining population Sunni Muslim (a little over 10 percent) and a small percentage Jewish. Populations of Orthodox Christians lived mainly around Serbia proper, while Catholics lived more around Croatia and Slovenia. Muslims lived largely in Bosnia-Herzegovina, as well as Montenegro, and Kosovo and Metohija. Over 70 percent of the population were peasants. While in the late 1930s approximately 40 percent of the population over ten years of age was illiterate, literacy rates varied dramatically by region. While over three-quarters of all Slovenes and Croats could read and write, only one-tenth of Kosovo's ethnic Albanian population was literate.[14] The interwar education system was delivered exclusively in Serbo-Croatian and benefited those who already spoke those languages. Illiteracy was considered a significant obstacle by later communists, who used written and visual propaganda to disseminate ideas.[15]

During World War II, Yugoslavia suffered significant and overwhelming civilian and military casualties, exceeded only by the those of the Soviet Union and Poland.[16] This was due to a variety of factors: occupying force brutality; civil wars fought by various warring south Slavic nationalities for ethnic and religious reasons; lack of life-sustaining resources, such as food, clothing, clean water, and medical services; the tactical Allied bombings of the final two years of the war; and significant emigration from Yugoslavia during the war years.[17] Axis invasions, combined with civil wars and later the Allied bombings, also destroyed infrastructure across the country, including hospitals, roads, bridges, factories, and warehouses, not to mention residential sites in major cities. The wartime birth rate also fell significantly compared to the interwar period and the years immediately following the war.[18] The historian Jozo Tomasevich argues that these factors compounded by the high loss of intellectuals across Yugoslavia significantly slowed economic and educational recovery after the war.[19] The material and human losses of the war created a foundation from which the communists' future pronatalist policies would grow, and Yugoslav women presented an opportunity to bridge significant demographic gaps in the population.

Interwar women suffered from a significant pay gap and discriminating family and marital policies, particularly regarding divorce rights and property inheritance, as well as ineligibility to enter certain professions and educational pathways. The Communist Party of Yugoslavia (CPY), led by Josip Broz Tito, was small and illegal during the interwar years, yet it was one of the few parties at the time that planned to alter gender and family policies and include women in political participation. The CPY enacted many of these plans during the early years of the war. The communist-led partisan movement that arose during the early war years included women within their rearguard, and over one hundred thousand mainly young rural women joined as soldiers in the partisan movement. The Communist Party's plans for reshaping postwar society began to take shape during the early years of the war.

The partisans aimed to erase gender differences by subverting traditional gendered roles in military life. Batinić argues that in the wake of WWII destabilization and turmoil, "women's mass military engagement took place ... posing a challenge to traditional gender norms."[20] The female fighter, according to Batinić, became the pride of the partisans, who proclaimed the "birth of the 'new woman' and, with her, the dawn of a new era of equality."[21] The Yugoslav socialist state was built on the foundations of those partisan ideals and strategies, and partisan women fighters were represented officially as unique across Europe. Women and women's social roles were key to gaining power, and once they were in power, women were crucial to maintaining the party's favor. Yugoslav communists rewarded women with constitutional rights in pursuit of equality of the sexes; however, they also became concerned with women because they needed them to fill out the labor force and because they perceived them to be more passive and backward than men and therefore more susceptible to "counterrevolutionary propaganda." They also knew that women, "as mothers and primary educators of future generations," were "indispensable to the success of the communist project."[22] Even though the Communist Party's vision of women's political participation was limited, communist women rose in leadership and enacted many important legislative changes that affected women's daily lives, such as policies regarding abortion, working life, and divorce.[23]

Once the Yugoslav Communist Party took power in 1945, leading communists aligned themselves with the Soviet Union and pursued the transformation of society through a social revolution. Immediately after taking over the

Yugoslav lands, the party began a long and protracted effort to claim legitimacy, especially among the vast and diffuse peasantry, constantly balancing its long-term revolutionary aspirations with immediate social, political, and economic needs. Yugoslav communists were aware of the dysfunction of what Sabrina Ramet terms the first Yugoslavia (1918–1945), which they put down to "exploitative capitalism" as well as the regime's failure to meet the demands of the different regions. While Croatia, Bosnia, Slovenia, and Montenegro wanted federalism, Vojvodina wanted autonomism, and Macedonians and Albanians wanted education systems in their own languages that acknowledged and supported their "distinctive cultures."[24] As they had as a resistance group during the war, the party continued to subvert ethnic differences by "championing a supraethnic patriotism in a region troubled by interethnic strife."[25] During the last two years of WWII, Yugoslav communists established republics and autonomous regions and provinces, juggling regional demands and placating local sensibilities. For example, in wanting to retain Serb support, communist leadership granted Kosovo status as an autonomous region under Serbia's jurisdiction. Communists granted Vojvodina the status of autonomous province, a higher status than that of Kosovo.[26] While they outwardly bought into the idea of a liberal state in terms of gender equality and neutrality regarding ethnic and religious differences, the reality of the situation was that deep divisions and inequalities persisted across the country. Access to health care and other services, employment, and education continued to be more abundant in urban centers, particularly in Serbia proper, Slovenia, and Croatia, and this continued to be reflected in the distribution of income and literacy rates.

Unlike other Eastern European states, Yugoslavia broke from the Soviet Union in 1948; Tito and Joseph Stalin clashed over Yugoslav foreign politics. Fueled by the split, Yugoslav communist leaders sought to pursue their own form of socialism which encompassed the "legitimating triad" of interethnic cooperation, which came to be known as *bratstvo i jedinstvo* (brotherhood and unity), self-management, and nonalignment.[27] Brotherhood and unity became the guiding principle for Yugoslav communists in maintaining the peace between different ethnic, religious groups. Ramet argues that Yugoslav "communists understood the importance of ethnic equality and gender equality, they understood the bitterness which could be stirred up by dwelling on grievances from the interwar and wartime periods, they understood that mutual tolerance (which they translated as 'brotherhood and unity') was essential to civil peace."[28] Self-management socialism was a system that was designed to be "emulated" by the international community.[29] According to the Yugoslav socialist theorist Edvard Kardelj, self-management represented a "new and direct democratic socialist right, which is possible solely in the conditions of the social ownership of the means of production and the ruling position of the working class in the society."[30] From the early 1950s, the Yugoslavs' socialist experiment encompassed a new, more temperate socialist style, typified by a more gradualist economic policy than its Soviet-style precursor and a dogged pursuit of foreign engagements. The state decentralized federal power, forging a governing system that would see the central state's function reduced and the country's workforce empowered through workers' councils and committees.[31] In forging a new socialism, the party represented itself as benevolent and altruistic, distributing control to republics, autonomous provinces, and local councils. The state also purported to be neutral in relation to religion of individuals, which "would remain an elusive virtue" owing to the state's bureaucratic management of religious communities.[32]

As in other nations, exceptionalism was the backbone of the Yugoslav socialist project, and the party used the state-sponsored women's press to gain legitimacy with the citizenry. State propaganda dominated mass media and popular culture—predominantly through periodicals and papers in the early Cold War period and later through film and music—where official propaganda constantly reiterated Yugoslavia's distinctiveness. A 1946 article from the state-sponsored women's magazine *Žena danas* (Woman today) confidently asserts that "no other people, apart from those of the Soviet Union, can praise themselves on their efforts in rebuilding their own land; no other people can say that they have achieved as much in this brief [postwar] period as have the people of Yugoslavia."[33] Patriotic messages about the new socialist country were bolstered by a cult of personality constructed around Tito. Reprinted and disseminated nationally, his speeches and those of his communist comrades promoted an image of the party's collective benevolence toward the Yugoslav people. Fostering political cohesion, the women's press emphasized women's gratitude for Tito's generosity: "Thank you to comrade Tito, who gave to us women the right to choose our freedom!"[34] Even though over time, the impassioned patriotic sentiment waned somewhat, as communist women leaders questioned the breadth of the state's commitment to public promises, these patriotic messages shaped perceptions of the state project beyond the life of Tito and of the country. As far as Yugoslav women were concerned, the socialist period created some "striking advances," particularly to do with women's literacy and education and in labor force participation. In 1948, 25 percent of the population over the age of ten was illiterate, with vast regional differences. Slovenia's illiteracy stood at 1.1 percent of that population, while Kosovo's was almost 57 percent.[35] Illiteracy rates for females older than ten were reduced from 56.4 percent in

1931 to 35.8 percent in 1953 and 28.8 in 1961, and women constituted 36.5 percent of all graduates of Yugoslav institutions of higher education in the period 1945 to 1977, compared to 19 percent in 1939.[36] Women's political participation and the traditional division of labor within the home remained largely unchanged during the socialist period.

Throughout the socialist period, Yugoslavia continued to be politically and economically linked with Western powers, while remaining socialist in political character. Tito saw the break with Stalin as an opportunity to dissociate his country from the West's Cold War enemy.[37] Amid the Cold War, the Yugoslav state presented itself as a unique socialist nation, one that existed outside of the East/West divide, taking simultaneously from East and West to produce its own version of socialism. As the historian Vesna Drapac argues, "Tito eventually emerged as the favorite of the European left. His split with Stalin . . . revealed to sympathetic outsiders that one could deviate from the Soviet path without betraying communist principles."[38] These moves gained Tito international praise and popularity among noncommunists in the West and brought Yugoslav communists into a closer relationship with the US, as compared to other socialist European states. Soon after the split, the US began to give significant financial aid to Yugoslavia, which contributed to the Yugoslav state being one of the wealthiest socialist countries in postwar Europe. Indeed, "the country went on to receive enormous amounts of Western material help, as well as political support and, even more importantly, developed its own, much more liberal and internationally open brand of socialism."[39] However, a relationship with the US was not the only foreign engagement that Yugoslav communists craved, and Tito energetically pursued affiliations with emerging independent countries of the Global South.

In its burgeoning relationship with countries that would eventually form the Non-Aligned Movement (NAM), the federal state aimed to do two things: present itself as a developmental model for those newly decolonized countries and serve as a bridge between those and Western countries. By 1961, Yugoslavia had become a leading force in the NAM, whose existence aimed to skirt Cold War tensions. According to the American historian of Yugoslavia Ramet, "nonalignment and self-management were developed as the central principles of foreign policy and domestic policy," and the combination of those policies opened doors for the state to engage with other foreign parties.[40] The distinctiveness of the Yugoslav way, attests Odd Arne Westad, helped Tito build "close relations with Third World revolutionaries who also wanted to be socialists without accepting the full Soviet package."[41]

The state aimed to bridge divisions between the Global North and South by way of its involvement with international nongovernmental organizations

(NGOs). From the late 1950s, the state established partnerships with multilateral humanitarian and health organizations, including the United Nations (UN), to establish itself as a leader in the provision of aid around the developing world. Yugoslavia's deliberate engagements with those global entities demonstrate a shift away from earlier Soviet-style socialist leadership in the first postwar decade, in pursuit of a new geopolitical position between the Global North and South. While it fostered its burgeoning relationship with the West, as a leader of the NAM, Yugoslavia also led the way for developing countries to adopt policies aimed at reducing their populations by influencing women's reproductive decisions. By becoming the vanguard of the production and expertise in fertility control, the state wielded the authority of science for its own benefit.

Reproductive regulation constituted one aspect of the state's broader strategy to construct a uniquely Yugoslav communist project. Reproductive regulation encompassed economic policies, social and cultural policies, and presented an opportunity to reach into the private lives of all citizens at every stage of life. As was common among the newly socialist postwar European states, Yugoslav communists adopted and implemented constitutional legislation, gender policies, and reproductive policies from the Soviet Union under the banner of the socialist commitment to gender equality. One of those measures included the 1946 constitution, which aimed to unify the Yugoslav citizenry across ethnic, cultural, and class divisions and ratified equality of the sexes. After the split, Yugoslav legislators set out to express their commitment to gender equality through new codes concerning abortion, contraception, and parental rights. They did so by drawing on examples from international humanitarian organizations, from their predecessors in interwar public health, and from other socialist states. From the federal decriminalization of abortion in the 1951 penal code through the 1960s as the Federal Assembly and the republican seats adopted the federal legislation, abortions were legally guaranteed for Yugoslav women.[42] Following the 1969 General Law, which legalized women's access to abortion "on demand" before ten weeks' gestation, the 1974 Yugoslav constitution affirmed parents' rights to decide on the number and spacing of their children.[43]

Literature: Yugoslavia and Gender

Yugoslav communists used the image of the New Yugoslav Man and Woman as a tool to distinguish between what was socially and culturally desirable, and gender played a central role in the construction of cultural representations. The sociologists Renata Jambrešić Kirin and Marina Blagaić argue that the evolving figure of the New Yugoslav Woman was "crucial for promoting urbanization, industrialization and consumption in the socialist Yugoslavia."[44] The Croatian historian Igor Duda in his work on the history of children and pioneers argues that the "new socialist man and woman started in childhood" and was developed through social institutions and cultural messaging.[45] In crafting a Yugoslav socialist character, Yugoslav authorities retained the traditional socialist identity that encompassed moral and physical health but added to it a particularly and uniquely Yugoslav flavor. Examining posters, magazines, and catalogs from the 1940s to the 1980s, Koraljka Vlajo has argued similarly that the image of the Yugoslav citizen was "shaped and reshaped" continually through "representations of men, women, and youth in order to consistently reassert the dominant state/regime narrative."[46] This book argues that the development of this idealized gendered version of the Yugoslav citizen was a central tenet and driving force of the state, and it is most clearly seen in the regulation of reproduction during the socialist period. Although the terms *New Yugoslav Man* and *New Yugoslav Woman* dropped out of use by the press by the mid-1950s, spurred by de-Stalinization, the essence of the idea of the New Yugoslav Man and Woman remained essential to the Yugoslav way.

Yugoslav feminists of the 1970s, 1980s, and 1990s questioned the discrepancies between state rhetoric and women's lived experiences in the domestic and public spheres. From the 1970s, these sociologists and historians critiqued the state's measures to legislate equality of the sexes by analyzing the spheres of home, public life, education, employment outside of the home, and intimate partner relationships. Much of that scholarship stems from the interests of Belgrade, Zagreb, and Ljubljana feminists who spearheaded studies that were borne of a combination of Western feminist principles and socialist ideology.[47] In an oft-cited 1989 review of women's invisibility in school history textbooks, the feminist scholar Lydia Sklevicky argued that the pervasiveness of patriarchal attitudes in constructions of the Yugoslav past meant that school children were largely taught about war and conflict. Consequently, horses, "man's steady companions in warfare," outnumbered women in the textbooks of the day.[48] While Yugoslav feminists were influenced by second-wave Western feminist ideology and applied it to their academic work in critiquing the status quo, their respective agendas differed. As one scholarly observer of Yugoslav feminism notes, the 1978 Belgrade feminist conference, which Sklevicky helped to organize and which attracted feminists from all over Europe, evinced the delegates' divergent concerns: "While Italian and French feminist movements were building their mass campaigns on themes such as divorce, [and] abortion," Yugoslav feminists argued that those rights already existed in Yugoslavia and did not constitute an issue.[49] Yugoslav feminists, like those of other Eastern European states, were more concerned about equality between men and women in terms of employment and promotion at work and with the issue of domestic violence.

Following in the footsteps of these feminists, historians and sociologists have of late begun to interrogate the disjuncture between state promises and women's everyday lives. The history of the family, including subjects such as intimate partner violence, continuation of religious rituals and celebrations, and gendered roles within the home, tells of the persistence of historically entrenched patriarchal attitudes within the private domain. For example, the Serbian historian Vera Gudac-Dodić contends that men's habitual abuse of their female spouses was "expected and inveterate" during the early twentieth century; it continued into the socialist period and, because of the state's avowed promotion of gender equality, remained "invisible."[50] The Slovenian sociologists Alenka Švab, Tanja Rener, and Metka Kuhar argue that socialist women exercised their rights within the public sphere through full-time employment and political participation. They could do so more successfully in those contexts than they could within the private realm of the family because "long term cultural structures of power and habitus," embodied within enduring patriarchal attitudes, negated women's abilities to challenge the distribution of power within families and gendered family roles.[51] Their arguments point to the ways that topics about private, family life stand to problematize the socialist state's measures to equalize the sexes.

Social scientists, rather than historians, have dominated the discussions of women's reproductive rights and health. Yugoslav-born scholars have led the way, with a steady stream of social science studies of abortion and maternal care in Yugoslavia.[52] They focus on the post-1989 period, with the topics including family planning services, contraception options and their use in certain sections of the population (such as university and high school students), the availability of induced abortion, and its widespread use by the population despite the availability of modern contraceptives and voluntary sterilization. In the wake of the Yugoslav wars, social scientists in each of the post-Yugoslav states have pushed to create better family planning services and education and to encourage changes in attitude toward contraception in the different areas of the populations. In the context of present-day conservatism, reproductive rights and abortion policies in socialist Yugoslavia are seen as examples of Yugoslavia's more permissive past: exemplifying socialist commitment to women's ongoing emancipation. Neda Božinović, a Serbian activist in her youth and political commentator and academic during the 1990s, praises the socialist laws on abortion in her seminal texts describing the social and political positions of women in Serbia.[53] The factors outlined above, combined with the germinal state of women's and gender studies across all disciplines in the region, illustrate why topics of reproduction and abortion under Yugoslav socialism have yet to receive the historically driven academic scrutiny that they deserve.

To the extent that historians have addressed socialist women's reproductive health and rights, their concern centers on the argument that reproductive legislation was an expression of the state's commitment to gender equality.[54] The Serbian historian Aleksandra Pavićević asserts that policies advocating for the limitation of births from the 1960s followed global demographic trends of lowering natality in pursuit of "better family life."[55] She, along with Ivana Dobrivojević, acknowledges that the state passed laws not so much to directly eliminate inequalities between men and women but to pursue a gradualist approach to social engineering.[56] They paint the Yugoslav government as fairly benevolent in its authority, contending, in concert with state propaganda, that gender policies evidenced the state's commitment to caring for women and uplifting their public roles. The sociologist Rada Drezgić argues that "liberal population policy and uninterrupted liberal abortion legislation in Yugoslavia, resulted, among other reasons, from the communist leadership's commitment to national and gender equality."[57] I, too, find that the bureaucracy was in accord with the ideological tenets of socialist gender equality and went some way toward expressing its commitment to that ideal. Regardless, the state's efforts ultimately fell short because it never fully endorsed or resourced initiatives that sought to realize equalizing ambitions, due to costs they were unwilling to cover, entrenched patriarchal attitudes regarding gender and women's sexuality, and a lasting concern over population growth, movement, and its regional discrepancies. As Rogić emphatically explained in his response to M. V., communist leaders viewed women's health and reproductive policies as the foundation of the evolving Yugoslav socialist system, but just as he did, medical experts were unable or unwilling to bring policy into practice.

The fall of Yugoslavia—in particular, the wartime rapes and ethnic cleansing that have come to typify its bloody end—along with conservative shifts in reproductive policies in the Yugoslav successor states have reframed analyses of reproduction, contraception, and abortion during the country's socialist period. Dobrivojević and Pavićević contend that the state never intended for reproductive laws to affect women's decisions about how many children to have.[58] Drezgić draws a line between demographic research and 1970s family planning policies, asserting that population policies replaced family planning policies starting from the 1980s. She contends that the socialist state did not aim to affect population makeup or distribution, at least not until the 1980s in the lead-up to the 1990s Yugoslav wars.[59] Drezgić is correct that state pronatalist population policies accelerated during the final decade of the socialist period. However, I argue that the state, even in its fragmented federal nature, was always concerned with the shifting tides of demographic change and that its concern manifested differently according to agendas, demographic research, and global movements.

Pertinent to the story of reproductive regulation is feminism, its contextualized definitions, and its relative merits within Yugoslav socialist society. Socialist ideology supports the ideal of equality of the sexes but considers organized feminism as a false consciousness and as ultimately detracting from the pursuit of the ideal classless society. The establishment of state-socialist women's organizations, such as the Antifascist Women's Front (Antifašistički Front Žena [AFŽ]), under the ideological banner of socialism, made mid-twentieth-century Western feminism seem bourgeois. However, as Jasmina Lukić wrote, "the term 'feminism' connotes very different things for different women, and there obviously is a certain stigma that goes with it in a number of regional countries. But what is often lost from sight in these positions are specific traditions of critical thinking that are local and regional, in which emancipatory actions and ideas are not necessarily recognized or named as 'feminist,' although they foreground in different ways general interest in women's issues."[60] Feminism and socialism are not mutually exclusive categories, and Yugoslavs navigated fluid definitions of both throughout the socialist period. Examining the sexual revolution of Croatia's 1960s and 1970s, Zrinka Miljan argues that similar processes that typified the sexual revolution of the West existed within Yugoslavia, and Yugoslav youth routinely utilized the rhetoric of sexual freedom. The availability and legality of certain contraceptives and abortion during the 1960s onward, argues Miljan, extended Yugoslav women's opportunities for sexual pleasure and free exploration afforded by the paradigm of the sexual revolution.[61] The prominent Slovenian lawyer Vida Tomšič (1913–1998) consistently and emphatically resisted the label of feminist because of its Western bourgeois associations and fought for women's reproductive rights under the banner of socialism. Within the dialogue of women's groups in Belgrade, Ljubljana, and Zagreb during the 1970s and 1980s, feminist rhetoric was adapted to socialist principles.[62] Female physicians, lawyers, academics, and activists agitated for more effective dissemination of education about contraception and family planning options, within the fabric of a socialist regime and on the ideological basis of socialism.

State-led efforts to regulate reproduction in Europe were in part a response to practical postwar realities, and Yugoslavia was no exception—though every country dealt with its own specific circumstances. In 1920, the Soviet Union was the first nation in the world to legalize abortion with the objective of offering safer medicalized abortions to women, believing that once it reached socialism there would no longer be any need for abortion.[63] The 1936 recriminalization of abortion, except in circumstances where it was deemed medically necessary, was overturned in 1955 under Nikita Khrushchev.[64] Abortion laws were applied throughout socialist Europe, with great variance. In 1950, East Germany relaxed strict antiabortion legislation to allow for cases other than when the mother's life was in danger; it was only fully legalized in 1972.[65] In 1976, West Germany followed suit. In 1992, after reunification, a new law was enacted that allowed access to abortion within the first trimester.[66] Some socialist nations enacted restrictions to abortion to encourage population growth within a socialist ideology that argued that every citizen had to contribute to socialist development and with a belief that socialism would increase the quality of life for all enough to void the need for abortions. Abortion was legal in Romania until 1966, when the notorious Decree 770 banned both pregnancy termination and the production and importation of contraceptive devices.[67] Twenty-three years later, after the overthrow of communism, Romania fully legalized abortion.[68] By contrast, the long-standing availability of legal abortion in Yugoslavia offers another example of the trajectories that nations took to deal with domestic population issues.

Socialist medicine, at its core, is available for all citizens, but because of isolation, especially in the first postwar decade, there were limits to how well or sufficiently the people were served. Susan Grant argued that a "lack of resources and lack of rigorous training meant that people often received substandard medical treatment and care."[69] As most medical authorities around the world did, socialists used health and hygiene to "cultivate the people and bring function to the state."[70] Socialist medicine differed from its Western counterpart "not in medicine or science per se, but in professional identity, the role of health care workers, and the structure of the health care system."[71] The socialist medical expert, from the nineteenth century onward, served to pathologize and heal not only the individual but the whole of society.[72] Medical professionals and scientists had less freedom than those in the West as they were in service of the state, but once there was more access to the West, socialist scientists and medical personnel caught up fast with developments in their specialties. The Yugoslav physicians interviewed for this book also reveal the ways in which individual medical professionals reconciled personal ideologies with institutional infrastructures and regulations, public health policies, and legal frameworks when it came to providing services to socialist women. Yugoslav state doctors benefited from the medical advances in the West, but their encounters with Western peers served to transfer knowledge and innovation outside the socialist world, too.

Even though socialism was purportedly about self-sufficiency and isolation to some extent, it also depended on what we understand now as a rather large gap in the Iron Curtain. Recent literature has established that the Iron Curtain was, in fact, highly permeable and that knowledge transfer and exchange among communist countries, and between them and the Western world, was prevalent.[73] Significantly, medical exchanges of knowledge occurred not despite state regulations urging against such interactions but because those exchanges were sanctioned by various socialist states. Narratives from various Eastern European contexts allows insight into different forms of socialist models of health, including importantly the centrality of the scientific expert to both developing and realizing the socialist vision. As in other Eastern European states, Yugoslav state socialist experts were central to "Eastern Europe's internationalization" from the 1950s through to the end of socialism in Europe. They served as "intermediaries between their states and other national, regional, and international environments."[74] Travel between communist countries was far easier than to the West, and regional networks in mental health knowledge and psychiatry, for example, ran regularly and worked to bridge gaps in knowledge established by isolation.[75] Tracing the development of polio vaccines in Hungary, Dora Vargha revealed "gaping holes in the Iron Curtain" through which expertise, people, and technologies traveled both within Europe and beyond.[76] Exchange of medical and scientific resources extended beyond the East/West divide as the case of Yugoslavia demonstrates. Yugoslav medical and scientific experts traveled beyond the borders of the communist world, into the West and Global South, in bids both to sow their influence and to acquire and exchange knowledge. The Yugoslav story also teaches us more about the socialist model and how, in some cases, it included geopolitics of the Global South. Yugoslavia also serves to further the argument that Cold War divisions were much more fluid than originally purported.

The dynamic relationship between the state, medical and scientific experts, and society has been key to studying reproduction in former state-socialist European nations. Over the last forty years, scholars have moved away from a totalitarian understanding of socialist regimes toward a more nuanced view that argues for complexity in the regimes' relationship with the population. In Eastern Europe, state rhetoric and scientific rhetoric complemented each other in seeking to regulate reproductive matters. Ulf Brunnbauer and Karin Taylor argue, in the Bulgarian context, that a medical community's backing, or the "guise of "science," was used by the regime to justify intrusion into private reproductive lives and into what women did with their bodies.[77] Historians have established that people internalized, advocated, resisted, and interrogated official legislation and scientific rhetoric on reproduction and abortion on a daily basis.[78] Harsch argues that East German women exerted persistent pressure onto the communist leadership to elevate the importance of domestic issues, such as childcare, reproduction, consumption, and family life, the cumulative effects of which saw the German Democratic Republic's transition from a productivist dictatorship to a welfare dictatorship.[79] Turning to Western contexts, Leslie J. Reagan contends that in the US the "continuing demand for abortion from women, regardless of law," influenced both doctors and state authorities to reconsider the procedure's illegality, fueling the revision of public policies dealing with abortion in the 1970s.[80] Extant sources on women's experiences in Yugoslavia are not as rich as those for Germany or the US, but physicians, public officials, and women as health care workers and health consumers demonstrate a comparably dynamic relationship within the Yugoslav context.

Women's relationship with medicalized childbirth, such as the turn to hospital-based childbirth, the use of pharmacological pain relief, and the shift in care from the hands of midwives to those of physicians, has been analyzed for its significance and meaning in contemporary feminist scholarship and within a transnational framework. By focusing on different topics within pregnancy and birth, scholars have analyzed debates about who should be involved in assisting pregnant women and women in labor, how much assistance and what type of intervention should be available to those women, and the role that parturient women themselves play in procuring, negotiating, or rejecting new technological developments and medical practices. This book situates the state's activities and agendas within a broader European and global shift in the medicalization of reproduction. Following in the footsteps of these scholars, I also incorporate the nuanced debates between medical officials and birthing women to present a more holistic narrative about the production and consumption of medicalized reproduction.

These layered histories fit within the landscape of two entwined global histories: the Cold War and family planning. In seeking to break down Cold War binaries, historians, since the 2000s, have stressed the importance of the Third World in the unfolding Cold War narrative. Decolonized nations of the Global South constituted a Cold War battleground, upon which the Soviets and the Americans fought to promote ideologically divergent development models for postcolonial revolutionaries seeking to remake their societies.[81] As an ideology, family planning was primarily a tool of population control by international US-led NGOs working in developing nations, with aims to, as Matthew Connelly argues, "coerce or control people to plan smaller families." Connelly explains that family planning as an ideology was born during WWII "and was meant to represent fertility regulation as both family friendly and essential to social planning... [with the proviso that] individuals could not plan their families without professional guidance to guarantee the greater good."[82] The narrative of reproductive regulation in Yugoslavia is instructive because of the individuals, institutions, and technologies flowing through and from Yugoslavia within this dynamic global landscape.

Yet Yugoslavia does not appear in recent histories of global population control even though it stands as an ideal case study. Connelly has urged historians to consider efforts to control global population change as "transnational phenomena" rather than as isolated national efforts to affect domestic population changes. The Yugoslav case can tell us more than already exists in the scholarship about the topography of this demographic landscape. Along with Mie Nakachi and Rickie Solinger, Connelly argues that international, Western, US-led NGOs have been instrumental in creating "a new kind of global governance," where "US government and American NGOs offered clients and even geopolitical adversaries" guidance in the sphere of population control.[83] These studies examine not only the international phenomenon of population control but also global efforts to stem the tide of demographic change. Starting from the 1950s, Yugoslav medical and legal experts engaged in global conversations about population and reproduction, incorporating the language of family planning into existing measures to affect reproductive behavior at home.

Engaging this expanding and disparate conversation about reproductive policies, health care and maternal medicine, and everyday life histories in socialist Yugoslavia, this book puts histories of women and their reproductive lives at the center of analysis. I draw on the methodologies and findings of academics of Eastern Europe and, unlike earlier studies, draw Yugoslavian women's history into the transnational turn in the scholarship.[84] The topic of women's reproductive health speaks to the story of daily life in Yugoslavia under socialism and elucidates the contradictory constructions of gender in the home, the persistence of local custom as separate from yet tolerated by socialist ideology, and the construction of gender and national identity within a global context.

Structure and Organization

I draw on diverse source materials and the methods of social and cultural history to tell the story of reproductive regulation in Yugoslavia. I balance public rhetoric and official government documents with everyday life narratives and popular culture. Government archives, the women's press, and scientific publications enabled me to explore the legislative and medical developments relating to women's health, as well as how changes were communicated to the public in both official and unofficial ways. These records have allowed me to build a layered narrative of the creation, evolution, and development of public policy and its integration into medical practice. Woven together, these sources construct a narrative of sweeping and broad government plans and directives, where individual voices of communist women, family planning advocates, and women's health professionals come through.

I look at legal, administrative, media, and medical discourses to reconstruct the dialogue between the state, health professionals, and the public about women's reproductive rights and responsibilities. In doing so, this project addresses questions of gender and national identity construction. A Foucauldian analysis of this discourse unmasks how the state, media, and medicine wielded power over women's (and men's) bodies and life courses. I interrogate knowledge production and how state officials used language and imagery to construct social norms and expectations through mass media.

Throughout the book, I draw on the testimonies of women and physicians and engage with them systematically in the final chapter on memory and remembering. Between September and November 2016, I interviewed twenty-nine former Yugoslavs: twenty-one private citizens who had experienced the medical system as patients and eight professionals who worked within the health care system. Of the professionals, all but two were women. The professionals included one social worker, five gynecologist-obstetricians, one midwife, and one academic and domestic violence activist. The rest of the respondents are in many ways similar to me and those in my networks: they are all educated, from urban, middle-class backgrounds, employed, and for the most part have had some experience traveling abroad. I initially recruited participants by word of mouth and through colleagues, friends, and family, which then led to snowball sampling as some particularly interested participants introduced me to their networks. Aspects of my analysis of oral histories are situated within the "post-war renaissance of memory as a source for 'people's history,'" where the purpose of oral histories is to bring forth lost voices and reclaim marginalized populations' place in history.[85] I follow the 1970s school of oral historians who "argued that the so-called unreliability of memory was also its strength," as I deeply read my sources for subjective and intersubjective clues about the construction of the past through the present.[86]

Transnational histories offer scholars new ways to explain the "connections and circulations" of ideas, knowledge, resources, and people, and I apply transnational methodologies to extend the analysis of Yugoslavia's state formation through its international engagements.[87] Patricia Seed explains that "transnational history does not threaten the traditional local or regional study that historians have always undertaken"; rather, it allows historians to consider their topics in a larger framework.[88] I demonstrate that the Yugoslav story represents one of myriad ways that state leaders responded to population shifts after WWII. Furthermore, I unearth the functions of the Yugoslav state in forging a unique self-management socialist vision that would serve as a key to Yugoslavia's entry onto the global political stage. Through its special relationship with Western powers and its leading role in the NAM, Yugoslav communists staked out a claim for a prime position as a developed leader of the developing world.

The book is structured chronologically and thematically to elaborate my arguments. By focusing on a different thematic subject, each chapter builds on the previous one to trace a narrative of the metamorphosis of the Yugoslav state through the lens of reproduction and the different layers that make up reproductive politics and health care. The book's structure reinforces the shift from state legal and medical infrastructures in chapters 1 and 2, to the development of the products and resources of reproductive regulation in chapters 3 and 4, and the ways in which these systems were consumed—internalized, negotiated, resisted—by ordinary women in chapter 5. First and foremost, this is a Yugoslav story. However, I tell it from the perspectives of the three main sites of Ljubljana, Zagreb, and Belgrade, urban capitals that housed well-resourced and financed research institutes, where the most prolific leaders in women's health operated. The decision to focus on these three locales was source driven. These histories were lived by women in all parts of Yugoslavia, though their experiences were not monolithic or static. Women's experiences of health care and their knowledge of their citizenship rights varied dramatically between the metropolises and villages, as well as from household to household. The historical actors, institutions, and the paper trail they left behind in the country's three urban centers offer a rich and diverse body of evidence. The body of evidence creates a largely institutional history, one that is very top-heavy. However, from various sources—including reports of village life and the testimonies of women and their families—we glean some insight into different regions and ethnicities and their practices, if only from the perspective of urban medical professionals.

The work of two establishments associated with the University Teaching Hospital in Ljubljana stand out above the rest in both the domestic and transnational elements of this history, and they cut through the entire book. Physicians working at the Obstetrical and Gynecological Department and the Institute for Family Planning comprise some of the most influential voices in this story. In part, this was because the Yugoslav Ministry of Public Health dubbed these establishments as central testing sites for all the developed and imported reproductive and fertility control technologies coming through Yugoslavia. Before a resource could be prescribed, dispensed, tested, or employed, medical and scientific staff at these two clinics vetted it for safety and efficacy. As a result, those physicians held clout and were sought out for research collaborations at home and abroad and featured regularly in scientific, medical, and popular journals. The Slovenian Republican Health Council founded the Institute for Family Planning in 1961 as one section of the larger institution, the Hospital for Birth and Women's Illnesses. By 1967, the newly named institute became the central point of research, development, and testing of contraceptive, abortion, and reproductive technologies. The department and the institute collaborated on research and innovation and worked together to increase public acceptance of contraception, to decrease abortion numbers overall and per woman, and to make legal medical pregnancy termination more accessible and safer for women. From the 1950s until the end of the socialist period, these and other Yugoslav physicians and scientists engaged with representatives from multilateral health and humanitarian organizations and smaller philanthropic agencies, collaborating on research, development, innovation, and dissemination of knowledge and products relating to family planning. Organizations concerned with population growth and development, such as the International Planned Parenthood Federation (IPPF), Population Council, and the Pathfinder Fund, among others, aimed to affect global populations, and Yugoslav gynecologists worked closely with their representatives.[89]

Key gynecologists, social workers, sociologists, and directors tied to family planning institutions populate this book. Franc Novak (1908–1999), WWII partisan fighter, renowned gynecologist, and former director of the Obstetrical and Gynecological Department in Ljubljana, and second husband to Tomšič, lobbied fiercely throughout his career for legislative and institutional change to women's health, including the provision of free contraception. His views on abortion changed over time. While he was not always supportive of abortion laws becoming more open, he also did not support its recriminalization. He ultimately championed the provision of contraception to change women's attitudes and fertility control behaviors and to secure their future reproductive health and fertility. He wrote sex education literature, developed contraceptive and abortion technology, wrote manuals on gynecological methods that have been translated into multiple languages, and normalized new technologies that had been innovated in Yugoslavia across the Western world. I have also made liberal use of private collections and papers from particularly influential individuals to scrutinize official papers. Tomšič herself was a member of the outlawed Communist Party in Yugoslavia before WWII. In the 1940s, she agitated for legislation relating to women's reproductive rights; she continued to fight for women's rights under socialism, representing Yugoslavia at international conferences on the social position of women, human rights, and population control. Personal archives reveal a glimpse into public opinion and how individuals in the public eye, including academics, leaders, and politicians, negotiated and interrogated official government ideologies and directives.

Chapters 1 and 2 cover the structures and systems that the state put into place to regulate reproduction considering the postwar disaster. They broadly deal with the state's Soviet links and the ongoing impact of Soviet influences as Yugoslavia sought the third way of socialist self-management. In chapter 1, I examine the foundation of the state's reproductive policy and analyze the tension between the letter of the law and an implicit pronatalist policy bias, by comparing state documents with state propaganda. From the end of WWII to 1953, the year of Stalin's death and the introduction of Yugoslav self-management, the state established a legislative foundation that was more pronatalist than scholars and contemporary commentators have previously acknowledged. In chapter 2, I interrogate how the state forged a bureaucratized medical system to unify the Yugoslav people and to entrench its political power throughout the regions. Responding to medical experts' research and to women's demand for safer medicalized abortions, the state aimed to build a comprehensive health care system, free for all citizens. Despite ambitious plans to rehabilitate the health of women and children and to establish an interconnected web of clinical services that would unify, modernize, and industrialize the peasantry, the Ministry of Public Health faced multiple hindrances that ultimately led its efforts to fall short of expectations and promises.

Chapters 3 and 4 concern the ways that Yugoslav gynecologists and family planning advocates developed tools of reproductive regulation, for domestic consumption and international exchange. These chapters also explore how the state engaged with human rights and population control movements, both with global humanitarian organizations and in its pursuit of new international alliances with newly decolonized African and Asian countries. Here, I plait Yugoslav archival and published scientific sources with documents from the Population Council, Pathfinder Fund, and Rockefeller Foundation Archives, to build a layered transnational narrative about international collaboration in the area of population control, family planning, and the international development of human rights. Chapter 3 contextualizes the development and testing of contraceptive intrauterine devices (IUDs) and vacuum aspiration for first-trimester pregnancy termination within global efforts to stem the perceived population explosion raging through the developing world. Chapter 4 analyzes Yugoslavia's sex education tradition within the global formulation of human rights. Together, these chapters demonstrate the ways in which Yugoslavia not only responded to global ebbs and flows but had a hand in their manufacture. They also explore the international ambitions of self-management socialism, showing how Yugoslavia was simultaneously motivated to connect with the US, the Global South, and multilateral humanitarian and health organizations. This section demonstrates how Yugoslav communists utilized international connections to innovate domestic products—specifically abortion and contraception technology and sex education material—and disseminated them abroad. It is in this section that I most explicitly analyze how the state positioned itself as a conduit between East and West and the developed and developing worlds through the model of socialist self-management.

In chapter 5, I balance official and scientific histories and narratives with women's recollections to retract the narratives of the "nonhegemonic classes" of ordinary female citizens and the physicians who provided health care services.[90] These testimonies allow me to examine the ways that individuals experienced the medicalization of reproduction and its institutionalization and how the perception of socialism in the wake of the Yugoslav wars and the demise of the Yugoslav state has shaped popular perceptions of the recent Cold War past. Rather than reviving voices lost to dominant narratives, I use contemporary oral history theory to interrogate the memory of my subjects and to better understand what can be attributed to the distinctive nature of Yugoslav socialism and what cannot. These sources demonstrate that women's memories of their experiences as patients in the socialist medical system show a continuation from the past rather than a dichotomy between the socialist and postsocialist world. Furthermore, two significant events—the fall of European socialism and the violent and traumatic breakup of Yugoslavia—affected how academics and the general population remember Yugoslavia and construct it and its events in the present day.

Like its socialist neighbor states, Yugoslavia evolved in response to extreme domestic hardships of war, souring political alliances, internal population and demographic dynamics, and the international political landscape. Certainly, the state experienced factors unique to it, such as a much earlier break with the Soviet Union and a financially beneficial relationship with the US, as well as the extremely violent nature of its 1990s collapse. Nevertheless, the case of Yugoslavia highlights the pervasiveness and long-lasting nature of socialist legacies. In Yugoslavia we also see how scientists and clinicians transcended national and ideological boundaries when it came to scientific discovery and clinical care, further underlining the fragile, porous, and mercurial nature of European socialism. Post-WWII nation building in Yugoslavia and abroad was complex and in constant flux; gender, especially as it is expressed in the regulation of reproduction, was a key tool in the evolution of the socialist Yugoslav state.

Notes

1. Davor Rogić, "Vi ste nas pitali: Bojim se pobačaja, što da radim" [You asked us: I am afraid of abortion, what should I do], *Svijet* [World], September 1958, unpaginated.
2. Ibid.
3. Morokvasić, "Sexuality and Control," 199.
4. Massino and Penn, *Gender Politics*, 5.
5. Clements, "Birth," 4.
6. Public art and architecture also fed into the idea of nation building. See, for example, Idiceanu-Mathe and Carjan, "Architecture."
7. Attwood, *Creating the New Soviet Woman*.
8. Ibid., 150.
9. Mead and Ghodsee, "Debating Gender," 18; Constantinescu, "How Women Made," 40.
10. Batinić, "Motherhood."
11. Ramet, *Three Yugoslavias*, 2.
12. Ibid., 3.
13. Ibid.
14. Curtis, *Yugoslavia*, 113–114.
15. Simić, *Soviet Influences*, 136.
16. There is no true consensus on the number of war casualties, and the estimation of those data have been in discussion and contention for the past eighty years. Jozo Tomasevich offers a thorough exploration and examination of these issues in his book *War and Revolution in Yugoslavia, 1941–1945: Occupation and Collaboration*.
17. Tomasevich, *War and Revolution*, 749.
18. Ibid., 750.
19. Ibid.
20. Batinić, *Women and Yugoslav Partisans*, 4.
21. Ibid., 5.
22. Ibid., 217.
23. Simić, *Soviet Influences*, 54.

24. Ramet, *Three Yugoslavias*, 163.
25. Batinić, *Women and Yugoslav Partisans*, 4.
26. Ramet, *Three Yugoslavias*, 164.
27. Ibid., 185.
28. Ibid., 603.
29. Ibid., 1.
30. Kardelj, *Pravci razvoja političkog sistema*, 119.
31. Ibid.
32. Ramet, *Three Yugoslavias*, 28.
33. "Za bolji život radnice majke" [For the better life of the working mother], Žena danas [Woman today], March 1946, 15.
34. "Novosti" [News], Nova Žena [New woman], July 1946, 7.
35. Breznik, *Population of Yugoslavia*, 35–36.
36. Batinić, *Women and Yugoslav Partisans*, 221.
37. Drapac, Constructing Yugoslavia, 206.
38. Ibid., 20.
39. Antić, "Pedagogy of Workers' Self-Management," 180.
40. Ramet, *Three Yugoslavias*, 5.
41. Westad, "Balkans," 358.
42. The gradual process of decriminalizing abortion began with the 1951 penal code and the 1952 Federal Law establishing the guidelines for performing medicalized abortions. "Krivični zakon" [Penal code], *Službeni list Federativne Narodne Republike Jugoslavije* [Official gazette of the Federal People's Republic of Yugoslavia] (hereafter, *Službeni list*), vol. 13, March 1951, 184–224; "Uredba o postupku za vršenje dozvoljenog pobačaja" [The law on the procedure for performing allowed abortion], *Službeni list* 4 (January 1952).
43. "General law on abortion," Službeni list 20 (March 1969); "Constitution of the Socialist Federal Republic of Yugoslavia with a constitutional law to enforce Constitution of the Socialist Federal Republic of Yugoslavia," Službeni list 9 (February 1974).
44. Kirin and Blagaić, "Ambivalence," 45.
45. Duda, "Uvod," 10.
46. Vlajo, "Designing a Socialist Man," 15.
47. For a recent account on the feminist movement in that context, see Lóránd, Feminist Challenge.
48. Sklevicky, "More Horses than Women," 70; Sklevicky, Horses, Women, Wars.
49. Bonfiglioli, "Belgrade, 1978," 84.
50. Gudac-Dodić, "Domestic Violence," 147.
51. Švab, Rener, and Kuhar, "Hajnal's Line," 432.
52. Milićević and Marković, "Srpska istoriografija," 145.

53. Božinović, Žensko pitanje, 158.
54. Dobrivojević, "Planiranje porodice," 83–98; Drakić, "Termination of Pregnancy," 533–542; Pavičević, Na udaru ideologija.
55. Pavičević, Na udaru ideologije, 186.
56. Ibid.; Dobrivojević, "Planiranje porodice u Jugoslaviji."
57. Drezgić, "Policies and Practices," 191.
58. Dobrivojević, "Za željeno roditeljstvo," 119–132; Dobrivojević, "Planiranje porodice u Jugoslaviji"; Pavičević, Na udaru ideologija, 186.
59. Drezgić, "Policies and Practices," 191.
60. Lukić, "Introduction," 165.
61. Miljan, "Seksualna revolucija."
62. Bonfiglioli, "Belgrade, 1978"; Lóránd, Feminist Challenge.
63. Nakachi, *Replacing the Dead*, 3–4.
64. Ibid., 4.
65. Grossman, *Reforming Sex*, 198, 213.
66. Ibid., 213.
67. Kligman, *Politics of Duplicity*, 33.
68. Ibid.
69. Grant, "Introduction," 5.
70. Starks, *Body Soviet*, 4.
71. Grant, "Introduction," 3.
72. Bernstein, Burton, and Healey, *Soviet Medicine*.
73. Bren and Neuburger, *Communism Unwrapped*; Ferber and Hutton Raabe, "Women," 407–430; Heitlinger, "Framing Feminism," 77–93; Hrešanová, "Psychoprophylactic Method," 534–556; Roman, "Gendering Eastern Europe," 53–66; Fidelis, "Are You a Modern"; Marks and Savelli, "Communist Europe"; Vargha, *Polio*.
74. Iacob et al., "State Socialist Experts," 146.
75. Marks and Savelli, "Communist Europe," 11–12.
76. Vargha, *Polio*, 74.
77. Brunnbauer and Taylor, "Creating," 301.
78. Albanese, "Abortion and Reproductive Rights," 10; Gal, "Gender," 256–286; Kligman, Politics of Duplicity; Heitlinger, Reproduction, medicine; Heitlinger, "Framing Feminism," 77–93; Harsch, "Society, the State."
79. Harsch, *Revenge of the domestic*, 11.
80. Reagan, *When Abortion*, 1.
81. See Westad, *Global Cold War*; Dockrill and Hughes, *Palgrave Advances*; Leffler and Westad, *Cambridge History*. In the latter, see particularly Bradley, "Decolonization," 464–485.
82. Connelly, Fatal Misconception, 5, 82.
83. Solinger and Nakachi, "Introduction," 14.
84. Bonfiglioli, "Feminist Translations," 240–254.

85. Perks and Thompson, "Introduction," 1.
86. Ibid., 4.
87. Iriye and Saunier, Palgrave Dictionary, 459.
88. Bayly et al., "AHR Conversation," 1463.
89. Established by Clarence James Gamble in 1957, the Pathfinder Fund was an American humanitarian organization that was prolific in both its distribution of contraceptives within developing countries and its work with those same countries to improve the efficacy of contraception. Unlike in other countries where the fund applied contraceptives to decrease population numbers, the need for contraceptive application in Yugoslavia was stated as being simply to decrease the number of abortions. Bernard, "International IUD Programme," 163–177. Other similar philanthropic agencies were also established. These were either bilateral, like the US Agency for International Development (USAID) or the American International Development Cooperation Agency, set up in 1961 by President John F. Kennedy, or multilateral, like the United Nations Population Fund (UNFPA), created in 1969. Major American foundations, such as the Population Council or the Ford and Rockefeller Foundations, also played a crucial role in funding the work of international multilateral and bilateral organizations.
90. Portelli, "What Makes Oral History," 56.

1

Establishing a Legal Landscape of Reproductive Regulation, 1945–1953

Abortion is harmful to society and society should fight to stop it. However, what gives society the right to fight against abortion? A society that abandons pregnant women and mothers with children to fend for themselves does not have the right to ban abortion. Women are leaving their homes in greater numbers and involving themselves in work and public life. For them, another child symbolizes a setback in their overall quality of life. They fear this so much that they will snuff their strongest instinct, the instinct of motherhood, to get an abortion, disregarding the law, illness, and death. That situation cannot be fixed merely by a law against abortion. When a woman is certain that she will have everything she needs during pregnancy, birth and breastfeeding, and that her children will have everything they need, when she sees that even after pregnancy her quality of life will not be affected, then women will abandon abortions.[1]

The main effort in our fight against abortion is our Five-Year Plan. The fight for the Five-Year Plan is the fight for socialism, and the fight for socialism is the fight for a better life. Then we have to bolster women's desire to fall pregnant, give birth and rear children. Our laws are the most progressive.[2]

Franc Novak

In 1945, the CPY prepared to govern a land burdened by population-related challenges. Novak captured the early postwar context aptly in the passages above. Like many of his contemporaries, he identified the double-edged sword that the Yugoslav state faced. As in other countries, the party was concerned about the war losses and demographic developments that signaled declining birth rates in the future, along with labor shortages. The problem was obvious: the CPY required more people to work and to build, to reproduce more citizens, and ultimately to carry forward the socialist cause. And it needed to plan ahead. The party's immediate obligations were to rebuild infrastructure, to reinvigorate agricultural production to feed the population, and then eventually to break all external dependencies by making the economy prosperous and self-sufficient. Running parallel to those obligations, the young administration aimed to unify the Yugoslav people and forge its own path for the newly communist country. The party-state apparatus anticipated future population growth that would be fueled by an increase in quality of life for all and that would fulfil the socialist dream of exponential growth in production.

In this chapter I analyze the ways that the state wielded federal legislation to influence private decisions about sex and fertility in line with evolving party requirements. In the first section below, I analyze the 1946 constitution, described patriotically at the time as "the first of its kind in free Europe," for the document sought to unify the Yugoslav people and to justify the party's recent assent to power, while appearing progressive, modern, and benevolent.[3] The constitution and the subsequent gendered laws that aimed to realize it afforded health and work protections for women during pregnancy and motherhood. In the second section, I argue that the 1951 penal code, which decriminalized abortion in some instances, reveals a new era in the state's pursuit of socialist utopia in postwar Europe. The state viewed the decriminalization of abortion as a way to distinguish the Yugoslav way from the Soviet way, since the Soviet Union's penal code still considered abortion a criminal act.[4] I examine legislation and expert debates and testimony that led to legislative change, alongside the women's press, which served as a transmission medium reaching a widely dispersed audience of women. Through periodicals, the AFŽ reported extensively on measures that reminded women of their expanded maternal duties, while failing to report on legislation that liberalized women's access to legal abortion. The state's pronatalist sentiment may not be evident in legislation, but it certainly is in propaganda.

In the wake of the catastrophe of WWII, how did the state reconcile its pronatalist intent with its explicit agenda of women's liberation? The administration adapted its position on population size, growth, makeup, and distribution between 1945 and 1989 in response to domestic requirements and international trends. For example, as demographers and government leaders from all over the world began considering population growth an issue that stemmed from the Global South and threatened the resources of the whole world, the Yugoslav state started to assess its own population demographics and distribution through that lens.⁵ Kosovo, for example, presented the Yugoslav government with concern. Though population growth had slowed over time, as it had in the rest of the country, the region's natality was still higher than all the other republics and autonomous provinces. The state and its demographic experts believed that the people of Kosovo and Metohija could never be truly uplifted if they were still having so many children.⁶ Underlying this, however, were religious and ethnic issues that came to eventually define the nationalist civil conflict of the 1980s and 1990s. This chapter centers on an earlier period when the seeds of future population policy and planning were sown. From the end of WWII to 1953, the year of Stalin's death, the state established a legislative foundation that was more pronatalist than scholars and contemporary commentators have previously acknowledged. The state was not passive in population matters. For example, demographic research came to be a significant aspect of the state's strategy to combat population devastation and to legitimize its pronatalist and population control policies. The Second World War left Europe grappling with population matters, and states employed policies concerning contraception, abortion, and pronatalism in subtle and not-so-subtle ways to manage widespread losses in population and infrastructure.

Through reformed reproductive legislation, the state prepared to enter the private lives of its citizens, a common move in the postwar era. The relationship between the state and society has been key to studying reproduction globally. Scholars studying state interventions into private lives have argued that states deeply affected women's options in private life and their decisions to obtain abortions through other, illegal methods.⁷ Newly socialist states enacted legislative changes early in their rule with family and reproductive codes evolving to follow the Soviet example. For the most part, lawmakers imbued legislation with pronatalist sentiment to varying degrees. In analyzing these processes in Czechoslovakia, Alena Heitlinger divided pronatalist policies into three categories: coercive measures that limited women's access to abortion and/or contraception, facilitative measures associated with the social protection of motherhood, and positive measures associated with fiscal incentives and rewards.⁸ Writing about a later period in Romania, Gail Kligman explains that states often combined such factors. Legal provisions in that country compensated families for "fulfilling their patriotic obligation to raise and educate children for the nation" and rewarded women for taking up their "predestined roles as workers, wives and mothers."⁹ Romania's 1966 law Decree 770 concerning prohibition of abortion, which Kligman designated one of the most "repressive pro-natalist policies known to the world," banned abortion in every instance except in the case that the mother's life was in danger, leading many women to seek help from backyard abortionists or self-aborting.[10] Prior to this law, Romania had fairly liberal abortion laws. By contrast, from the outset of the postwar period the Yugoslav state offered women social protections through legislation along with recourse to legal abortion.

The women's press represented a key factor in shaping the consciousness of ordinary women regarding their own fertility and in modernizing the citizenry. Complemented by imported foreign press and periodicals for women, Yugoslav women's magazines were a weekly or monthly presence produced and published by national, regional, and local arms of the AFŽ and its successors and financed by a combination of membership and subscription dues, fundraising campaigns, and the CPY.[11] The first periodical published by the state was *Žena danas* (Woman today), published between 1936 and 1953. The republic of Croatia published the extremely popular *Žena* (Woman). Published between 1957 and 1992, it had first operated under the title *Žena u borbi* (Woman in battle) (1943–1956). Editors initially intended for the magazine to be aimed at the everyday woman worker, mother, and housewife; however, the magazine evolved into an academic journal after 1967. Slovenia's *Naša Žena* (Our woman) began publication in 1941 and remains in circulation today. *Zora* (Dawn) was the periodical of AFŽ Serbia, Belgrade, and was in circulation between 1945 and 1961. The Bosnia and Herzegovina chapter of AFŽ in Sarajevo published *Nova Žena* (New woman) between 1944 and 1971. Available throughout Yugoslavia, *Svijet* was published in Croatia as a popular fashion, entertainment, and lifestyle magazine. Originally (between 1926 and 1936) a magazine aimed at the elite fashionable woman, it dealt widely with the question of women's emancipation in Yugoslavia. The magazine returned to publication from 1953 to 1994 and bore the mark of socialist ideology, focusing on matters of entertainment, family life, childcare, and pregnancy, as well as fashion. It introduced advice columns and began to engage more explicitly with housewives, mothers, and workers.

The state's endeavors to modernize the economy paralleled its aims to modernize the people, shaping the citizenry into the New Yugoslav Man and Woman. Communist leaders promoted unification that transcended historical, ethnic, religious, and geographical divisions to reach a modern communist ideal. The New Yugoslav Woman would ideally be politically minded, employed and educated, and atheist or at least discreet in religious belief; her appearance would reflect the latest Western fashions. The state did not suppress expressions of ethnic dress, music, and dance. In fact, in 1945–1946 the women's press swelled with images celebrating local dress and customs. In line with Terry Martin's argument about Soviet policy, the new government promoted what he called an "ostentatious" show of nationality in dress, cuisine, and music while demanding conformity in politics and economics.[12] Though only civil marriage would be recognized under the new legislation, for example, couples were free to marry again in religious institutions after their civil vows were formalized. When the press reported on new marriage legislation, reporters praised the state for its tolerance while encouraging women to aspire to rid themselves of religious marriages, which, according to one observer of the Bosnian *Nova Žena*, make "fools of [Moslem] women."[13] Although ethnic dress was embraced in early issues, designs and samples of more modern attire began to dominate the women's press from the early 1950s.

The Yugoslav state's efforts were at once progressive and problematic, promoting modern notions of gender based on cultural hierarchies in an ethnically, religiously, and culturally diverse state, efforts that took place in various ways across central and eastern Europe. Women's bodies, in the literal and symbolic form, presented an ideal space for gendered modernizing tactics. Writing about Romania, Kligman argues that "Marxist-Leninist regimes embraced scientific rationality as a means of legitimizing their modernization strategies; especially in Romania, the body was the favored vehicle through which success would be achieved."[14] Kligman explains that "race, gender, and ethnicity were all to be homogenized, as were spatial and other distinctions. Each body was to be molded into a productive member of the socialist masses."[15] Of course, the reality of this ambition played out differently across national contexts in Europe.

Scholars diverge regarding the Yugoslav state's intentions, as well as the AFŽ's unfolding role in negotiating state directives and party propaganda. Several historians, including Jelena Batinić, Ivan Simić, and Chiara Bonfiglioli, have explored early Cold War gender policies in Yugoslavia. The historian Ivan Simić argues that the party installed fresh gender policies not to simply "reinforce patriarchal ideas" but rather with the purported intention to improve the lives of Yugoslavs under a socialist system.[16] Even so, the new state was a powerful and not entirely benign entity. Batinić attests to the power of the party in that the "embryonic apparatus" of the WWII partisan movement evolved into a "full-fledged communist regime after the war."[17] The regime, she explains, used propaganda to design and disseminate its idealized version of womanhood in the postwar world.[18]

Scholars disagree about the agency of female communists operating within state-socialist women's organizations. Nanette Funk argues that European state socialist women's organizations were "transmission belts" for party agendas.[19] Simić concurs. Because the government was undemocratic, argue Simić and Funk independently, whatever agency women exercised within a segregated women's organization was limited.[20] Bonfiglioli suggests that communist women exercised a large degree of autonomy within the AFŽ during wartime and that throughout the Cold War era, communist women promoted women's emancipation within the AFŽ by way of literacy campaigns, access to work, and political participation.[21] To be sure, AFŽ activists and the women's press were not monolithic entities, and their relative evolutions were not linear. Communist women negotiated state directives, local issues, and personal ideologies on a daily basis. Nevertheless, through the women's press, AFŽ activists labored to fulfill their part of a larger mechanism of aggressive state-led modernization. During this period, the women's press was a testament to a collective yet heterogenous drive by communist women to work toward a common national goal. I emphasize that the AFŽ worked as a conduit, not necessarily as a transmission belt, between the federal and republic bureaucracies and the people. Writers combined reportage of state directives alongside efforts of local women. I also spotlight the enthusiasm that editors, journalists, and columnists held for the communist project, especially in the germinal years.

Constituting Equality: The New State, Women-Workers and the 1946 Constitution

The new party-state wielded reproductive politics and propaganda much as it did as a communist movement during WWII. While its wartime goals were to depose the monarchy, drive out foreign occupiers, and win national liberation for the Yugoslav people, the government's new goal was to unify Yugoslavs irrespective of long-standing regional, ethnic, socioeconomic, and religious divisions. In their campaigns during WWII, male and female partisans discouraged women from having children, as this could hamper women's wartime efforts. After national liberation, the CPY envisioned a new ideal. Batinić argues that the partisans had a long tradition of using motherhood, not fatherhood or parenthood, to package their social expectations. This in itself was not a unique exercise, as the well-documented case of the New Soviet Man and Woman springing from representations of 1920s Russia reveals.[22] Communists shaped the political ideals of womanhood and motherhood in line with changing political priorities alternatively "guarding women *from*" pregnancy during WWII when *partizanke* served in significant combat and strategic roles, through its first postwar decade during which the state "turned into a guardian of parenthood," promoting motherhood.[23]

The women's press played a significant role in representing the new Yugoslav people as one citizenry, working toward a collective goal, in the transition from war to reconstruction. In 1945 the ideal Yugoslav woman tilled the soil of the new socialist land, reinvigorating that land for agricultural production (figs. 1.1 and 1.2). She was celebrated for her role in the revolutionary war and praised for the sacrifices she made for her people and Tito. This was also the case around central and eastern Europe, such as in Romania, where military attire and workers outfits were a common feature of female depictions in the immediate postwar years.[24] Bulgaria's *Zhenata Dnes* (Woman today) and the Hungarian *Asszonyok* (Women) were public forums for the transfer of ideas.[25] Through regular "news from the Soviet lands," authors encouraged Yugoslav women to aspire to that example. Cover imagery relayed visions of national unity, while content disclosed local narratives.

Gendered representation in other socialist states followed similar trajectories, even though their legislative frameworks differed. Analyzing the Romanian *Femeia* magazine, the only media outlet targeting women, Sorana-Alexandra Constantinescu argues that the state used magazines as propaganda, deploying "stereotypical views of womanhood, [weaving] them together with ideological ideal images and the necessities of State planning, in order to create in the minds of the audience an image of women."[26] In Romania, a notable shift in representation of women occurred around the time of Ceaușescu's assumption of power in 1965, wherein "images of burly tractor drivers and plain-looking textile workers" were replaced by "images of female laborers [who] became increasingly beautified and glamorous."[27] As was the case in Yugoslavia in the early 1950s with the break from Stalin, "glamorization of the female laborer signified a new stage of socialism. Like the cosmetics and fashionable dresses advertised in department stores and magazines, the glamorous, modern worker signified progress without sacrifice" and signaled a shift to a more progressive socialist style, much like that of the Yugoslav state.[28] In Romania, this was coupled with blatant pronatalist policies, which was not the case for Yugoslavia.

While *Femeia* was one of two publications specifically aimed at women, Yugoslav women had access to a variety of magazines that were regionally specific, as well as limited international fare in the later decades. AFŽ chapters employed a hierarchical and cyclical propaganda model through the women's press to encourage women to participate in postwar reconstruction efforts. The press was largely intended for consumption by ordinary women, since communist leaders believed that "uplifted women read the daily paper, not women's periodicals."[29] The federal periodical *Žena danas* provided an example for republic and district publications. Editors relayed images and messages of communist party women as leaders, ushering in a new generation of educated, employed, and enfranchised women. Over time, the periodicals came to include more content about entertainment and fashion, even including dress patterns in the

Figure 1.1 *Naša žena, glasilo protifašistične ženske zveze* (Our woman, the newsletter of the antifascist women's union), no. 2–5, 1945.

Figure 1.2 *Naša žena, glasilo protifašistične ženske zveze*, no. 10, 1946.

back of each magazine.³⁰ Reporting on Yugoslav women's attendance at national and international conferences on the status and social position of women set the tone for local activists, who in turn reported on district meetings where local village women received information about their legal rights. Above all, the AFŽ viewed women's health as central to the overall uplifting of the Yugoslav woman, as seen by the oft-repeated instruction to women's press editors nationwide: "Health content has to take top billing."³¹

Regional magazines espoused national unity and equality, while reporting on the local situation. For example, in Bosnia and Herzegovina, where long-held ethnic animosities had led to wartime civil conflicts, authors represented women fighting side by side and rebuilding side by side. Authors blamed "foreign fascists" for pitting historically warring people against each other to unify citizens against a common, sometimes fictional, external foe.³² In the very first issue of the Bosnian *Nova Žena* (New woman) after liberation, Dušanka Kovačević, the influential Bosnian prewar communist and then AFŽ politician, wrote about the lead-up to the Bosnian AFŽ first women's congress: "At the congress, Serbian, Muslim, and Croatian women will talk about their children who together are freeing their country, about their collective tasks, about Serbian women who are gathering seeds to give to the charred Muslim villages, about Muslim women who bring gifts to hospitals and are dying in camps for freedom. Our unity will be the most beautiful gift for the women of the congress, to our young country, for her happiness and future."³³ To ameliorate ongoing tensions and to refocus people toward the task of rebuilding, regional papers utilized idealized scenes of cooperation. Furthermore, periodicals dubbed women's participation integral to the success of the rebuilding effort as the partisans had with women's wartime contributions during the revolutionary battle. Authors invoked narratives that, like the one above, positioned Yugoslav women in a long line of loyal fighters, whose efforts would translate into prosperity for future generations.

The 1946 constitution represented an important milestone for the newly minted ruling communist party. Party officials viewed constitutional change as an opportunity to unify Yugoslavs, to liberate women from enduring systems of oppression and inequality, and to justify their new regime to the population. The historian Rory Yeomans argues that Yugoslav women did not legislatively exist prior to the 1946 constitution and that the constitutional change reflected a political necessity to unite Yugoslav women.³⁴ Prior to 1946, women labored under total legal, economic, social, and educational disempowerment. Women became enfranchised only in 1945; partisan women, in 1942 with the Foca Ordinance; they were unable to participate equally in education and employment, and discriminatory inheritance laws kept female children from inheriting land.

Socially conservative rhetoric held that women should remain in the home, bearing children and taking care of the household. Under the new constitution, the state constructed the identity of the New Yugoslav Woman: she was now an educated voter (votes could be cast "regardless of sex, nationality, race, creed, degree of education or place of residence"), a politically minded worker, and a mother who could rest easy knowing that her female children would be guarded by the state, a privilege previously reserved solely for male children.[35] However, instead of fostering equality in all spheres of life, the constitution saddled women with the dual responsibility of worker and mother.

The party promoted constitutional change as reward for its female supporters, *partizanke*, who were loyal during the war. Since women were implored to participate in antifascist resistance through military participation, it promised women equality with their male comrades once they took power: "The people's revolutionary victory brought about measures to annul the domestic enslavement of our women and to ensure their active and full engagement in social and cultural life."[36] The content of the women's press in these early years emphasized the fulfilment of the state's promise to women that they would be rewarded with the right to vote and equality with their male comrades after the sacrifices they made during the war. The editor of the federal AFŽ periodical *Žena danas*, Blaženka Mimica, wrote with patriotic sentiment about these constitutional changes, describing how the editors searched for this declaration of their equality with men in the constitution with anticipation, "as we were not entirely certain where it would be written." They claimed, however, "We were certain that it would be there because we know that our people, women now included, fought for that declaration and for full democracy."[37] Readers were to understand that the state was building a new Yugoslavia and that women would be a central part of that vision. Through rhetoric that included women under the definition of citizen, the state also distanced itself from its predecessors.

Section 24, article 4, of the 1946 Yugoslav constitution that pertained to the rights and duties of citizens, ratified equality of the sexes. Legislating gender equality was a common move in the socialist world, according to Kligman, who argues that equality was among the "fundamental ideological tenets of socialist states."[38] Yugoslav women fought in the revolutionary war, "determined to dissolve their earlier bleak position, and their young socialist country rewarded them by assuring their equal membership in society."[39] Of the new constitution, the communist leader Mitra Mitrović opined that "if it is at all possible to confirm that old saying that the culture of one country can best be characterized by the legal position of its women, then in terms of its political standing, our new republic of Yugoslavia has risen above all other European countries, apart from USSR."⁴⁰ Mitrović was a prewar communist and held a number of leadership roles during the war, including as editor of *Borba* (Battle), the party's newspaper. She was married to Milovan Djilas, party ideologist as well as a member of the AFŽ central committee and the Serbian Republic's government after the war. In the same speech, Mitrović explains that gender equality is an expression of modernity, describing Yugoslavia as a "civilized country." She pegs equality between men and women as a unique aspect of socialist modernity, unlike its Western capitalist equivalent.⁴¹ Tomšič argues that Yugoslav women would only reach equality with men if they followed the Soviet model through revolution and transformation of the entire society.⁴² According to Simić, the state based post-WWII gender policies not only on the Soviet example but also on wartime gender policies.⁴³ The government firmly aligned itself with the Soviet Union and within the Eastern Bloc and, more importantly, as opposite to, or separate from, the West.

In step with Soviet policies, the Yugoslav state reinforced women's maternal roles, anticipating their eventual return to maternal responsibility. It helped create a public image of women as "naturally" predisposed to motherhood. Mitrović, who regularly championed state ideology, wrote that the constitution had eliminated the "old notion that called the duty of motherhood, women's most sacred duty. Instead, the party has turned its attention to the ways that the state can protect mothers and children, since maternity is something that women would not and could not rid themselves of."⁴⁴ According to Simić, from the end of the war, "Tito inseparably tied womanhood with maternity," with women's biological duty eventually surpassing their duty to industry.⁴⁵ The headlines, visual imagery, and focus of reporting reoriented women's roles and returned them to motherhood (figs. 1.3, 1.4, and 1.5) from the late 1940s, in a similar way to what occurred in Romania in the mid-1960s. Women workers held rights alongside responsibilities to the state that allowed women to "serve their natural role as mothers, along with their responsibilities to their state as workers."⁴⁶ Writing in 1946, Mimica underlines the link between motherhood and women when writing about socialist responsibility: "When we talk about women's equality, we have to talk about motherhood as those two are closely linked. The notion of woman cannot be separated from the notion of mother."⁴⁷ Because family policies were gender-specific, the primary parent was always the woman.

The constitution's gendered language and sentiment saddled women with additional responsibilities explicitly demarcated within social protection articles. Women became the primary focus of the state's social protection policies, including maternity leave, health care, and childcare to support their dual positions in society. Although legislators may have framed these as benefits

Figure 1.3 *Naša žena, glasilo protifašistične ženske zveze*, no. 11, 1950.

Figure 1.4 *Naša žena, glasilo protifašistične ženske zveze*, no. 6, 1948.

Figure 1.5 *Naša žena, glasilo protifašistične ženske zveze*, no. 5–6, 1950.

of socialist citizenship, gendered laws—maternity leave rather than parental leave, for example—left women solely responsible to take up such social protection policies. Policies operated in tandem with an impetus to work outside the home, which the state also presented to women as a benefit of being a Yugoslav. Writing about Eastern and Central European socialist nations broadly, Massino and Shana Penn argue that "although women were legally recognized as men's equals, protective legislation restricted women from participating in certain jobs, and gender-specific family policies—such as maternity leave—reinforced rather than challenged essentialist notions of gender."[48] While the state promoted legal changes as supportive of gender equality, as testament of the state's modernizing mission, and a sign of the Yugoslav state's close link to the Soviet Union, these legal measures set women up for a complex task of juggling domestic and work responsibilities. In analyzing Romania's *Femeia* magazine, Massino argues of Romania that "the ability to successfully combine the role of worker, wife, and mother was the most important quality of a modern woman.... By presenting the modern woman as someone who could 'do it all,' the state sought to transform women's multiple burdens (or roles) into something validating and ennobling."[49] Conversely, fatherhood, Batinić observes, does not appear in the constitution, and if men are specifically referred to, it is in their roles as "proletarian laborers, shock-workers, and revolutionary heroes."[50] While the bureaucracy presented the constitution as serving to "dissolve women's domestic enslavement," that did not entirely come to fruition.[51]

Furthermore, though the constitution endorsed national unity and equality, the state's reporting on the constitution reveals a constructed ethnic and cultural hierarchy. Spanning the women's press, authors uniformly describe Slovenian women as the most advanced and Albanian women as the most culturally backward. Authors connect being advanced to being educated, atheist, and urban, and "culturally backward" peasants should aspire to reach that ideal. In the Serbian magazine *Zora* (Dawn), Albanian peasant women of Kosovo and Metohija, known as *šiptarke*, are represented as grateful to Tito for giving them their freedom: "One can often hear how a *Šiptar* woman, with contentment, says 'Thank you Tito for freeing us.'"[52] "Kosmet women,"[53] the author writes, work tirelessly to rebuild their new country because they are so pleased to be gaining enlightenment.[54] The term *Šiptar* was a transliteration of the Albanian *Shqiptar*, which Albanians have historically used to call themselves. Although used before the war, *Šiptar* was adopted by the CPY after 1945 in the pursuit of national unity to name Yugoslav Albanians. Since the 1960s, Albanians in Yugoslavia have agitated for official rhetoric not to use *šiptar*, but rather *Albanci*, or *Albanians*, to recognize national over ethnic identification. The term *šiptar* in Serbian, Croatian, Macedonian, and Slovenian has since acquired a derogatory meaning, associating Kosovo Albanians with racial and cultural inferiority.[55] AFŽ activists were also focused on different types of women within an urban or rural area. They wanted to promote the "enlightened"—meaning literate, for the most part, but also women who were on board with the messages being disseminated around the areas—women to positions within the leadership of the AFŽ, so they could help "uplift" others.[56] The authors of the women's press describe the process of disseminating information throughout the country as a civilizing mission. The state employed multiple efforts—press, conference, teams, lectures, and multiday workshops—which, they claimed, "penetrated even the most remote (zabačeno) villages and have become integrated in the masses."[57] Authors in the Bosnian magazine Nova Žena (New woman), write that all Bosnian women are now included through the constitution in the same standards as Serbian and Croatian women.

Reporting on the constitution suggested that the New Yugoslav Woman was educated or at least literate, able to partake in communist politics and society, and able to pass on socialist ideology. Literacy was a key campaign during the first few postwar years as communist leaders encouraged women to set up and participate in "reading groups" and intensive literacy workshops to learn to read and write (fig. 1.6 and 1.7). However, illiteracy was rife among the population. In 1948, 25 percent of the population over the age of ten was illiterate, with vast regional differences. Slovenia's illiteracy stood at 1.1 percent, while Kosovo's was almost 57 percent.[58] Literacy rates differed greatly by sex, too, and they did not improve over the first five years after the Tito-Stalin split. Comparing the 1948 and 1953 censuses, illiteracy rates for women over fifteen years of age increased slightly from 36.7 to 38.1 percent, while men's illiteracy decreased from 16.2 to 14.9 percent.[59] By 1961, demographers observed reduced rates of illiteracy (9.9 percent for men and 28.8 percent for women).[60] Literacy campaigns targeted women in particular because illiteracy was higher among women than men and because women, in their role as homemakers and mothers, were the primary educators of the future socialist generation. Literacy courses, run by local chapters of the AFŽ, were often delivered alongside courses regarding motherhood and domestic hygiene, which inadvertently perpetuated gendered divisions within the home.[61]

Women's magazines convey the state's ideal hierarchy in their characterization of women in their efforts to rebuild and learn. Reporters often called for unity yet highlighted cultural hierarchy. In the first issue of Nova Žena, the reporter Jela Bicanić proclaimed solidarity among Mostar Muslims, Serbs, and Croats, and wrote that "for Muslim women, who had previously been in the most difficult social position and who were the most backward, battle has created a

Figure 1.6 Unknown, "Žene Jugoslavije u izgradnji socijalizma" (Yugoslav women in the construction of socialism), AFŽ Arhiv, https://www.afzarhiv.org/items/show/224.

Figure 1.7 Unknown, "Analfabetski kurs" (Literacy course), AFŽ Arhiv, https://www.afzarhiv.org/items/show/181.

new Muslim woman—fighter, warrior, worker, learner. Muslim women have not only helped bring our people to unity, they have also experienced their own rebirth."[62] In Mostar, at one of the local AFŽ meetings, the women of Mostar—Serbian, Croatian, and Muslim—were observed "working together."[63] However, the author's commentary on the meeting's atmosphere demonstrates the perceived hierarchy between the three representative groups: "At those meetings, we read in the eyes of old Muslim women the desire to beat their backwardness. We see Serbian women listening intently to the descriptions of the Constitution, and we hear the Croatian women discuss it."[64] In line with interwar reporting, the reporter designates Muslim women as targets of civilizing missions, while Croatian and Serbian women lead the way.

The women's press established not only an ethnic hierarchy but, more importantly, a class one. If the New Yugoslav Woman lived in a village and worked the land, her family should aspire to what Pavičević defined as "urban-family models."[65] Visual cues supported the conflation of ethnic and class hierarchies. From reporting in the magazines, it becomes obvious that leading communists perceived that city women had already achieved a sense of modernity and shed their local ethnic dress and other markers of backwardness in the process of urbanization. As we can see in figures 1.6 and 1.7, village women were women who were not modern as they had not yet divested their particular ethnic dress and, presumably, customs.

Soon after the constitution came into effect, the state ratified legislation aimed at regulating private family life, human reproduction, and industry in the pursuit of socialist utopia. Legislation aimed at keeping women in industry incentivized motherhood in combination with employment outside of the home. The structure and content of laws changed over time, as did their public and private aims. By 1947, the state began strengthening constitutional benefits through laws that gave women more rights at work while pregnant or breastfeeding. Subsequent family and labor policies, underpinned by the new Yugoslav constitution, strengthened the veneer of women's equality. Like the 1946 constitution, subsequent laws were modelled on or were a direct copy of Soviet laws (not until the 1951 penal code is there a departure).[66] Between 1946 and 1951 the state enacted legislation both to support women's reproductive capabilities and to offer them resources to combine work with motherhood.

Laws on marriage, inheritance, and legitimate children served two purposes in that the state was able to offer women freedoms and assurances that had previously been unavailable to them, while also serving its own goals of unity and population growth. The law on marriage declared that only secular marriage would be recognized from 1946, while permitting people to have religious weddings after the secular one.[67] The state had taken marriage under its wing because the old church regulations were outdated and treated women unequally, returning "to a married woman her human dignity."[68] This law, along with laws protecting illegitimate children, buttressed the secularization processes at the core of socialist ideology, while also uniting women under a legal framework that aimed to protect them against spousal abuse. Legislation that assured citizenship status and state protections for illegitimate children also served to fuel population growth by decreasing abortions, as women did not have to fear that their illegitimate children would be excluded from citizenship privileges. In her study on the 1944 Soviet Family Law, Mie Nakachi analyzes the language used in the laws and the ways in which reproductive policy translated into political realities, arguing that "the law instituted the legal category of 'single mother' and vastly increased the number of illegitimate births. It forged a new set of gender relations."[69] The move to support single mothers was not universally or uniformly undertaken across Europe. Single motherhood remained taboo in Poland even though out-of-wedlock children were granted the same rights as those born within marriages from 1950, while the German Democratic Republic followed the Soviet cue and officially supported single motherhood from the 1950s and encouraged it to be socially acceptable.[70] Inheritance laws enabled women to prosper economically and to assure that future generations of women would be able to seek independence from male family members.

Laws protecting mothers at work appeared supportive of equalizing men and women within the workplace yet were not entirely pragmatic. Similar parental benefits laws were enacted across Eastern Europe, in countries like Poland, Hungary, Romania, and elsewhere, which provided incentive for women to remain workers even if they took a break to take care of children. In 1948 the state passed a new "law on the protection of employed pregnant women and breastfeeding mothers."[71] The law set out more specific stipulations aimed to uphold constitutional promises. It allowed for ninety days' maternity leave, to be taken forty-five days before the due date and forty-five days after birth, at full pay based on her earnings during the previous month of work. The division of forty-five days on each side of the due date was strict in the first place; however, after debates this was at the discretion of the employer. The law also allowed breastfeeding breaks for mothers of children under eight months old. To receive full maternity pay, women had to have been employed for the preceding six months prior to taking maternity leave or for at least eighteen of the preceding twenty-four months, meaning that women would need to have been employed for most of the postwar period. Breastfeeding breaks were to be permitted every three and a half hours and were to be limited to two hours including travel to and from her baby. There were also provisions to fine employers who did not accommodate these stipulations.[72] A revised social security law also included some provisions for working parents, to help them mitigate working life and parenthood. Working fathers could take up to fifteen days' paid caregivers' leave to help care for an ill child, while breastfeeding mothers who fell ill would also have their incomes topped up through social security.[73] Traveling to and from babies for breastfeeding two to three times throughout the day would essentially mean that women could be away from work for four to six hours in the working day. As new mothers were limited to shorter shifts and were not permitted to work in the evenings or overtime, this did not equate to a practicable solution. This was compounded by the dearth of childcare services available to women close to their work.[74] Women across Eastern Europe were expected to return to work at some point after birthing children, but in reality their return would not be for a number of years (usually daycare services started at three years), and if women were to return to work sooner, they would not have the state support to do so because of a lack of childcare institutions to service their family needs.[75]

Beyond improving the daily lot of Yugoslav women, the state also aimed to affect future demographics by influencing women's reproductive decision-making. This was not necessarily an effort enacted by only men to dominate women, as many leading communists were women and they shared these sentiments. The state was also concerned with getting the population healthy, and women's reproductive health was one aspect of that motivation. While the state needed women to permanently step into the workforce, it also needed families to be prepared to have more children—if not immediately, then in the near future. Socialist leaders considered these policies as a temporary stopgap measure. Party supporters, like Novak, were convinced that socialism would inevitably lead to an increase in the quality of life for its citizens, so much so that there would be no need to regulate reproductive matters. In the state's vision, Yugoslavs would eventually simply want to have more children.

The Yugoslav state wanted to deliberately reconstruct the Yugoslav family, ridding it of its "economic and domestic functions, which the Communists considered artificially imposed by capitalism and harmful to the 'primary' functions of the family: procreation, education in communist values, and participation in the construction of socialism."[76] Recent historical and social scientific scholarship has emphasized the significance in both Eastern and Western Europe of the family for state policy and as a vehicle for buttressing conventional family values and ideals. Kligman argues that the post-1945 laws constituted a political restructuring of the family, which was crucial to the construction of socialist transformation.[77] A two-child family structure became the norm in Poland through an entanglement of religious and state-socialist strategies. Natalia Jarska and Agata Ignaciuk argue that in the Polish context, "limiting family size became embedded in understandings of modernity, related to economic considerations and conditioned by women's individual goals."[78] Socialist states mobilized the family unit to undertake modernizing efforts; the Yugoslav example demonstrates how nuanced the state's approach to family life could be.

Since after the 1950s Yugoslavia sat somewhere between East/West divisions, the Yugoslav example helps us to see that the political restructuring of the family was not only a socialist tool. Angela Y. Davis argues that the specific social, medical, and political context of postwar Britain helped to construct the notion of motherhood, especially in terms of the role of women in the family and the relationship of the family and the state.[79] The Yugoslav family was not meant to exist in isolation from society, but rather, "all of its problems could be solved only through the collective."[80] True Yugoslav socialism, for Tomšič, was the incorporation of socialist principles into the everyday life of the family, to create a family that was unlike the Soviet family and unlike any Western permutation.[81] Taken together, the Yugoslav constitution aimed to affect the bodies and actions of women workers, and it aimed to change the face of the Yugoslav family. Women were expected to exit the home and to take up employment in industry, administration, and service, while their domestic domain was to be divvied up and delegated to other women.

Women were essential to the national economy and to the building of Yugoslav socialism. Ideologically coaxing women from the home, ostensibly freeing them of their domestic demands, meant that they could do the state's bidding. Their presence in the workforce, in significant numbers, was paramount to the success of Yugoslav socialism, and the state depended highly on their ability to distance themselves from domestic commitments that the state was professionalizing, such as laundry, cooking and cleaning, and childcare. By endorsing the building of an entire workforce to carry out domestic tasks, the state went some way to achieve this goal. The state opened training facilities for child educators and caregivers that would see women (almost exclusively) in those roles. However, it also had to ensure that women would follow what many commentators called their "natural imperative" to become mothers, while remaining in full-time employment in industry. There was a fine line between encouraging women to eschew their domestic duties to join the labor workforce and simultaneously paving the way for them to take up their reproductive duties. This was not unique to the Yugoslav context. Legal provisions compensated Romanian families for "fulfilling their patriotic obligation to raise and educate children for the nation" and rewarded women for taking up their "predestined roles as workers, wives and mothers."[82] The uneven distribution of power and labor within the home continued to be an issue throughout the socialist period in Yugoslavia, despite these early legislative measures. Tomšič platformed the issue at every public domestic and overseas event, arguing that through modernization and development, women would eventually be freed from domestic duties to engage more meaningfully in public and political life, which in turn served society and the state. Women's positions within a socialist society also became the benchmark of global economic development, another aspect of state foreign interests.

From the late 1940s, the women's press demonstrates that the state had already begun to reposition itself geopolitically, all the while asserting its position as a leader in women's rights, gender equality, and economic development and as a model for developing nations. As colonized Asian and African countries struggled for independence, authors charged them to "revolt against their oppressors" in pursuit of "freedom and a better life."[83] As the state began talks with those countries regarding a neutral nonaligned position, the women's press echoed the potential to align with countries such as Burma, "which does not belong to any bloc and keeps fighting for peace."[84] Throughout the early 1950s, the women's press features articles about socialist movements in Asian countries, where leading communists were "looking to socialism to increase the rights and position of their women."[85] In 1949, as a result of the Soviet-Yugoslav split, Yugoslavia was expelled from the Women's International Democratic Federation (WIDF), the main organization federating antifascist, communist, and socialist women. Chiara Bonfiglioli argues that to "overcome international isolation, Yugoslav representatives established their own bilateral connections with women's organizations internationally, particularly in the Global South," of which the communist women's leader Vida Tomšič was a key figure.[86] Tomšič wrote about a goodwill mission that she was a part of that was sent to India, stating that "though Indian women are represented in parliament, they are still not equal. This, as we know from our own experience, will take them a long time to reach."[87] At the All Indian Women's Conference in Madras, India, in 1952, AFŽ representatives were praised for their work on women's equality and the building of socialism through legislative measures, which the Indonesian delegates called "priceless" examples for their own communist-building project.[88] Communist women constituted essential cogs in the state's international positioning, and the women's press served as a sound communication tool for domestic audiences.

1951 Penal Code: Divesting of "Unscrupulous Charlatans"

The laws and policies that the state enacted between 1946 and 1951 constitute one half of the narrative about the establishment of reproductive regulation in socialist Yugoslavia. Pronatalist laws that fostered women's dual roles of mother and worker were amplified by the state's early restrictions on abortion access. The provision of services for birth and abortion was stretching the state's resources, and women were stuck in a cycle of relying on abortion for controlling fertility and remaining in work. After the CPY took power and before the Tito-Stalin split, the state only permitted abortion on very strictly defined medical grounds. This criminal code was based on the Soviet code that at the time banned abortions; it initially stated that women who sought illegal abortions would be punished along with abortionists.[89] New laws, the subject of the following section, changed this legislation, expanding the reasons that a woman might seek an abortion and not punishing women in the case of illegal abortions. Laws that facilitated reproduction and those that permitted individuals' fertility control after 1951 worked in tandem to buttress the state's position as a modern and progressive state, especially regarding gender politics and the rights of the woman worker.

Scholars of women's health have aptly asserted that legality and the medical provision of abortions have been only part of manifold factors that influenced women's ideas about sexual health.[90] Abortion practices and methods have always existed outside of legal or medical systems, long before the first legalization of abortion in Europe. In much of eastern and southeastern Europe, those methods, generally practiced by local wise women, continued to thrive throughout much of the socialist period over more hygienic and safe medical methods despite the legalization and availability of abortion in many instances.[91] Liubov Denisova explains that, in rural Russia, the combination of long-held and enduring stigmas around abortion, the lack of access to medical facilities, and the unaffordability of "legal" abortions meant that women's use of nonmedical abortion methods and abortifacients continued and thrived.[92] This was certainly the case for Yugoslav women who, as I elaborate in the next chapter, procured their own abortions using feathers, knitting needles, and homemade remedies that served as abortifacients. The state argued that nonmedical abortion methods jeopardized women's physical health, especially their reproductive systems.

The many negative effects of illegal abortions were reason enough to design the new penal code; however, the change also presented the state with an opportunity to move away from the USSR. The medical historian Ana Antić argues that the use of psychotherapy and psychoanalysis were both examples of "Yugoslavia's early experimentation with alternatives to Stalinism."[93] She argues that even as psychotherapy was applied to reeducate pro-Stalin dissenters in the wake of the Tito-Stalin split, it also signified a "connotation of personal growth, development, and ultimate liberation."[94] Legislation and policies having to do with reproduction were, as psychotherapy was, important for Yugoslavia's ideological evolution and geopolitical positioning. During the first postwar years, the state followed the Soviet example and viewed abortion as a social disease, reasoning that women sought abortions because their material circumstances inhibited their desire to have another child. The state's solution was twofold: criminalize abortion, as in the USSR, and then initiate a five-year plan designed to improve the quality of life to passively remove a woman's need for abortion. However, over the span of the next five years, criminalization failed to have the desired effect, and women continued to self-abort or to procure illegal abortions in other ways, just as they had for generations. The party leadership had hoped that by the end of the first five-year plan, due to end in 1952, the overall quality of life would have improved enough to dissuade women from wanting to terminate their pregnancies. As the state began moving away from the Soviet Union, it aimed to design its penal code so as to safeguard women's health by consulting with medical experts about the best ways to proceed.

Yugoslav medical experts argued that early restrictions to abortion access had to be overturned because they did not dissuade women from terminating their pregnancies. According to Novak, during the period 1946–1950, women, in fact, sought "abortions in higher and higher numbers and many were started by criminal means."[95] He reasoned that "[health professionals] know that those types of abortions are much more harmful to the health and welfare of the woman, as compared to legal abortions. We also want to highlight that this phenomenon has economic impacts as well. The maintenance of healthcare facilities, cost of medication and sanitary equipment on the one hand and women's decreased working potential on the other, present a substantial material loss."[96] Concerns over women's health are conflated with concerns about the economy and the financial losses that abortions generated. To more effectively safeguard women's health as well as ensure state goals of decreasing abortion rates and increasing numbers of women in industry, gynecologists felt compelled to argue for decriminalization.

In the pursuit of a new framework for abortion care, medical experts contributed significantly to legislative debates. According to Miroslav Perišić, the state's overarching strategy for changing tack in terms of its geopolitical orientation was the "insistence on expert opinion," as "knowledge was awarded over ideology."[97] In 1949, the Ministry of Justice, prompted by the impending expiration of the penal code, sought feedback from medical and legal experts and administrative bodies regarding the current state of abortion in Yugoslavia and suggestions for legal amendments. In 1950, the Committee for the Protection of Public Health and the Directorate for the Protection of the Health of Mother and Child responded and came up with some initial conclusions: "Abortion is a dangerous operation, even when it is performed under the most ideal circumstances. Its performance should be limited to only those situations where the mother's life and health is at stake."[98] Experts agreed that abortions should only be undertaken in clinical settings, preferably hospitals, by specialist gynecologist-obstetricians and that requests for abortions should be regulated by a commission appointed by the Ministry for Public Health. Experts also agreed that the law must change because "strict legal restrictions do not dissuade women from seeking abortions, they simply turn women over to unqualified 'unscrupulous charlatans.'"[99]

Medical and public health officials disagreed, however, on whether regulations should allow provision for social indications for legal abortion. Many experts offered patriotic reasons for their objections. A report from a group of gynecologists submitted to the committee states that all gynecologists and forensic pathologists from the medical universities of Belgrade, Zagreb, and Ljubljana who have worked in the area of abortion law, believe that

> to legalize non-medical social indications would be a sign of moral and material calamity, a sign that we are incapable of securing the existence of all of our citizens. In our country, that certainly is not the case. In our socialist Yugoslavia there do not exist socio-economic reasons that would justify the need for having an artificial abortion. Our country is improving economically, and her essence is the care and protection of mankind. The average standard of life has really increased in the hardest of situations, and besides that, the country offers help to pregnant women, women in labor, mothers and children, such that social indications are unfounded.[100]

By pinning all hopes to the state's legislative overhaul, many experts refused to acknowledge that legal changes to protect all citizens, including mothers, would not automatically equate to immediate and significant changes to material circumstances of families and the overall state of the country five years after total war. Furthermore, by attesting that Yugoslav women did not have socioeconomic reasons to apply for an abortion, attendee consultants implied that women who wanted to abort for nonmedical reasons would be shirking their maternal roles and responsibilities to the state. Although the 1951 Penal Code did concede to "other justifications," the code and subsequent laws were vague, leaving the final decision to case-by-case interpretations.

Gynecologists also debated whether eugenic indications should be taken into account, and the resulting conclusion against them demonstrates the state's experts' desire to remain popular in the public eye. While discussion notes only medical grounds, not racial, ethnic, or cultural considerations, proponents agreed that the potential well-being and health of future generations, as well as the strain that ill or "defective" children have on the health system and society, should be considered. Novak argued that "for our health system to be able to focus on the protection of healthy children and on improving the lives of capable children, it should not be burdened with children of unwed mothers, or of mentally or morally defective mothers. Furthermore, the number of abortions that would be completed under such circumstances is not great and would not impact on our natality."[101] Another gynecologist's report argues that abortion should be done in cases of hereditary illness, because those illnesses "represent a burden for the individual, their family and the socialist society."[102] While the state wanted to take on the responsibility of caring for its citizens, it also debated which citizens were worthy of its protection. The report authors conclude that including provisions for eugenic indications would be tricky and potentially unpopular.

The state and its medical experts had wanted to dissuade women from seeking abortion by increasing the overall standard of living and by alleviating some of women's fears having to do with pregnancy and labor. However, in pursuit of preserving women's reproductive capabilities long-term, many gynecologists argued that birth was not something that should be forced onto anyone. Ultimately, lawmakers wrote in provisions for pregnancy and birth care, and, in theory, institutions were meant to be established for the provision of services for pregnant women and birthing mothers. The state made massive efforts to educate the public about the advantages of hospital births over home births and of proper diet and exercise during pregnancy. However, the state's efforts had not yielded the results it had hoped for due to resource limitations. In 1952, in Montenegro, for example, there were no full-time permanent gynecologists to serve approximately seventeen thousand women in their reproductive years. In Kosovo and Metohija, there was one serving almost forty thousand women.[103] When discussing medical justification for legal changes, one expert argued that "we understand that even with the best clinical assistance, no-one can guarantee a woman a good birth, and women should be protected from the distress that may come from a difficult birth, which tend to lead to complicated operations. In any case, a woman should be given the choice to decide whether she wants to gamble with her life, because we know that many pathological presentations are likely to arise again in future pregnancies."[104] This choice, this excerpt hints, may also preserve women's future birthing capabilities. The debates outlined so far demonstrate that medical professionals felt the weight of a dual responsibility to their patients and to the state.

In 1951, the state enacted new abortion legislation.[105] Article 140 effectively decriminalized abortion, permitting abortion to protect the "life and health" of women and in "other justified cases," leaving indications for legal abortion fairly unclear.[106] In early 1952, the Ministry of Justice passed a federal law, "The law on the procedure for performing allowed abortion," setting out new stipulations for its regulation.[107] Pregnant women had to present their case to a commission composed of a gynecologist, internist, and a social worker who would determine the outcome of their request. Each hospital and clinic had its own abortion commission and the makeup of these commissions varied, with some hospitals including a psychologist. This bureaucratic arrangement was fairly common across Eastern European nations at the time, and the public nature, biased views, and uncertain outcomes made women want to avoid commissions if they could. Kateřina Lišková wrote that, similarly to Yugoslavia, abortion commissions were "despised" by Czechoslovak women, and they, too, were very keen to avoid them if possible.[108] The Ministry of Public Health expected physicians to take turns serving on commissions. Physicians could only perform abortions in clinical settings, preferably hospitals, and physicians should have specialist training in gynecology and/or obstetrics. The state expected women to pay for the procedure, which was also common in other socialist states. After the penal code change, they were no longer liable to prosecution if they procured their own abortion outside of the medically regulated system, although unlicensed practitioners were still liable for prosecution if caught.[109] In "exceptional circumstances," women's abortion requests could be approved if "the woman finds herself in particularly difficult material circumstances, or if, due to the birth, her health and livelihood would be affected in other ways, such as if the child was born with significant physical or mental defects."[110]

Immediately after the Ministry of Justice passed the law that regulated what constituted legal abortions, heads of hospitals, clinics, and gynecological departments raised concerns about how to interpret the guidelines.[111] The main issue appeared to be with indications for approving abortion requests. In the lead-up to the writing of the new law that would regulate abortion provision, experts submitted extensive lists of indications that could be used to approve women's requests for abortion. Instead of offering these as an appendix to the law, experts suggested that specific indications, especially social indications, be left out and that each abortion committee be permitted to approve requests under social indications on a case-by-case basis and at their discretion. Although the report's author does not offer any reason, he writes that examples of social indications should also not be made known to the public.[112] That legislators planned not to release information about social indications implies that they may not have trusted women with all the information pertaining to their personal health, and they must have feared that women might falsify records or provide false information to obtain abortions under these circumstances. If women did not know about the possibility of applying for an abortion based on their financial or material circumstances, they might also be less likely to even apply for an abortion in the first case.

At the behest of the Gynecological-Obstetrics Division of the Medical Association of Croatia, the Council for the Protection of Public Health and Social Politics of Yugoslavia held a conference in May 1952 to discuss aspects of the law and to refine guidelines. The conference sought to clarify where abortions could be done, by whom, and under what circumstances.[113] Some of the issues that attendees raised concerned material conditions and human resources. For example, abortions were only to be performed by specialist gynecologist-obstetricians, which attendees agreed was appropriate. However, there were few gynecologist-obstetricians practicing across Yugoslavia, as I discuss in the next chapter, which meant that the ones who were qualified would be overburdened under those regulations. Some experts took issue with the fact that there was no plan for the provision of contraception in the regulations, which would inevitably lead to women's reliance on abortion as a birth control tool.[114] Debates between experts, held at elite conferences and through correspondence, directives, and reports, did not invite the opinions of the consumers of those services; nor was the breadth of these deliberations communicated to women.

The women's press did not report on the penal code and subsequent law regulating abortion care, which highlights the state's pronatalist intent, or at least the fact that experts did not rate women's abortion access as highly as their access to maternity care.[115] Forums between AFŽ and party doctors in the early 1950s demonstrate how significantly the issue of infant mortality and maternal health monopolized discussions about women's reproductive health and legal rights. In one such consultation in 1951, whose minutes run for more than seventy pages, the provision of abortion care is mentioned only once by a female gynecologist who says that "so far, no one [in the room] has touched on the topic."[116] According to the minutes, nobody else speaks about it or responds to her point, focusing instead on various strategies for increasing maternal and infant health among the peasantry.

Even after abortion was decriminalized in some instances through the 1951 code, the legislation remained invisible within public discourse. It was not until the mid-1950s that abortion came to be featured in the women's press. Even then, however, the reporting differed significantly from that of the reporting on maternity leave and marriage laws. While the state charged the AFŽ to educate women of the country about the new rights and privileges that the state had given them in work and society, there was no such directive in the case of the new abortion regulations. When authors did discuss abortions, it was to say that abortions were dangerous, no matter who conducted them but especially so when completed by "unlicensed individuals." In practice, this was also related to rural *vračare*, fortune tellers who were also healers in the countryside (the topic of the next chapter). The women's press presented information about abortion through cautionary tales. Physicians wrote that "short- and long-term consequences of abortion, included issues with fertility, ongoing pain and discomfort and a changed rhythm of menstruation."[117]

In fact, it was around this time that women's magazines began featuring more and more children on their covers, and the enclosed articles began to take on a more instructional tone regarding child rearing. This happened in Yugoslavia much sooner than in Romania and other Eastern European states because Yugoslavia distanced itself from Stalin much earlier than other socialist states. In Romania, while in a period of relative abundance, "articles on family, parenting, and maternal and infant health proliferated in the magazine after the passage of Decree 770 in 1966, which recriminalized abortion."[118] While initially, Yugoslav magazine covers displayed women working the land or in other professions, from the late 1940s through the early 1950s, images of children and mothers begin to dominate covers (table 1.1). In *Zora*, we see a steady rise in images of children and mothers from 1946 to 1950 with a sharp increase in 1951 and 1952, potentially pointing to an overall stabilization of the society and economy. This is reflective of proportions in other republic magazines, too. Children playing outside, with female caregivers and statues of women holding babies, dominate covers. Photographs of women within the pages of the magazines often depict them with children. Children are either being cared for by their mothers or by professional female caregivers. Birth rates were increasing at the time, so editors may have been acknowledging the demographic increase.[119] The state highlighted for women the social protections

Table 1.1 Number of covers of children or mothers with children per year.

	1946	1947	1948	1949	1950	1951	1952
Zora	0 of 8	2 of 9	3 of 10	3 of 10	4 of 10	8 of 10	8 of 10

that came with Yugoslav citizenship, at the expense of informing them about new abortion legislation and services.

The Yugoslav state's legal changes between 1946 and 1951 officially prompted the transfer of abortion out of the hands of illegal abortionists and into the state-regulated hospital setting. Along with other aspects of reproduction, such as contraception, pregnancy, birth, childcare, and child development, the state deemed abortion a medical procedure. The procedure operated within legal and institutional regulations and bureaucratic processes and procedures, and it was subject to the personalities and power of individual medical professionals. Legal changes placed the procedure within the bounds of scientific innovation and medicine, leaving medical professionals responsible for the lives of women who underwent abortions. While the law still played a part in regulating access to the procedure, control lay with the medical community, who could ultimately decide a woman's fate.

Conclusion

Legislative change encouraged women to seek employment outside the home while planning for the inevitability of motherhood. According to legislation, women could take control of their own fertility and choose when to have children, enjoying the protection of the state and its medical institutions. Legislation was passed quickly and with extensive expert consultations. Nevertheless, new regulations were not clear enough to avoid broad interpretation and confusion. Furthermore, the approval criteria for legal terminations were poorly defined, leading to inconsistencies in decision-making and an increase in illegal abortions. Legislation was also gender-specific, which meant that it was not parents who were burdened with the need for inevitable childbearing, but rather, it was mothers.

Laws that facilitated reproduction for working mothers underwent numerous revisions and interpretations. The state introduced child benefits aimed at supplementing family incomes, allowing women more freedom to use state childcare facilities. However, this inadvertently led to many factory directors dismissing women or not hiring them in the first place.[120] Mothers received money for nutrition during pregnancy, for child-rearing equipment, monetary awards that increased with every child, and regular child benefits until the child turned seventeen years old. In 1954, a working-class family of four would be entitled to 25 percent of their monthly income from child benefits.[121] The state said that women had to use their benefit to pay for kindergartens, but in fact there was subsequent decline in the use of these childcare centers because many women left work to look after children instead.

While the state sold legislative change as an expression of its commitment to women's equality, state propaganda told a different story. Presumably fearing that women would have even more abortions, authors of the women's press did not trust women with the information they needed to make more informed choices about their own bodies and fertility. The state also faced a complex task of addressing falling natality and realizing its own promises to women. In theory, the state protected women's ability to terminate an unwanted pregnancy. In reality, the state's propaganda set out new expectations for Yugoslav women, whose rights of citizenship authors injected with pronatalist sentiment, if not necessarily coercive measures to ban birth control measures. This strategy allowed the state to remain benevolent in the eye of the public and the international community. It also constructed a gendered citizenship for Yugoslav women who were expected to wear many hats in the building of the new Yugoslavia: continue to work outside and inside the home, birth children, and arrange care for them, while also becoming educated participatory citizens of the new socialist state.

Legislative and constitutional changes coaxed women to adjust to the new requirements of the state. Scholars of gender and political theory have established that while the overarching ideology of gender equality may have formed the foundation of socialist policy and public rhetoric in state-socialist European countries in the twentieth century, it was not effectively established within the private, everyday domestic sphere.[122] Yugoslavia was no exception. Starting from the 1960s, magazines bemoan the failure of legislation and rhetoric to penetrate the life of the everyday Yugoslav family. One such article in 1963 from *Svijet* highlights that many communist officials thought that declaring women equal citizens and ensuring their rights to education and employment would naturally trickle through into the domestic space. However, as the article states, equality had not yet been established within the home.[123] Despite the state's legislative and institutionalizing efforts to equalize women's roles with those of men in the new Yugoslav society, patriarchal attitudes prevailed, and private behavior was slow to change. In fact, as one Croatian gynecologist in her sixties at the time I interviewed her told me, "The patriarchal tendency smoldered over everything. It still does."[124]

The state's self-constructed image as a progressive, modern, and benevolent entity serving the needs of its female population extended beyond legislation and into the arena of institutions. Public officials continued to use the weight of medical and scientific authority to enact the state's agenda to both rehabilitate the population and unify Yugoslavs beyond ethnic, religious, and class divisions. As I have argued in this chapter, the state used the propaganda machine to shape social expectations, even if laws themselves appeared benevolent. The Yugoslav example demonstrates the subtle ways in which pronatalist messages could be conveyed to large audiences of urban and rural women. While Polish, Hungarian, and certainly Romanian public policies having to do with family, reproduction, and women seemed outwardly to be in stark contrast to those of Yugoslavia, there are certainly comparisons to be made across a variety of different socialist countries in the wake of WWII. Yugoslavia continued to do so with more vigor in its pursuits of medicalizing reproduction through institutions designed both to serve the myriad health care needs of the population and to civilize and colonize its citizens.

Notes

1. Arhiv Jugoslavije [Archives of Yugoslavia] (hereafter, AJ), 636-22-7/1949, Savet za Narodno Zdravlje i Socijalnu Politiku Vlade FNRJ [Council for public health and social policy], Odeljenje za zdravstvo [Department for health], 22–23.
2. Ibid., 28.
3. Ana Božić, "Šta nama osigurava ustav?" [What does the constitution assure us?], Zora, February 1946, 2.
4. Batinić: "The old prewar Penal Code, which permitted pregnancy termination only for strictly defined medical reasons, remained in effect until 1951. For illegal abortions, the old code stipulated harsh penalties: imprisonment of up to five years for the pregnant woman and ten years for the person who assisted her. This was in sharp contrast to the Partisan practice during the war, when abortions were routinely performed by Partisan physicians. Once in power, the communist leadership could have been reluctant to decriminalize pregnancy termination on request in part because it initially modeled its policies on those of the Stalinist Soviet Union, where abortion was prohibited at the time; the Yugoslavs moved toward a more liberal policy only after the Tito-Stalin break. A decree promulgated in 1952 made "sociomedical" reasons acceptable grounds for pregnancy termination." Batinić, *Women and Yugoslav Partisans*, 217–218.
5. Macura, Problemi politike obnavljanja stanovništva. For more recent historical analysis, see Bracewell, "Women, Motherhood," 27–28.

6. Bracewell, "Women, Motherhood," 27–28.

7. Albanese, "Abortion and Reproductive Rights," 10; Gal, "Gender," 256–286; Heitlinger, Reproduction; Heitlinger, "Framing Feminism"; Harsch, "Society."

8. Heitlinger, Women's Equality, 130.

9. Kligman, Politics of Duplicity, 71–72.

10. Ibid., 2.

11. Majstorović, "The creation of the new Yugoslav woman," 91.

12. Martin, Affirmative Action Empire, 13.

13. Stanka Todorović-Šubić, "Žene o ustavu" [Women on the constitution], Nova Žena, December–January 1945–1946, 11.

14. Kligman, Politics of Duplicity, 12.

15. Ibid., 33.

16. Simić, Soviet Influences, 3, 11.

17. Batinić, "Motherhood," 259.

18. Ibid.

19. Funk, "Very Tangled Knot," 345.

20. Simić, Soviet Influences, 11; Funk, 345.

21. Bonfiglioli, "Revolutionary Networks."

22. Similarities in changes to representation can be found in the Russian example as well because the state constructed a very ambiguous character: "The magazines continued to celebrate women's achievements in the work-place, but held up motherhood as their most important function. They glorified the family, but encouraged the single mother. They insisted that the era of self-sacrifice was over, but demanded self-sacrifice on the part of wives of wounded veterans." Attwood, Creating the New Soviet, 150. This was also not unusual in other parts of the world, as war-ravaged countries required a new workforce.

23. Batinić, "Motherhood," 269.

24. Fidelis, "Are You a Modern," 172.

25. Lóránd, "International Solidarity," 103–129; Ibrosheva and Stover, "Bulgarian Woman."

26. Constantinescu, "How Women Made," 40.

27. Fidelis, "Are You a Modern," 172.

28. Ibid.

29. AJ, 141-9-32/1951, Antifašistički Front Žena Jugoslavije [Antifascist women's front] (AFŽJ), Sekreterijat Centralnog Odbora AFŽ Jugoslavije [Secreteriat of the central committee of AFŽ Yugoslavia], 1951, br 32/1951, "Zapisnik broj 2 sa sastanka sekreterijata centralnog oddbora AFŽ, 31 January 1951" [Minutes 2 of the meeting of the central committee of AFŽ], 3. By "uplifted," communist leaders meant educated, politically literate women.

30. Ibid.

31. Ibid.

32. Bogomir Brajković, "Hrvatice Bosne i Hercegovine" [Croatian women of Bosnia and Herzegovina], Nova Žena, February 1945, 3–4.

33. Dušanka Kovačević, "Pred prvi kongres žena Bosne i Hercegovine" [At our first congress of the women of Bosnia and Herzegovina], Nova Žena, January 1945, 6.

34. Yeomans, "Fighting the White Plague," 389.

35. Section 23, Constitution of Yugoslavia 1946.

36. Blaženka Mimica, "Ravnopravnost u ustavu Federativne Narodne Republike Jugoslavije" [Equality in the constitution of the Federal Republic of Yugoslavia], Žena danas, November–December 1947, 2.

37. Ibid., 1.

38. Kligman, Politics of Duplicity, 43.

39. Veljko Šarić, "Prava i zaštita žene nekad i danas" [Rights and protection of women in history and now], Žena u borbi, March 1957, 3.

40. Mitra Mitrović, "Žena, djeca, brak i porodica u novom ustavu" [Women, children, marriage, and the family in the new constitution], Nova Žena, December–January 1945–1946, 1.

41. Ibid.

42. Simić, Soviet Influences, 26.

43. Ibid.

44. Mitrović, "Žena, djeca, brak," 2.

45. Simić, Soviet Influences, 65.

46. Božić, "Šta nama osigurava ustav?," 2.

47. Mimica, "Ravnopravnost," 2.

48. Massino and Penn, "Introduction," 3.

49. Massino, "Something Old, Something New," 233.

50. Batinić, "Motherhood," 260.

51. Mimica, "Ravnopravnost u ustavu," 2.

52. S. Kovačević, "Rad žena Kosmeta u izgradnji" [Work of Kosmet women in rebuilding], Zora, April 1946, 5. Between 1945 and 1963, the official designation was the Autonomous Province of Kosovo and Metohija. The designation is highly contested at present.

53. The Serbian paper writes "Kosmet" instead of "Kosovo and Metohija." This was a commonly used abbreviation at the time, which was interpreted by many Albanians as derogatory.

54. Kovačević, "Rad žena Kosmeta u izgradnji," 5.

55. Neofotistos, "Cultural Intimacy," 288. See also Neofotistos, "Postsocialism," 884–891.

56. AJ, 141-36-234/1947, Materijali kongresa i organa republika, pokrajina i oblasti [Materials of congresses and republican, provinces and areas], "Consultation between AFŽ and doctors about the issue of protection of mothers and children and in eradicating infant and child mortality."

57. Nada Grkinić-Vukšin, "Žene o svojim pravima" [Women on their rights], Zora, October 1946, 7.
58. Breznik, *Population of Yugoslavia*, 35–36.
59. "World Illiteracy at Midcentury: A Statistical Study, 1957," https://unesdoc.unesco.org/ark:/48223/pf0000002930.
60. Farmerie, "Education in Yugoslavia," 146.
61. Simić, *Soviet Influences*, 136.
62. Jela Bicanić, "Muslimanke u borbi" [Muslim women in battle], Nova Žena, January 1945, 8. "Rebirth" is a common trope when describing Muslim women.
63. Nadžida Hadžić, "Kako radi mostarska organizacija AFŽ-a" [How the Mostar section of the AFŽ works], Nova Žena, December–January 1945–1946, 23.
64. Ibid.
65. Pavičević, Na udaru ideologije, 209.
66. Simić, Soviet Influences, 93.
67. "Osnovni zakon o braku" [The basic marital law], Službeni list 29 (April 1946).
68. Božić, "Zakon o braku vraća ženi ljudsko dostojanstvo." [Law on marriage returns to a married woman human dignity], Zora, March 1946, 5.
69. Nakachi, "N. S. Khrushchev," 42.
70. Jarska and Ignaciuk, "Marriage, Gender," 148–149.
71. AJ, 141-15-81/1947-52, Propagandna i kulturno-prosvetna sekcija [Propaganda and cultural education section], "Iz uredbe o zaštiti trudnih žena i majki—dojilja u radnom odnosu [About the law on protection of employed pregnant women and mothers who are breastfeeding].
72. Ibid.
73. AJ, 25-13-27/1946-1951, Ministarstvo Rada FNRJ [Ministry of Labor of the Socialist Federal Republic of Yugoslavia], Odeljenje za radne odnose, zaštita žena, majki i dece [Department for work relations, protection of women, mothers, and children], Committee for Social Welfare, "Obrazloženje o uredbi o socijanom staranju" [Explanation of the law about social security].
74. Simić and Simić, "'Who Should Care," 145–158.
75. Fodor et al., "Family Policies," 480.
76. Brunnbauer, "'Most Natural function,'" 84.
77. Kligman, *Politics of Duplicity*, 42.
78. Jarska and Ignaciuk, "Marriage, Gender," 142.
79. Davis, *Modern Motherhood*.
80. Mimica, "Equality in the Constitution," 2.
81. Vida Tomšič, "Suvremena porodica i njeni problem" [The contemporary family and its problems], Žena, January 1959, 11.
82. Kligman, Politics of duplicity, 71–72.
83. "U Indiji, Burmi i Malaji" [In India, Burma, and Malaysia], Žena Danas, January 1949, 17–18; "Borba za osnovna prava, za slobodu, za sreću svoje dece" [Fight

for basic rights, for freedom, and for the happiness of their children], Žena Danas, May 1948, 27–30.

84. Marković, "Burma," 9.

85. Krista Đorđević, "Povodom konferencije socijalista Azije" [Regarding the conference of Asian socialists], Žena Danas, February 1953, 9–10.

86. Bonfiglioli, "Women's Internationalism," 446.

87. Tomšič, "Susreti sa ženama Indije" [Encounters with women of India], Žena Danas, December–January 1953, 5.

88. "Sastanak žena Jugo-Istočne Azije" [Meeting of the women of Southeast Asia], Žena Danas, November 1953, 4.

89. Batinić, Women and Yugoslav Partisans, 216.

90. Evans, "Communist Party," 757–775.

91. Denisova, Rural Women, 176.

92. Ibid., 181–182.

93. Antić, "Pedagogy of Workers' Self-Management," 181.

94. Ibid.

95. AJ, 49-39-71/1948-1951, Ministarstvo Pravosuđe Vlade FNRJ [Ministry of Justice of the Federal People's Republic of Yugoslavia], Pravno odeljenje, zakonodavnopravni poslovi [Legal department, legislative affairs], Novak, "Stav ginekologa u pitanju legalnog arteficialnog abortusa" [Position of the gynecologist regarding the question of legal termination of pregnancy], 5.

96. Ibid., 9.

97. Perišić, "Yugoslavia," 292.

98. AJ, 36-27-70/1951, Savet zaštitu majke i dece, materijali delokruga rada saveta za zaštitu majki i dece [Council for the protection of mother and child, materials for the scope of work of the council], Dražen Sesardić, "Odgovor Ministarstvu Pravosuđa o indikacijama za prekid trudnoće" [Response to the Ministry of Justice about indications for termination of pregnancy], 1.

99. Ibid., 9.

100. AJ, 49-39-71/1948-1951, Novak, "Stav ginekologa u pitanju legalnog arteficialnog abortusa," 6.

101. AJ, 36-27-70/1951, Sesardić, "Odgovor Ministarstvu Pravosuđa o indikacijama za prekid trudnoće," 8.

102. AJ, 49-39-71/1948-1951, Novak, "Stav ginekologa u pitanju legalnog arteficialnog abortusa," 7.

103. Žena u društvu i privredi Jugoslavije" [Woman in Yugoslav society and industry], Statistički bilten [Statistical journal], 298 (1964): 77.

104. AJ, 49-39-71/1948-1951, Novak, "Stav ginekologa u pitanju legalnog arteficialnog abortusa," 5.

105. 1951 Penal Code.

106. "The law on the procedure for performing allowed abortion."

107. Ibid.
108. Lišková, *Sexual Liberation, Socialist Style*, 125.
109. "The law on the procedure for performing allowed abortion."
110. Ibid.
111. AJ, 36-27-70/1952, Savet zaštitu majke i dece, materijali delokruga rada saveta za zaštitu majki i dece [Council for the protection of mother and child, materials for the scope of work of the council], "Council for Public Health and Social Politics of the Government FNRJ."
112. AJ, 36-27-70/1951, Sesardić, "Odgovor Ministarstvu Pravosuđa o indikacijama za prekid trudnoće," 6.
113. AJ, 36-27-70/1951, Proceedings from "Konferencija po pitanju predloga za propize o sprovođenju Krivičnog zakona po pitanju pobačaja održana u Komitetu za zaštitu narodnog zdravlja 9-III-1951 [Conference about the suggestions for implementing the criminal code on abortion, held at the Committee for the protection of national health, March 8, 1951].
114. Ibid.; AJ, 36-22-56/1951-1953, Odeljenje za zdravstvo [Department of health], "Referat sa konferencije ginekologa-akušera održane u Zagrebu po pitanju dozvoljenog pobačaja" [Report from the gynecologist-obstetric conference held in Zagreb about legal abortion], May 22, 1952.
115. "Medicinske posljedice pobačaja" [Medical consequences of abortion], Žena, April 1964, 34.
116. AJ, 141 9-32/1951, "Savetovanje centralnog odbora AFŽ-a sa lekarima po pitanju zaštite majke i djeteta i suzbijanje smrtnosti djece" [Consultation between AFŽ and doctors on the issue of protecting women and children and eradicating infant and child mortality in Belgrade], September 13, 1950, 43.
117. Rogić, "Vi ste nas pitali, recite mi istinu o pobačaju" [Tell me the truth about abortion], Svijet, April 1958, n.p.
118. Massino and Penn, *Gender Politics*, 234.
119. Similar increases in representations of childhood and child-rearing in magazines were seen in the USSR alongside the legalization of abortion. See Randall, "'Abortion Will Deprive You.'"
120. Simić, Soviet Influences, 107.
121. Ibid.
122. Kligman and Gal, Reproducing Gender, 5.
123. "Stvarna ili deklarativna ravnopravnost" [Real or ostensible equality], Svijet, March 1963, 4.
124. Jelena Grubič, interview with the author, Zagreb, September 17, 2016.

2

An Infrastructure to Medicalize Reproduction, 1945–1965

Stana—"Where are we going?"
Mother-in-law—"To the barn, where else?"
Stana—"Not the barn, God help me! Let us go to the house."
Mother-in-law—"We have to. That is our custom."
Stana—"I have to give birth in such filth?"
Mother-in-law—"You have to. I did, and so have all of our women. It's what we do."[1]

Dialogue from *Svekrvin Grijeh* [The mother-in-law's sin], 1937

In *Svekrvin Grijeh* (The mother-in-law's sin), a 1937 educational film produced by the Croatian School of Public Health in Zagreb, Stana goes into labor on a busy farm. Despite Stana's appeals to her mother-in-law to take her inside the house to give birth, her mother-in-law shuts them both in a barn, where she is to give birth away from the men of the household, whom we see drinking *rakija* (brandy) at the kitchen table. The birth is brief, and the viewer watches from the other side of the barn, as if hiding behind a cow. The animal's udders and legs frame the shot, likening woman to cattle. Stana dies in childbirth, but her baby survives and is taken care of by her bereaved husband and his family. Sometime later, the mother-in-law attends local seminars about hygiene, sanitation, and safer medicalized childbirth. She learns that hospitals, birthing centers, or at least clean well-ventilated rooms in the family home are a more suitable setting for childbirth than the barn. She also discovers that even the most straightforward birth should be attended by a medically trained professional. In time, her son remarries, and when his new wife gets pregnant, the mother-in-law does not make the same mistake again. Although she does not take her daughter-in-law to the hospital, she, under a nurse's guidance, sets up a clean space inside the house for the birth to take place. She constructs a single bed so that her daughter-in-law could be raised off the ground and reserves fresh sheets and blankets to be used for birthing purposes alone. Her husband protests their daughter-in-law giving birth inside the house, demanding to know why the women are not following the usual custom of birthing with the farm animals. The mother-in-law shakes a fist at him, contending that "these are new traditions," explaining that "better our traditions are destroyed than we lose another life."[2]

The film, which predates the period in question, captures a number of key themes pertinent to this chapter and to understanding the nascence of a socialist reproductive medical system in Yugoslavia after WWII. Though the film dates from the interwar period, it demonstrates the customs and attitudes surrounding births in the countryside. The film hints at the tension between folk customs and medical science during the rise of public health in interwar Europe, and its relevance in the socialist period highlights how open Yugoslav communists were to borrowing from their predecessors when it came to science, medicine, and public health even though they culturally and politically disassociated from them. It also speaks to the Yugoslav state's enduring battle against ethno-medical healing practices.[3] And it reiterates the abiding role of women in both the older and the newer system; it is the mother-in-law, not the husband, who is newly educated in the story. As the film demonstrates, the medicalization of childbirth and reproductive health care prefigured Yugoslavia's time as a socialist state. However, it was after the socialist revolution that the state systematically merged principles of preventive and curative health care with social welfare and health education to create an integrated socialist Yugoslav health service. Even as the state embarked on its own path away from the Soviet Union, it continued to mirror aspects of the health system's structure and governance model beyond the Tito-Stalin split.

This chapter analyzes the institutionalization of women's health care and argues that biomedical health care models constituted modernizing efforts on the part of the state, tracing the state's multilayered approach from 1945 to the mid-1960s. Bearing in mind that the medical service was more fragmentary than comprehensive between 1945 and 1965, what factors drove and hindered the institutionalization of women's health? In those twenty-odd years, medical and public health officials made significant leaps toward establishing an interconnected web of reproductive services across the country, which sat within the larger health care network. Though the state's health agencies fell short of expectations in some ways, particularly in modernizing peasant attitudes and overhauling ethnomedical healing customs,[4] the state's most significant achievement was its establishment of world-class health research institutes that led innovation throughout the socialist period and beyond. Driven by a desire to rehabilitate population health and by its commitment to "brotherhood and unity," the state measured the lives and health of individuals against its agenda to unite Yugoslavs as one socialist people.[5] The state experienced numerous roadblocks on the path to a bureaucratized medical system. Yugoslavia of 1945 was a largely rural country, and health services existed mostly in towns and larger cities. The devastation of war also meant that modes of transport and infrastructure were almost nonexistent, meaning that peasants who lived in remote areas as well as cities could not easily reach doctors' clinics. Bosnia and Herzegovina, Montenegro, Macedonia, and Serbia (including the autonomous provinces of Kosovo and Vojvodina) had an agricultural population of just over 70 percent; Croatia had 62 percent, and Slovenia had the lowest agricultural population of 44 percent. Kosovo alone had a nearly 81 percent agricultural population at the time.[6] As expected, citizens continued to use health treatments outside of the medical system. These practical aspects were coupled with peasants' distrust of medical authorities, who threatened their community healing customs. Rivalries and long-standing animosities between the Ministry of Public Health and the AFŽ also stood in the way of the state's ambitious plans.[7]

The state's fraught relationship with its female citizens underpins this narrative, and the figure of the New Yugoslav Woman highlights the disjuncture between public policy and private practice. On the one hand, the state's measures to bring private birthing and fertility control practices into a biomedical health care system represented the state's commitment to socialist gender equality.[8] If we consider the process of institutionalizing women's health as one that took place over time, the state was in many ways responding to demand, as more and more women utilized legal abortions performed within the medical system. On the other hand, medicalizing strategies deliberately threatened community-based processes that had been passed down generationally woman to woman and censured folk healers, who stood as entrusted community members. These modernizing efforts also strengthened the divide between urban and rural populations. Ethno-medical healing practices were, of course, not without their flaws. However, the forceful nature of overturning those practices demonstrates how intent the federal state was on achieving a unified biomedical model at the near-complete expense of local custom. Furthermore, by devising ways to entice women into biomedical health care institutions, medical authorities inherently questioned women's personal instincts, autonomy, and prior knowledge in pursuit of a bureaucratized service. Ultimately, the idealized image of the New Yugoslav Woman, one who entrusted medical professionals with her reproductive health, would also prove unachievable in practice since promises of medical infrastructure accessible by all women across the country were not reached.

This chapter takes a chronological approach, weighing factors that motivated and impeded the state's medicalization of reproduction. First, I survey the pre-1945 context of ethno-medical birthing, contraception, and abortion practices women employed across the region, some of which survived throughout the socialist period. These healing customs represented one of the main driving factors for the state's efforts to medicalize reproductive health care. Communist officials, like their interwar predecessors, strongly believed that ethno-medical healing practices were to blame for the poor state of women's health and that of their infants and small children. Furthermore, such community-based practices existed outside of the scope and control of state health authorities and represented a threat to state unification goals. The new government anticipated that integrated biomedical reproductive health care would rehabilitate the population and unify and modernize the Yugoslav citizenry. Following the Soviet example, the Yugoslav state constructed a "civilizing mission" to realize its vision of the New Yugoslav Man and Woman and to entrench its political power throughout the regions.[9] I then analyze state strategies to coax peasants out of their communities and into biomedical health services. In section one, I rely largely on published ethnographic accounts of village life throughout the first half of the twentieth century, along with fragments from socialist archival documents wherein concerned physicians and AFŽ activists communicate their observations of women's practices in villages. In section two, I make use of AFŽ documents and the women's press to retrace the propaganda machine in operation, analyzing how the state utilized different communication tactics intended to encourage peasants into the state-led medical system. In section three, I use Ministry of Public Health records to reconstruct its plans for a hierarchical "bureaucratic pyramid" of a health service designed to eradicate peasant practices and to create state-of-the-art research institutions.[10]

As in other twentieth-century states around the world, Yugoslavia's building of its medical infrastructure became part of a broader system of modernizing the nation. Interwar and postwar public health campaigns in the United Kingdom, for example, focused on epidemiology and the establishment of services, as well as promoting newly available health knowledge to prevent disease.[11] Strategies to educate and train staff in the latest scientific methods were also of high importance, particularly when it came to nursing and midwifery. Medicine also offered a mechanism for spreading Western biomedical models around the Global South. Modernization efforts in colonial India brought (usually male) medical experts to the realm of women's health care and brought women into public clinical institutions for their health care, at the expense of (almost exclusively female) "skilled practitioners" with whom women and their families were familiar.[12] When it came to vaccinating against tuberculosis in India, Western medicine clashed with local practices.[13]

Though state authorities claimed to have devised a singular system, Yugoslav medical authorities based their plans for the new socialist medical infrastructure on several examples: the Soviet model at the outset; ideologies and practices from other non-Soviet examples, including global health and humanitarian organizations; and from their own recent past. Kligman asserts that "Marxist-Leninist regimes embraced scientific rationality as a means of legitimizing their modernization strategies."[14] Writing about Stalinist Russia, Frances Lee Bernstein, Christopher Burton, and Dan Healey argue that "science, and medicine, were yoked to the industrialization project."[15] The process of modernization through medicine was a common goal among postwar communists across Europe, and states entrusted medical experts in realizing that project. Kateřina Lišková explains that medical experts in the psychological sciences ushered in the Czechoslovak sexual revolution of the 1950s "from above," which was utilized "by the people below," in a continuation of interwar modernization efforts.[16] The application of science, personified by medical experts, represented a common modernization tactic.

Scholars of Soviet Russia are divided on whether state-led modernization projects aimed to entrench political power across the non-Russian periphery and Russian countryside represented internal colonization or empire building. Traditionally, historians have looked to industrial technologies and infrastructure, such as railways and steamships, to understand empire and globalization.[17] Historians of the Soviet Union have recently begun interrogating the systematic application of biomedical health care in a bid to exert dominance over far-flung regions and their populations.[18] Yuri Slezkine argues that communist leaders deployed colonizing mechanisms in the same way in the Russian countryside as they did in the non-Russian empire, denying the interethnic dimension that typified the dynamic between mainland Russians and the people within the non-Russian peripheries.[19] Placing Kazakhstan at the center of her analysis on Soviet medicine, Paula A. Michaels argues that the state used "medical and public health systems to reshape the function, self-perception, and practices of individuals, both patients and practitioners," in a fashion not dissimilar to the Yugoslav case.[20] Although the Yugoslav state utilized comparable processes to spread its influence, the Russian case reveals potentially sharper divisions between urban/rural and interethnic dimensions than are present in the Yugoslav context. The Yugoslav state did not hold overland or overseas empire-building ambitions, where interethnic elements would have to be neutralized to realign allegiances. Nor was it solely concerned with diminishing the urban/rural divide at home. The state often conflated the two elements, as I demonstrate throughout this chapter, and a clearer demarcation between the two would only arise later in the socialist era.

The state's seemingly altruistic efforts in installing free public health care throughout the country to raise the overall health of peasants and the quality of life of all Yugoslavs did not mean that they did not aspire to those goals without ulterior motives. Melissa K. Bokovoy argues that after the war, the party had to enact land reform measures, at the same time as it had to "find a place in the new state for its peasant allies and build institutions that would bind them to the state."[21] The medicalization of reproduction constituted one such institution-building strategy, one that would enable party officials entry into the private domain of the peasantry. Throughout the first two postwar decades, Yugoslav administrators energetically pursued science-fueled modernization to fulfil their own ambitions to consolidate and entrench power throughout the regions. They also relied heavily on the women's press to disseminate modernizing ideas to readers and persistently shaped the idealized New Yugoslav Man and Woman according to state agendas. Even so, the process also reveals that individuals welcomed, negotiated, internalized, and sometimes rejected new health and social structures at a local level.

Women's Ethno-medical Healing Practices in Pregnancy, Fertility Control, and Childbirth

Scattered ethnographic scholarship on village life in Yugoslavia has produced some knowledge of diverse ethno-medical healing customs that existed within communities. Aleksandar Petrović studied the districts of Rakovica, Serbia, and Banjane, Montenegro, in the 1930s with a focus on peasant life, hygiene, and health, aiming to uncover trends in population health and local practices.[22] During and after WWII, Yugoslav refugees to the US prompted new research into Yugoslav ways of life. The US-based Croatian ethnographer Vera Stein Erlich published the first significant English-language study of village life in Yugoslavia based on research she conducted between 1937 and 1943 by way of interviews and questionnaires.[23] Joel and Barbara Halpern visited and studied villages all over Yugoslavia during the 1970s and 1980s, and the two were prolific in their English-language publications.[24] The Halperns' Western cultural bias likely colored both how respondents engaged with them and their interpretation of evidence. Erlich, on the other hand, lived in Zagreb from 1897 until 1951, when she moved to the US and published *Families in Transition* the following decade. Though she resided in the country at the time of the interviews and surveys, her urban perspective likely influenced her motivations, interactions with participants, and the resulting analysis within the monograph. The project took her almost thirty years to complete. By then, Europeans had experienced total war for the second time; Yugoslavia had survived foreign occupation and civil conflict and had undergone a socialist revolution, followed quickly by rapid industrialization. Inspired by the deveiling campaigns of the 1930s across Yugoslavia, Erlich set out to better understand the nature of the Yugoslav family and women's social position. Through her ethnographic work, she aimed to accelerate the social, economic, and political uplift of Yugoslav women who lived on collective farms, *zadrugas*, across the region.[25] In *Families in Transition*, she frequently highlights the isolating and at times life-threatening nature of women's experiences of pregnancy and childbirth, and in controlling their fertility, to bring the focus on the need for more work to equalize the sexes in village communities.

In the context of reproduction, Yugoslav families depended on local wise women, *vračare*, to help them conceive, to abort unwanted pregnancies, to give birth. In concert with village wise women, couples depended on wisdom passed down generationally, woman to woman, and within extended farming families. However, according to ethnographers, women also often carried their pregnancies without much discussion or preparation for birth or baby's first few weeks; they sometimes birthed alone, though these seem to be peculiar incidents; and birth always occurred in private and away from men.[26] In light of those realities, the state targeted village wise women in an effort to destabilize peasant trust in folk practices.

According to local and foreign ethnographers, pregnancy, childbirth, abortion, and fertility control were all associated with shame and disgrace, and this representation of women's reproductive lives extended state efforts to eradicate or at least decrease ethno-medical healing practices. Folk healing, understood alternately by outsiders as exotic or magical and by communities as "common" and "routine" aspects of daily life, segregated women's reproductive lives from the input of men. Religious beliefs, coupled with regional particularities and long-standing gender divisions, meant that women were largely isolated during birth. Women and their female attendants operated under secret all-female circumstances.²⁷ Since peasants considered birth a shameful and dirty event, community beliefs inevitably led to silence around the topic. Because of connotations of shame, women tended to give birth in barns, as we saw in Stana's case, or in basements or cold storerooms, which were readily available in rural areas.²⁸ This was very much a rural practice as such environments were not accessible in the urban areas, and urban women were able to utilize what limited public health care options existed locally. Women retreated at the first signs of labor to find a place away from other people, especially men, and would give birth with livestock or sometimes alone. In doing so, they avoided befouling commonly used parts of the house, and they avoided alerting others of their condition.²⁹ In some villages, wise women attended the birth, and would visit new mothers soon after birth to give them advice. In many instances, as we saw in Stana's case, family matriarchs would attend to the parturient woman. In Erlich's account, one subject describes finding a sheltered space outside near the family farm behind a wall of boulders where she gave birth alone without making any noise because men were nearby.³⁰ These accounts or anecdotes may very well be extreme examples of practices common to some villagers and village communities in Yugoslavia during the mid-twentieth century. More significantly, however, they point to a collective understanding of pregnancy and birth as furtive women-only events. They also point to the prevalence of patriarchal structures within village families that ostracized pregnant and birthing women, which Erlich highlighted to challenge those systems.

We have learned from ethnographers of Yugoslavia and elsewhere that women held and safeguarded knowledge about fertility control, keeping it secret from male kin and larger communities all while developing their technical skills for ending unwanted pregnancies. The shaping of gendered expectations of female citizens into modern, urban workers was designed to disrupt many of these knowledge links and place those practices within the hands of state doctors. Yugoslav women controlled their fertility usually through abstinence before conception or via abortion after conception, habits that continued into the socialist period. Women used a variety of methods to abort, and according to Erlich, these methods were always quite secretive. Erlich writes that women who procured abortions were seen to be very clever but also magical and therefore worthy of suspicion.³¹ Many of her male respondents adamantly claimed that no one in their villages would ever abort a pregnancy; nor "would anyone even know how to do that."³² The discord between the narratives of villagers points to a segregation of knowledge, and the common response—"that doesn't happen here"—did not reflect practice or reality.

Even so, according to Erlich, when villagers spoke more openly about fertility control, they described different abortion methods. Methods included physical measures, such as lying over a wooden fence or a turned-over trough and rocking back and forth on their stomachs or binding their bellies with ropes and lengths of cloth.[33] They also used herbal remedies made from local roots, such as *kukurek* (hellebore), and herbs or concoctions of brandy and vinegar, which women would drink to induce abortion.[34] Other naturopathic abortifacients include the use of gunpowder, various nitrates, or red mercury sulfide, as well as other herbal concoctions.[35] Women also inserted foreign objects into their uteruses to induce abortion, including sewing needles, goose feathers, and wire.[36] One woman described her self-abortion: she used soap and water to wash every instrument and her own body, after which she folded a length of wire several times to the length of forty centimeters. She then inserted the makeshift tool through her vagina and cervix and into her own uterus and turned it two or three times: "When the wire entered the uterus I knew because up until that point there is not really any pain." Bleeding would continue for about a week.[37] Denisova, writing about abortion in rural Russia, describes analogous practices among women whose pregnancies were still barely noticeable: "Miscarriages were provoked by tightly binding a woman's belly, then pulling robes around it and placing heavy weights on top of it." She writes that "chemicals were used as well to 'improve' chances of a miscarriage, and especially common were gunpowder, various nitrates, kerosene, cinnabar powder (red mercury sulphide), and arsenic."[38] In Yugoslavia, other methods included piercing the uterus using spindles and knitting needles.[39] Though women may have sought the guidance of local *vračare* as they did for many other events in their lives, according to Erlich and the Serbian historian Momčilo Isić, women often procured their own abortions. Eventually, Yugoslav postwar legislation came to protect women from prosecution in such instances, which meant that the only people singled out for punishment were local wise women.

Women, ordinary or wise, were shrewd and fostered shared expertise. The state viewed these practices and the knowledge held by wise women as a threat because they were out of its sphere of influence. Whether intentionally or not, the work of ethnographers advanced the state's case for modernization. Medical professionals perceived ethno-medical healing techniques as threatening to women's reproductive health and future fertility. The state held that such reproductive practices, compounded by widespread poverty, unhygienic living conditions, and terrible nutrition, contributed to Yugoslavia having the highest infant mortality rate in Europe in the first few postwar years.[40] Given that 70 percent of the Yugoslav population were peasants, the communities ensnared

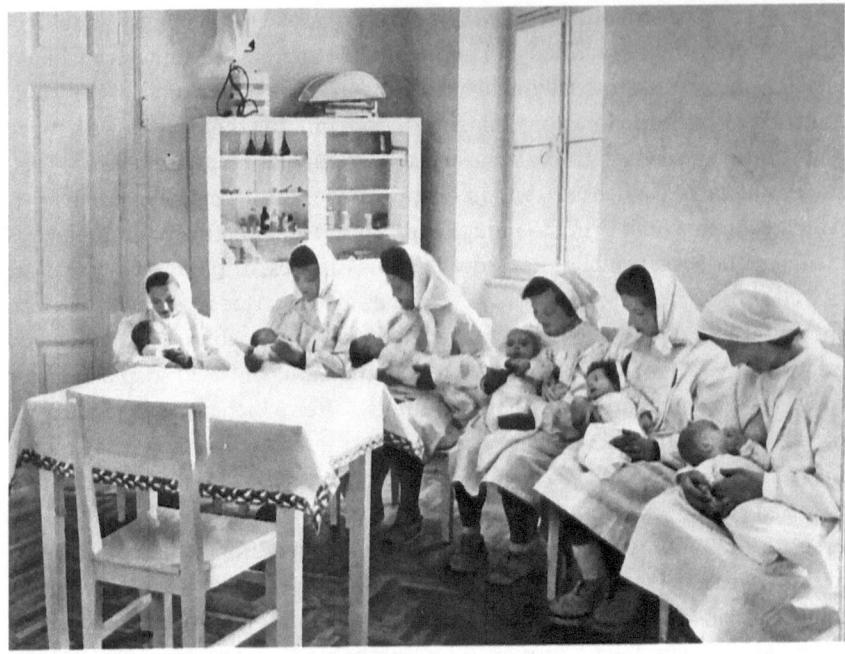

Figure 2.1 Unknown, "Žene Jugoslavije u izgradnji socijalizma" (Yugoslav women in the construction of socialism), AFŽ Arhiv, https://www.afzarhiv.org/items/show/219.

by the methods of local independent wise women constituted a large proportion of citizens outside the control of state services.[41]

As I demonstrate in the following sections, some women and their communities and families vigorously resisted state biopolitics. However, many women also wholly welcomed medicalized procedures, along with the clinical facilities and techniques that the state offered within the realm of free institutionalized health care (fig. 2.1). The opportunity to receive free health care sweetened the prospect of state unification. Abortion numbers are notoriously difficult to track and interpret. However, in Yugoslavia, as regulations permitting abortions expanded, abortion numbers increased. The rise of official numbers might reflect legal changes, whereby women felt safe to seek out abortions through the medical establishment, or it may suggest that clinics and hospitals improved their systems of tracking and reporting abortions. Either way, women were, at least in part, agents in the process of medicalizing reproductive health, especially when it came to abortion care.

"Even the Most Backward Villages": State-Led Modernization and Public Health, 1945–1950

In 1945, Tito and his party prepared to respond to the war's devastation of the land and population. The government's first tasks included delegating responsibility to fixing the issues of population health, rebuilding infrastructure, and planning for the future of an integrated health service. The state mobilized several branches of the government to serve these agendas. To begin the process, the state charged the AFŽ with the task of eradicating local healing customs in favor of state-led medical services. This was an extension of the AFŽ's other duties of helping homeless children and establishing orphanages, tasks that the state gave to AFŽ activists because they saw them as naturally maternal. The AFŽ was an easy choice as the organization already connected the federal administration with the regions and community groups. Given that the prewar medical service was largely destroyed during the war, the state also enlisted the Ministry of Public Health to draw up plans for a new medical system that would soon span the entire country and to work with the AFŽ to reopen hospitals and clinics. The administration also initiated an overhaul to statistical research and analysis. From 1921 to 1939 various religious and municipal local government registrars took on the job of collecting data on births, deaths, and marriages, though their data was patchy and summarized.[42] The new socialist state established an administrative body to launch a science-based and integrated national effort to track demographic data. The state wanted to better understand its populations in terms of quantity, composition, distribution, and health condition. It charged state demographers with tracking natality, morbidity, mortality, and fertility rates across the regions and began gathering data from state hospitals and clinics about women's use of those facilities during pregnancy, birth, and eventually abortion.

The socialist state's interwar predecessors had been dealing with high infant mortality rates and poor maternal health and had made some attempts to medicalize reproductive health care and encourage women to use public health services. Leading physicians, particularly specialists trained in women's health, had already begun the process of medicalizing reproductive care by the early 1900s in Serbia, Slovenia, and Croatia. In 1904 and 1911, Serbs formed two societies to battle high infant and maternal mortality in the region.[43] While *Materinsko Udruženje* (Mother's society) catered mainly to the needs of orphaned children, *Srpska Majka* (Serbian mother) offered medical services to mothers and young children.[44] Zagreb's School of Public Health conducted campaigns to introduce peasants to biomedical health care models and encouraged them to abandon local customs. Presocialist birthing facilities were not always purpose-built. Instead, many emerged in an ad hoc manner springing from facilities aimed to serve a different population.[45] The first bespoke gynecological-obstetric clinic opened in Belgrade in 1923, and by 1939 there were fifty-eight facilities for women's health with 953 beds across Yugoslavia.[46] Though relatively significant, these developments were insufficient in number and geographical distribution, and they lacked specialist professionals trained to provide medical services; this issue hampered those who followed in their footsteps. Furthermore, the health system was already stretched before the war. Prior to 1945, Yugoslav medical administrators identified issues in staff numbers, staff capacity, and the distribution and availability of cadres and services across the regions.[47] Hospital department heads and heads of medical training establishments repeatedly wrote to the wartime health administration even before 1945 to ask for continued and increased funding to support growing demand.[48]

Resources remained thin after the war, and the state instigated various tactics to stretch finances and specialists. Starting from 1946, health administrators sent pediatricians and gynecologists to underserved areas—"into the interior"—where the local populations had no such specialists.[49] Serbia sent 34 of 53 Belgrade-based pediatricians to the regions: 22 to Serbia proper, 9 to Vojvodina, 3 to Kosovo.[50] Their tasks were not only to provide care but also to set up clinics and help local groups get set up for offering services.[51] The ministry also began educating new cadres almost immediately after the war.[52] Combined with the previous administrations' efforts, between 1939 and 1951 public health officials trained 488 new midwives, upskilled 45 general practitioners to work in children's clinics and hospital departments, and educated 40 nurses.[53] The AFŽ was to use what resources it had on hand, and communist women across the country instituted funding campaigns to ensure that services could be opened and women could attend for free.[54] Furthermore, international humanitarian and health agencies, such as United Nations Children's Fund (UNICEF) and the Yugoslav Red Cross, started providing financial aid to support the country's postwar recovery.[55] As the ministry reinvigorated hospitals, the Red Cross donated new equipment and medical resources. The state's early dynamic and manifold efforts kick-started extant measures aimed at rehabilitating population health.

Meanwhile, the state began designing extensive long-term schemes for a free bureaucratized national service; demographic research was one way to legitimize state efforts—and this was common across the world in the postwar context. The Federal Institute of Statistics began operating in December 1944, and the new department was commissioned to modernize the process of data collection and analysis in Yugoslavia and in turn to enhance prewar efforts to modernize the peasant population. Along with this administrative body, special interest departments also led research in their areas. The state targeted efforts at reaching remote rural areas and the peasants who held fertile yet neglected lands. Peasants constituted a significant proportion of the population; however, physical distance and cultural differences meant that many villagers and city dwellers did not lead similar lives. Statisticians deduced that demographic and economic change was "sluggish" in that agricultural production was not transforming according to the needs of an increased urban population.[56] Furthermore, education levels did not reflect those of a developed nation; though illiteracy fell from 51 percent to 45 percent during the interwar years, postwar illiteracy rates, according to demographers, made Yugoslavia "one of the most backward countries in Europe."[57] In 1948, after almost four years of intense literacy education led by the AFŽ and the Youth League, a quarter of the total Yugoslav population over ten years old was illiterate.[58] Demographers blamed the peasantry for being reluctant to change and continued to do so in the coming decades. According to Dušan Breznik, one of the state's leading demographers, who observed the situation at a later date, the economic and educational determinants of the interwar Yugoslav population existed because of peasants' resistance to industrialization efforts and local customs that "had only barely begun to be sloughed off with industrial progress."[59] Peasants followed religious rituals, ceremonies, and community customs that were outside the state's sphere of influence and that the state, therefore, deemed backward.

In a renewed effort to address issues of the economy and population, socialist demographers began compiling, collating, and analyzing data with a view to understand how to address poor health outcomes and how to prompt a cultural and demographic shift in the peasantry. Demographers began tracking statistical data nationally and by region. They used annual natural population growth data, which was published in two Federal Institute of Statistics periodicals after WWII: *Vitalna Statistika* (Vital statistics) from 1945 to 1955 and *Demografska Statistika* (Demographic statistics) from 1956 until 1977. They compiled census and statistical data and combined them with hospital and institutional data.[60] Demographers provided analyses of those data to the state, informing state ministries about population numbers, makeup, general health, employment, and the state of services across the regions. Amid general maladies such as postwar trauma and physical injuries, tuberculosis, and malaria, the population also suffered from epidemics of endemic syphilis and rampant sexually transmissible infections (STIs). Considering the catastrophic human loss sustained during war, the cause of most concern for the new socialist state was the extremely high infant and child mortality and morbidity rates, which state doctors attributed to poor maternal health.

State demographers were not simply concerned with numbers when it came to infant mortality but also the ways that regional and socioeconomic factors impacted mortality and morbidity rates. Infant mortality rates showed a cataclysmic increase compared with prewar statistics. Demographers found that in the years 1936 to 1939 there were almost as many infant deaths in the first year of life as there were in 1949 alone.[61] One Slovenian AFŽ activist lamented, "In our Slovenia alone, we excavated 4,000 graves a year for our infants before the war; just think of how many more we have lost since the war!"[62] However, Slovenia was not the only place where high infant mortality rates abounded. In 1949, infant mortality was high across all of the republics and autonomous provinces. Doctors debated the best ways to tackle the explosive issue of infant mortality at expert forums on the topic. Angelina Mojić, a doctor close to the party, argued that the only way to reduce mortality rates among infants was to focus on the health of women during pregnancy, childbirth, and early parenthood. "Women's connection to their children starts with conception and lasts well beyond pregnancy and birth," she attested, and therefore investing in women's health was essential to overhauling mortality rates.[63] The women's press reflected this idea by highlighting that motherhood, in conjunction with active participatory citizenship and employment outside the home, was imperative for the image of the New Yugoslav Woman. Mojić, like other party doctors, viewed women's health beyond the gynecological specialty and made the case that caring for women meant providing affordable childcare, relief from domestic chores, and access to gainful employment. Tending to the needs of peasant women, she concluded, was paramount.[64] Such expert opinions constituted the foundation for unfolding social welfare policies that helped address mortality and morbidity rates across the country. In 1950, across all of Yugoslavia, there were 116.3 infant deaths per 1,000 live births, a figure that was reduced by 50 percent over the course of the next twenty years.[65] Compared to North America and the rest of Europe, the 1950 figure was relatively high. In 1950, there were 72 infant deaths per 1,000 live births across all of Europe and 29 across North America.[66] Though Yugoslavia's infant mortality rates declined, they did so at different rates regionally over the coming decades.

State demographers constructed and perpetuated an ethnic and cultural hierarchy at the national and republic levels. The urban/rural divide was always a primary issue for the state and its health ministries, but as the urban population grew, demographers focused more on ethnic elements. Over the next twenty years, demographers observed that poor infant and maternal health was far more pronounced in Kosovo and Metohija. Demographers bemoaned that those "more backward regions" had not risen to the rate of improvement they observed in the "more developed and advanced" regions of Serbia proper (which excluded the autonomous provinces of Vojvodina in the north and Kosovo and Metohija in the south), Croatia, Vojvodina, and Slovenia.[67] Specific religions and ethnic groups, such as Muslims and Albanians (particularly ethnic Albanians in Serbia and Kosovo), were of particular concern due to a relatively high fertility rate among those populations and their disdain for utilizing the public health service where it was available.

Prompted by dismal health indicators, the party expected help from communist women to care for regional populations. The party's official instructions to the AFŽ at the organization's first congress in 1945 was the four-pronged task of reconstruction: consolidating government, caring for expectant mothers and children, "consolidating brotherhood and unity," and reconstructing the country's civil infrastructure.[68] The administration enlisted the AFŽ to address poor hygiene and diet in pregnancy, unsterile birthing conditions and practices, and unscientific methods of caring for newborns, which were among the factors that the state saw as contributing to increasing rates of disease, illness, and death among new mothers and young children across Yugoslavia. By subverting local customs, the AFŽ aimed to resolve poor health in the peasantry, establish common ground irrespective of ethnic or regional differences by way of a science-based medical practice, and realign peasants' allegiances to the state.[69]

Advocating for a biomedical approach to health care, AFŽ activists responded to the immediate needs of local women and families. Biomedicine held the key for the state to enter isolated communities and disseminate socialist propaganda. The AFŽ, the Red Cross, and the Ministry of Public Health worked together to open clinics while others were established by local groups in an ad hoc way. These combined efforts were substantial. In Serbia, in 1939 there were 3 birthing centers; by 1951, there were 120.[70] Alena Heitlinger and Ema Hrešanová have independently described similar processes in the context of medical services in Czechoslovakia. The AFŽ in Bosnia and Herzegovina opened 30 centers during 1946–1949, despite ongoing shortages of midwives and doctors.[71] Some centers had to be closed when doctors returned to the cities, while many villagers were left completely unattended when doctors refused to make visits throughout the countryside. In Brčko (Bosnia), in 1950, there were five local doctors, none of whom had visited any of the villagers for the past two years, and they failed to send vaccination teams in to provide smallpox vaccination to almost half of the regions' more than seven hundred children.[72] From the outset, the government entrusted the AFŽ with constructing a foundation for change across the regions, and the women's press played an important role in relaying the party's directives. In the eyes of the state, folk and traditional cures and practices were symptomatic of a greater social division that stood in the way of a unified communist Yugoslavia. State physicians also understood these practices as uniformly damaging for women, their bodies, and their reproductive capabilities. The eradication of folk practices was not just about stamping out religion and local customs in favor of state allegiances to modernize the state. It was also about dissolving rural and urban divisions and bringing about more migration into the cities where the most services were housed.

Considerable efforts to establish clinics did not speak to quality of care or to women's partaking of newly opened facilities. The organization employed a complex strategy to both pull women into the system and push them away from their old ways. Since women were reluctant to attend services, the AFŽ used the women's press to communicate with women about how exciting new establishments were and what they offered women. Regular columns on regional news reported on the ways that New Yugoslav Women had built small birthing centers that could accommodate "3 women in labor" or "care for women for 3–4 days after they have given births."[73] Local activists also set up orphanages, children's kitchens and bathing facilities, childcare facilities, laundries, and immunization stations. AFŽ chapters held district-wide Labor Day (first of May) competitions that rewarded groups for innovative or particularly exemplary work: "In order to get a better result in the Labor Day competition, the women of the village Pejkovac opened a birthing center where under proper hygiene methods and under the guidance of a qualified midwife, the women of that village can birth. In this way, women are protected from various discomforts and infections, from which they otherwise may have paid with their lives."[74] In cities, AFŽ groups also founded larger maternity centers. For example, a local women's group in Vič, Slovenia, established a residential facility for women from seven and a half months gestation, where they could await their babies. During their time at the center, which usually spanned approximately six weeks, women gained child-rearing skills and spent time doing charity work for aged-care institutions.[75] Though the AFŽ opened many new centers and piloted various new models of community health care, women were not always interested in changing their practices to attend those centers. Nevertheless, on the surface, the women's press represented a bustling state-led effort to build a medical infrastructure to accommodate both city dwellers and villagers, and it painted the ideal Yugoslav woman as participating in both the establishment and servicing of that medical infrastructure.

At the same time as the AFŽ began praising state efforts in fulfilling its promises to women, the state and AFŽ realized that much of their readership and audience was largely illiterate and therefore not entirely privy to mass communication techniques. In a bid to encourage women to learn to read and write at the same time as encouraging them to go to women's health clinics, reporting from the early postwar years constructed a new ideal of Yugoslav womanhood. The organization also ran thousands of reading groups around the country in which women would read articles with teachers. Often those who were literate would read aloud. These social spaces were important and offered one of the few women-only forums outside of housework and childcare. The women's press built on the ethnic and class hierarchy established by demographers. Collectively, state women's magazines exhibited educated, politically participatory, urban elites as aspirational models for the Yugoslav peasantry. Authors of the Serbian magazine *Zora* describe how Kosovar women were "improving" themselves through lectures, courses, and workshops, as well as through the work of rebuilding and establishing women's health centers. The two—literacy and health literacy—went hand in hand.

Though the state initially welcomed cultural displays, it also expected participation in the economic industrialization of the country, which could not happen if peasants were not fully abreast of developments and the state's new expectations for them. One AFŽ activist opined that "our fight for the liquidation of illiteracy remains the main obstacle on the path towards cultural rebirth."[76] Through such messages, modernity was equated with women eventually divesting of ethnic dress and embracing education, literacy, and, therefore, political participation in the state. Furthermore, authors described programs through which city dwellers could instruct peasant women in urban behaviors. One such program, *selo-grad* (village-city), connected city women, who shared household goods, clothes, books, and propaganda about medical services, with their village sisters: "Peasant-women from all corners of the republic awaited eagerly in an effort to learn as much as they could from their city friends."[77] By the late 1940s, AFŽ activists and state physicians agreed that a more targeted approach where activists and teams from the central office would enter the villages, offering information, education, and resources, would be the only way to spread health literacy throughout the countryside.[78] Unsurprisingly, such programs did not intend for city women to, in turn, learn anything from peasant women.

The building of services was irregular—so as AFŽ activists were encouraging women into services, the state also was not filling the necessary quota to make this meaningful, impeding combined efforts to realize the goals of a unified biomedical service. AFŽ activists rationalized the slow nature of the growth of state services and made excuses when state efforts fell short of expectations and promises. While formal state facilities to help women were certainly being planned, it was clear to all that "in the first year after revolution and reform, the state would not be in a position to create" enough facilities to service every Yugoslav woman.[79] Socialist women were expected to make allowances for the state as it failed to fulfil its promises to them.

Communist women used the press to highlight the work of the state in establishing the services that they could open. The women's press expressed patriotic sentiment: "In the old Yugoslavia, nobody cared about women. Nobody thought about those difficult moments for women bringing a child into the world. The least care was given to peasant-women who were often given over to unskilled wise-women."[80] Ultimately, authors wrote, women's groups were waiting for the rebuilding of the nation before the state could achieve the high standard that women deserve. One Vera Nikolova wrote about a new birthing center, which contained a new school for midwives in Skoplje, Macedonia: "Do not imagine these birthing centers as brand new buildings with several departments, and multiple doctors and midwives. Those are the centers that we hope to open in the future, when we have renewed our land and when it yields economic growth. For now, we are creating small and humble, yet still very useful centers so that women can deliver under better conditions."[81] While the school on its own might not have seemed so special, she wrote, compared to the pre-1946 situation and the extreme shortage of doctors, midwives, nurses, and maternity care establishments, the school marked the beginning of a new supply of professional midwives who would be able not only to support women in birth but to travel to all areas of Macedonia to provide ongoing local community support to mothers and children as they grew.[82]

Despite energetic efforts to build adequate maternity services, AFŽ activists and some physicians admitted that most people's reproductive practices would not change overnight, if ever. Some medical experts were vocal about the fact that women should be given practical advice about childbirth that would give them the minimum levels of hygiene to get through a birth safely. At one expert forum on women's and infant health in 1954, Mojić argued that a more holistic effort, beyond the biomedical health system, needed to be employed to reduce mortality rates. She explained that medical professionals needed to acknowledge reality, especially since 70 percent of women still gave birth at home by the 1950s. By providing women with useful practical information about not cutting the umbilical cord with a dirty knife, for example, she explained that AFŽ activists held the potential to help women achieve a basic level of hygiene during childbirth.[83] Following the advice of experts such as Mojić, the women's press complemented publicity encouraging villagers into clinical settings with practical advice to women regarding safer, more hygienic practices for births at home. Two early columns, "Care of Newborns" and "Care for Birthing Mothers" offered instructions for hygienic births at home. Since "little attention is being paid to the care and cleanliness of newborns, which is one of the main causes of death in infants," authors shared medical wisdom.[84] Infant death was the scourge of medical professionals, "especially in the villages, where there are no doctors or midwives, and as such it is a common occurrence."[85] Aiming at birthing women and their attendants, authors advised the use of clean instruments to combat "women in the villages [who] cut the umbilical cord with unclean instruments."[86] Authors, directed by medical experts, recommended cleanliness, warmth, and good ventilation in the room chosen for home births.

In a desperate bid to legitimize the socialist state's efforts, journalists writing for the women's press routinely wrapped health enlightenment within patriotic sentiment that compared the new and improved Yugoslavia with the old. Coverage combined issues on the activities of women rebuilding roads or bridges with patriotic propaganda that also encouraged women to trust the state's offerings of biomedical healthcare. Authors recounted women's alleged inspirational tales to coax peasants into clinics: "Peasant-woman Mara gave birth recently in the birthing center in Bačka Topola, of which she said that 'I gave birth to my first children at home in the hay, but I gave birth to my son on white sheets, with a doctor beside me. I never dreamed that I would live to see the day that that would happen to me.'" Her neighbor remarked that "before [socialism] we gave birth to children and we cried because we thought that their lives would also be dark, full of humiliation and anguish. Now we all rejoice with each new life because we know that life will be even better for our children than it is today, when even today our live is unrecognizably better than before revolution."[87] As Bokovoy explains, the party sought to capitalize on the momentum of the national-liberation battle, during which many peasants joined the fight against occupation.[88]

Furthermore, while the AFŽ was bolstering state efforts, it also had to break down loyalties to ethno-medical healing practices. The press vilified folk healing through personifications of the medical system. The state systematically excoriated folk medicine and criticized knowledge that families passed down through generations. In one of many such articles, the *Svijet* columnist Štefanija

Grossmann declared that "our mothers often learn about childcare and nutrition from their grandmothers, mothers, and mothers-in-law, who learned it from their forebears. Most of the harmful customs that are gained through such transactions stem from backwardness, ignorance, and incorrect understandings about the functions of a healthy and unhealthy organism."[89] Introducing her column as a way to rectify faulty assumptions and practices, Grossman writes that "as clinicians, even today we fight against many prejudices and incorrect habits when it comes to the care and nutrition of children. Many of these customs are so deeply entrenched that it is very difficult to correct them."[90] Medical experts eschewed family traditions in favor of socialist-backed scientific education, and they expected young Yugoslav women to do the same.

Architects of modernization projects in Yugoslavia and in other countries employed destabilizing maneuvers to eradicate the work of local folk practitioners, which they viewed as the antithesis to modern industrialized nations. "Our villages need a significant cultural rebirth," opined one AFŽ activist, explaining that "women especially need to learn about various illnesses and what causes them. In that way they prevail against superstition and all harmful misconceptions, because of which thousands of young children and birthing mothers have died."[91] Nevertheless, rituals and the healers who practiced them endured as an aspect of community life in Yugoslavia and the rest of Europe, coexisting with various attempts to centralize biomedical health care models. Writing about the Bulgaria of the 1960s and 1970s, Galia Valtchinova argues that free biomedical health care, along with the "aggressive" vilification of religion in that context, led many postwar Bulgarians to abandon folk medicine.[92] However, individuals' desire for privacy and long-standing familiarity with ethno-medical healing practices led many to incorporate aspects of folk healing with state-funded care.[93] Natalia Jarska and Agata Ignaciuk write that Polish women's memoirs and testimonies reveal both "modernization and the persistence of more traditional practices, plus a complex relationship between population policies and individual choice," leading to the widely accepted model of the two-child family despite 1960s and 1970s pronatalist policies and enduring Catholic influences.[94] Given the low rates of peasants seeking clinical services and the persistent use of illegal abortion across the country, it seems likely that a similar situation existed in the Yugoslav context.

Local communities depended on folk healers for assistance in all areas of life, including pregnancy, fertility control, and childbirth; one strategy for shifting women's attitudes toward biomedicine was to demonize the bearers of that expertise. The juxtaposition of the modern doctor and the old crone embodied the confrontation between biomedicine and folk healing. Articles and advice columns by Grossman and others served this agenda. Just as Soviet *babki* represented a threat to the new "social order" in Russia, *vračare* were the targets of the Yugoslav state's anti-folk-medicine propaganda.[95] Campaigns extended to wise women or family matriarchs, such as the mother-in-law, as we saw in the opening.

Expanding an Integrated Biomedical Health System, 1950–1965

The state's expansion of a Soviet-inspired integrated national medical system served three purposes, each of which held the potential to win over the Yugoslav people. The new medical system went some way toward fulfilling the first five-year plan, which aimed to expand the economy while fighting supposed economic and social "backwardness." First, the state aimed to address poor health standards of its citizens, including nutrition, through the expansion of free medical care. Compared to interwar public health officials, communists tried hard to make it universal to all and free. Entitlement initially came through employment, and then in the early 1950s, the state included "agricultural workers" into health care insurance schemes. Second, the new administration wanted to consolidate power across the regions through a network of state-affiliated services that connected administrative centers with remote localities. Theoretically, all citizens contributed to and received the benefits of social insurance, coming under the care of the state. Third, the state aggressively aimed to modernize the country's economy and population, to put them on par with other socialist nations who were establishing similar networks. The administration also aimed to collectivize farms in order to feed the population and to boost agricultural production.[96] The state was driven to create a homogenized system with a center that held power, and the figure of the New Yugoslav Woman represented a suitably homogenic ideal.

An abundance of official state documents points to a concerted effort by health ministries to plan out the way that a countrywide infrastructure should look. According to state propaganda, the entire countryside was busy building clinics, opening maternity homes, and learning to read. As the AFŽ responded to local community needs and attempted to engage the masses in a unified rebuilding effort, the ministry set about creating a hierarchical administrative bureaucracy across Yugoslavia that oversaw clinical and research facilities. Similar processes occurred in neighboring socialist states. Kligman explains of Romania that "official policy was instrumentalized through a constellation of public institutions and organizations whose administrative and political activities were intercoordinated."[97] While a similar model existed in Yugoslavia before the socialist grassroots takeover, the socialist version added provisions for the social protection of mothers and children across the country.[98] In pursuit of these goals, the Ministry of Public Health modelled its service on that of the Soviet Union. Socialized medicine emphasized preventive medicine in combination with therapeutic services.[99] Other Soviet bloc countries, such as Czechoslovakia, followed similar paths in building a nationalized health care system, aiming to address population health and to serve as a "tool of the state's biopolitics."[100]

The early 1950s were a hotbed of activity in the establishment of an integrated health service across Yugoslavia, and these bureaucratic processes both hampered and aided future efforts. The Ministry of Public Health had already begun reopening or reinvigorating existing city hospitals and clinics, and they had started to establish new training programs for the next generation of Yugoslav physicians. However, the era saw a significant change in the landscape of biomedical care and research. For one, the various state bodies involved in the provision of health care changed between 1950 and 1953. From 1950, the Ministry of Public Health began asserting its position as the leader in health care, as the state gradually reduced the AFŽ's role in leading health care provision in regional areas. As the state stabilized and as new state institutions were built, the role of such mass organizations as the AFŽ and Youth League also decreased. The medical and public health leadership began to enact plans that they had been constructing for the establishment of what was to be a uniquely Yugoslav health service. However, even though Tito had severed his ties to Stalin by the early 1950s, the evolving medical system continued to resemble Soviet-style bureaucratic governance that oversaw a combination of preventive and curative principles. Even as it was establishing the Yugoslav way, apart from the Soviet Union, Yugoslav officials mirrored the Soviet concept of holding power over finances, plans for medical curricula and cadre training programs, and the assignment of medical staff and medical supplies.[101]

The different organizations involved and the clashes between them hindered state efforts. During the early 1950s the Ministry of Public Health and AFŽ met on multiple occasions to discuss the medical system and the health of the population, as well as the role of each administration therein.[102] While the ministry planned a unified system of health care, women's groups associated with local AFŽ chapters worked to allay immediate issues of health care infrastructure, including staffing, housing, and care. The ministry argued that the AFŽ had not been communicating effectively with them regarding what services were needed where, while the AFŽ retorted that their efforts were underresourced.¹⁰³ AFŽ groups also pushed for the establishment of services that had been promised to women after liberation, both during such meetings and in the women's press.¹⁰⁴ During one such meeting held in 1951, the ministry suggested that AFŽ activists should help women in their local communities by providing them with information about available services, bringing experts to them, holding seminars about pregnancy and childcare, and overall by assisting in the "fight against backwardness and against harmful traditions."¹⁰⁵ One aspect of the ministry's relationship with the AFŽ was that it expected and relied on the AFŽ to bring local women out of their backward ways, "convincing birthing women and their families that birth is natural and that there only needs to be technical help, and that there does not need to be any magic involved," which activists did through visual and written descriptions of women utilizing services that were on offer.¹⁰⁶ They also expected the AFŽ to provide immediate response to urgent needs in their regions. However, AFŽ activists had already, since before the war ended, been helping women, children, and families in this way across the regions.

One significant meeting, held in 1950 and called by the AFŽ, whose members sought the advice of medical experts about the regional health care situation, illustrates the seething conflicts between party doctors and AFŽ leaders and disagreements within each group. AFŽ leaders voiced concern that in most regions women still had insufficient resources to safely deliver their babies, criticizing the ministry for failing to deliver on its promises. The ministry's medical representatives in turn expressed disappointment at the fact that they did not know about the state of affairs in the regions and that women were still birthing in barns and doing heavy work up until they went into labor.¹⁰⁷ They blamed AFŽ activists for not alerting them to that fact earlier on.¹⁰⁸ In turn, the Slovenian lawyer and communist leader Tomšič openly argued against party doctors, saying that AFŽ activists were not the only ones to blame for the status quo. She, along with her fellow activists, pointed out that one of the reasons that the regional situation was such was because physicians refused to come to the remote districts, and they certainly did not want to live there with the communities they served.¹⁰⁹ She defended the work of the AFŽ, asserting that "we can freely say that there is no basis on which our organization has not been involved in the uplifting of society in one way or another, and no way that we have not been involved in the protection of mothers and children."¹¹⁰ AFŽ leaders expressed further disappointment because the ministry had other priorities, such as fighting tuberculosis or endemic syphilis, which meant that it could not provide sufficient resources for maternity wards. Maintaining the image that women listened to ministry advice on reproductive hygiene and accessed services provided a reassuring veneer over a disjointed and insufficient health care infrastructure.

Irrespective of tensions between the ministry and AFŽ, the state's democratization and decentralization project advanced.[111] As an extension of the Yugoslav way, the state envisioned that the new socialist health service model would theoretically see leadership and governance responsibilities shift to districts and towns. State officials anticipated "that the governance and leadership of the health service be transferred, as much as possible, to the counties and towns as self-sufficient administrative-territorial units."[112] However, the state retained the pyramidal administrative hierarchical layer that negated the agency of local health services. At a local level, each town or district that had the means and resources to do so would set up a center for public health. The center would serve as the go-to place for all the medical needs of the local community and peasants from the surrounding villages. Consumers could attend distinct clinics that specialized in children's health or women's health, and they could attend the specialist antituberculosis clinic or dental clinic.[113] The center would offer diagnostic and therapeutic services, too, including x-ray imaging, laboratory services, and physiotherapy. Above this comprehensive structure, the state installed three administrative layers: At the very top was the Council for Public Health and Social Policy under which sat the relevant Republican or Provincial Council alongside the larger health institutions, such as hospitals and research institutes, that oversaw clinical provision and research. The town or district Council for Public Health and Social Policy would fit below those tiers and oversee the local situation (see table 2.1).[114] The ministry also established the Institute for Women's and Children's Health, which bore responsibility for researching and gathering statistics on women's and children's health.

In addition to intra-agency conflicts, the state faced several challenges in installing an integrated medical service, the most pronounced of which was a dearth and geographically uneven distribution of medical cadres and services. Correspondence between the Ministry of Public Health and regional chapters of the AFŽ reveals that they shared a common frustration because of the low number of doctors.[115] The state charged demographers to track women's attendance at clinics, their use of maternity wards for giving birth, and how many clinics and specialist gynecologists and obstetricians were employed in each clinic and region. By tracking the number of births taking place in state hospitals, the state used Federal Institute of Statistics data to legitimize its position—more clinics needed, more state efforts needed to uplift the peasantry. Demographers determined that Kosovar women were least likely to give birth in hospitals because of insufficient numbers of clinics in Kosovo to serve them:

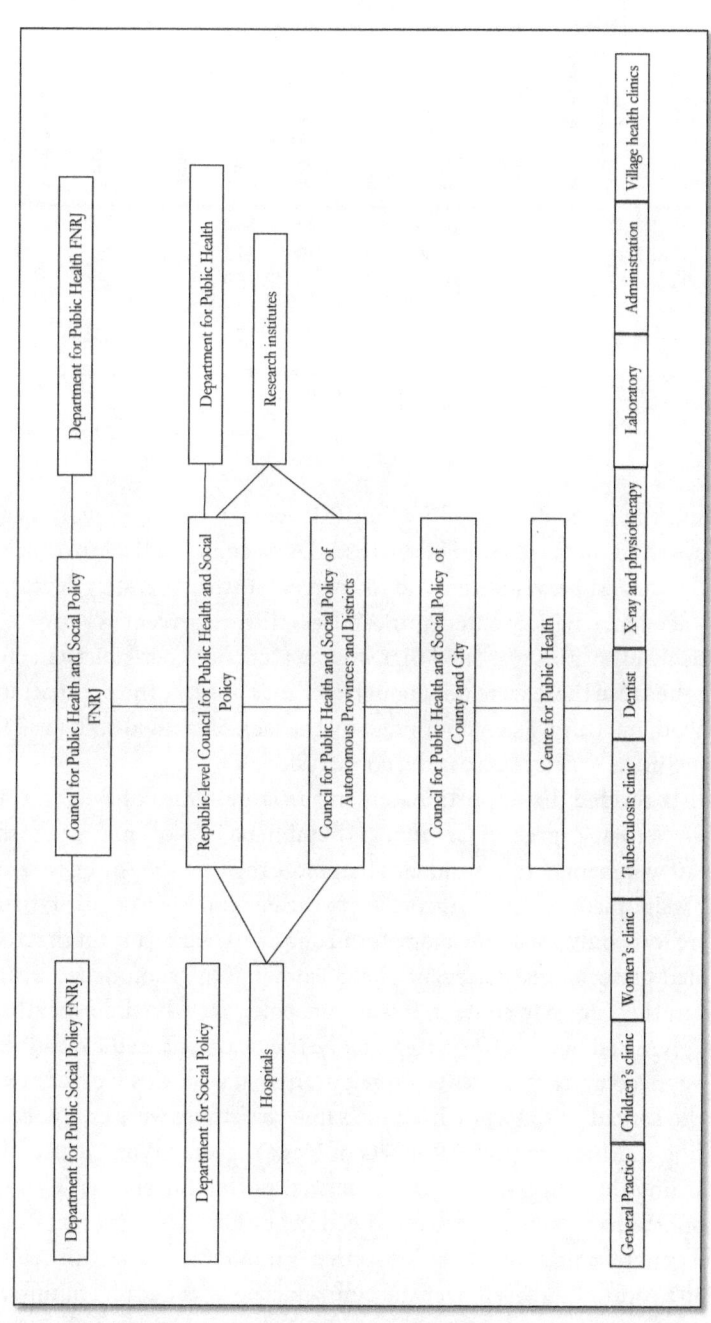

Figure 2.2 AJ, 36–22, "Plan for health service."

Table 2.1 Number of gynecologists and per capita for women in Yugoslavia per year.

	Total across country	Bosnia and Herzegovina	Montenegro	Croatia	Macedonia	Slovenia	Serbia			
							Total	Serbia proper	Vojvodina	Kosovo and Metohija
1952	209	11	0	61	11	26	100	77	22	1
1955	266	16	2	76	16	39	115	91	22	2
1961	480	50	10	125	28	69	197	148	42	7
# women per doctor	13,988	21,390	16,706	12,954	15,032	8,990	14,236	12,191	17,213	39,598

Source: "Žena u društvu i privredi Jugoslavije," 77.

"Although in the more developed regions (Slovenia, Croatia, Vojvodina and Serbia Proper) 80–99 percent of all births take place in medical institutions under professional supervision, only 50–60 percent do in moderately developed regions (Macedonia, BiH, Montenegro), and less than 30 percent in Kosovo."[116] State medical authorities reasoned that women were not giving birth in clinical settings because there were not enough facilities to serve the population of pregnant women. This was compounded by the lack of trained staff available to conduct clinical services across the countryside.

Specialists resided disproportionately in the larger cities of Belgrade and Novi Sad in Serbia, Zagreb in Croatia, and Ljubljana in Slovenia. Even when medical staff were sent to take residence in remote regions, they often returned from their assignments early.[117] According to the Federal Institute of Statistics, in 1952 there were only 209 gynecologists in Yugoslavia, which meant that there was 1 trained gynecologist for every 13,988 women. One should also bear in mind that in the Yugoslav context, it was gynecologists who did everything: checkups, giving advice, delivery. Regionally, the dearth of medical cadres fit to provide gynecological services was obvious. In that year, Kosovo had 1 gynecologist who served 39,598 women. In the same year, there were no gynecologists residing in Montenegro.[118] Reports of New Yugoslav Women attending clinics, learning about hygiene and child-rearing, and birthing in sterile clinical spaces supported by trained staff were anecdotal rather than representative of any actual general shifts in women's practice. From table 3.2 we can see that each region's cadres increased over the course of the next decade. Simultaneously, the Federal Institute of Statistics recorded the number of physicians, specialist gynecologist-obstetricians, and clinical services available in each region. Demographers established that since women could not or did not want to attend birthing centers, low attendance led to those regions' enduring higher rates of infant mortality.

The state responded by expanding its institutional presence in more remote regions of the country. The ministry set up new departments within universities with revamped training programs that enabled physicians to specialize in gynecology and obstetrics, with an aim of seeing the country's gynecological, obstetrical, and pediatrician cadres increase. Recognizing the geographic disparities in medical personnel, the ministry opened new departments at universities in Skopje, Macedonia, and Sarajevo, Bosnia, to encourage young people to pursue medical training in an effort to "lift those areas from backwardness."[119] The effectiveness of this was uneven and never really fully realized as most specialists sent to regional areas did not want to remain there, returning to their urban lives sooner than expected.[120] Medical personnel's unwillingness to remain in rural areas caused a significant source of conflict between doctors and AFŽ activists.

To further alleviate the paucity of medical professionals, the AFŽ organized teams made up of housewives, nurses, midwives, AFŽ activists, and educators who visited locales identified as in need of most "cultural uplift" and "hygiene education."[121] Peasant women from small remote villages were apathetic about the medical system and any encouragement heaped upon them to attend prenatal checks and give birth in maternity centers. Party doctors held high hopes for these traveling teams, believing they could successfully reach regions that existed outside of the purview of existing clinics.[122] To boost the efforts of traveling teams, local activists also encouraged well-known members of the central council of the AFŽ to be seen traveling with the teams, as they saw central members' presence in the villages as essential to building trust with local communities.[123]

Traveling hygiene teams found villagers living in overcrowded and unventilated conditions, sharing small spaces in dangerous conditions, and they also found that women's and children's health was suffering due to women birthing in those environments and without assistance. Reports from traveling teams found that in 1950, 90 percent of women across Serbia, Macedonia, and Bosnia and Herzegovina were birthing without any professional assistance and in unhygienic circumstances, and although women's mortality during birth was not overly high, they found that women and their children continued to experience health issues as a result of their poor birthing conditions and their early postnatal care.[124] In a summary report of early findings from the village traveling teams, Dr. Angelina Mojić wrote of the "familiar type of 'sickly woman,' who was pale and sunken in face, with long and irregular periods, chest pains, prolapsed reproductive organs," and lamented that newborns were faced with utmost adversity, from the dirty cloth or hay "that waited for it upon birth" to its umbilical cord cut with rusty scissors and the wound filled with spiderwebs.[125] Abortions also featured in doctor summaries "of which there were many," according to one report from Brestovac (Serbia) in 1951: "Abortions were begun by pregnant women themselves or by a midwife who practices such things."[126] AFŽ leaders who joined the hygiene teams traveling around villages also reported on the housing conditions in general, making observations regarding different approaches to household operations based on religion or ethnicity: "In all houses, families cook over fire without a chimney. Families sleep on the floor which in Muslim homes is carpeted and in Orthodox houses is dirt. In Orthodox houses families sleep on hay usually, while in Muslim houses families use a type of rudimentary mattress that is then propped up in a corner after use without airing."[127] Peasant practices were observed extremely closely in both the general function of the area and its population, as well as how individual households operated, and how women and children were cared for. Traveling teams displayed genuine concern regarding living conditions and the dismal health of women and children due, in large part, to village birthing practices; however, they did not report on these visits in the women's press. Teams used these expeditions as data-gathering opportunities, and reports were typed up per village and the information collated and reported on by region.

Each AFŽ chapter approached this task differently, but they shared an objective to help cultivate new habits of hygiene and domestic cleanliness within isolated families. Some teams stayed in villages or districts for fifteen days, while others remained for three to six months.[128] Teams were charged with providing educational seminars to the public about hygiene and sanitation in the home and on the farm; pregnancy care, childbirth, and childcare; and proper nutrition for families, especially regarding starting solids before the first year of life. In Bosnia and Herzegovina, the AFŽ, Red Cross, and Ministry of Public Health set up a bus with a projector so that teams could travel through remote villages. Hoping to decrease infant morbidity and mortality rates, they spent fifteen days painting and cleaning homes during the day and showing health education films in the evening.[129] This was one of many such programs to educate villagers in the absence of medical professionals. The Ministry of Public Health formed similar teams to travel through Kosovo, employing medical cadres from other republics to serve the population: medical staff and AFŽ activists trained people to go into remote areas and translated information pamphlets into Albanian.¹³⁰ In addition to seminars and information sessions, they were to visit pregnant women and sign them up for midwifery services, perform exams, and take stock of each household regarding general hygiene and the state of children's and adults' health and cleanliness.¹³¹

Despite ambitious plans and myriad meetings aimed at strengthening the campaigns, the teams were successful in some regions but not in others. Some activists reported that local women were open to receiving visits in their homes, especially when teams offered to help with household tasks, such as cleaning rooms and bathing children.¹³² Warm welcomes were not common, however. One activist reported to the central council of the AFŽ that teams faced significant resistance. According to her report, one team encountered such defiance from locals that in almost all of the eight villages they had visited, not one woman came to the meetings. She explained that in many cases, local women reported that their husbands would not permit them to go to meetings where there might be men.¹³³ The teams aimed to encourage women to travel to their local clinics for checkups during pregnancy and after birth; however, as another activist explained, women were discouraged when they would eventually come to clinics and there was neither space for them nor staff ready to meet their needs.¹³⁴ However, in the press, they continued to elevate and highlight the image of women genuinely attending and adopting services, even if they were reluctant to do so at first. They also continued to use the women's press as a tool for disseminating education regarding hygiene and health.

Due to inadequate numbers of physicians and clinics, the state faced the additional problem whereby women and families had little faith in the medical system when it came to childbirth in hospitals, as demonstrated by their lack of attendance at clinical visits and a rejection of the interjections by traveling education crews. This was particularly apparent in Jajac, while in Vojvodina, for example, reports state that literacy, crafting, health promotion, and political education were well received by women and very well attended.¹³⁵ Since 1945, state propaganda had promised women clean and well-equipped medical birthing centers, along with specialists qualified to guide them through birth. Since these promises had not been fully realized, when a visiting doctor or hygiene team would come through the more remote areas, local families remained skeptical. Furthermore, because of inconsistent services and the physical barriers of travel and time away from their farms and existing children, women did not attend the temporary clinical facilities and maternity homes established in nearby villages.¹³⁶ Rural women continued to rely more on home remedies and ethno-medical healing practices, which the state blamed for high infant and maternal mortality.¹³⁷ In attempting to eradicate folk practices, the state attempted to override culturally and socially ingrained norms. While folk practices were more commonly observed in rural families, urban-dwelling couples retained elements of traditional attitudes about gender, marriage, contraception, pregnancy and childbirth, and science and put traditional knowledge into practice when all other options failed. The same went for abortions.

The Yugoslav state's legal changes from 1951 officially prompted the transfer of abortion into the state-regulated hospital setting. With decriminalization in 1951, abortion became a topic of discussion in medical circles, however not yet within the popular press. Along with other aspects of reproduction, the state deemed abortion a medical procedure, moderated by legal and institutional regulations, bureaucratic processes, and procedures, as well as subject to the personalities and power of individual medical professionals. The historian Johanna Schoen argues about the US context that "if the illegal or only quasi-legal nature of abortion had previously stifled research on the topic, legalization opened the procedure to scientific inquiry and debate."[138] The legality of abortion in Yugoslavia also opened new avenues for the state to interfere with aspects of private life previously deemed outside the bounds of public discussion. From 1951, the state backed physicians to become the new face of reproductive care, and that included abortion and eventually contraception. The ministry incorporated abortion care and contraceptive provision within the growing web of women's health services. However, abortion was the only procedure not covered by the state health insurance scheme, and women had to pay a fee to get a termination.

Legal changes placed the procedure within the bounds of scientific innovation and medicine, leaving medical professionals responsible for the lives of women who underwent abortions. During the socialist period, both AFŽ successor organizations—Savez Ženskih Društava (Union of Women's Societies [SŽD], 1953–1961) and Konferencija za Društvenu Aktivnost Žena (Conference of the Social Activity of Women [KDAŽ], 1962–1975)—and the Ministry of Public Health nurtured the relationship between the physician and the patient, constantly devising new ways of bringing the two together. The medical administration aimed to replace independent folk healers with state-educated science-driven physicians and health professionals, who would not only heal the population but carry forward the socialist cause. Experts agreed that abortions should only be undertaken in clinical settings, preferably hospitals, by specialist gynecologist-obstetricians, and that requests for abortions should be regulated by hospital commissions appointed by the Ministry of Public Health. Each hospital and clinic had their own abortion commission, and the makeup of these commissions varied. Before 1969, commissions had to approve each abortion application before a woman could access the service. After the laws changed in 1969, when abortion was available on demand up to ten weeks' gestation, commissions continued to operate for pregnancies beyond ten weeks' gestation. From 1951, physicians were expected to take turns serving on commissions and eventually reported resentment at how much of their time was taken up with this work due to the high demand for abortions across the country. While the law played a part in regulating access to the procedure, control lay with the medical community, who could ultimately decide a woman's fate. Abortion regulations were unclear at the outset, leading to inconsistency in decision-making; however, even as the laws were more clearly defined, the decision over women's access to abortion were still made at a subjective level.

Efforts to medicalize abortion were not as successful as the state had envisioned, and the flaws in the system manifested in women's attendance at medical services to terminate pregnancies. Although the Ministry of Public Health governed each hospital's commission, individual decisions still depended on subjective choices and panelists' personalities. Although commission panelists approved the vast majority of abortion applications, the process was lengthy and public. Women had to line up in the morning to submit their paperwork, which included evidence of their reasons for applying for an abortion, wait to pay their fee, and see a social worker before they were given an appointment with the commission. They had to attend a gynecological exam to establish pregnancy and gestation, and they had to visit specialists to procure the necessary evidence to support their claims of needing to access an abortion.

Campaigns to encourage women to seek abortions through official medical channels were successful in that they convinced women that doctors, not laypersons or wise women, were best placed to perform abortions. In 1962, eleven years after decriminalization and two years after the state passed legislation to include social indicators for legal abortion, only 50–55 percent of all abortions in Serbia were performed legally.[139] In 1964, that percentage rose to 60–70 percent; however, so did the overall numbers of abortions.[140] Demographers gathered abortion statistics from institutional data. The statistical office's annual publication on population trends never mentions abortions. Institutions' statistics on abortions came from their own internal documentation on approved abortions; however, they often surmised that some women who came into hospitals with miscarriages had procured their own abortions elsewhere. By the 1960s, women increasingly sought illegal abortions through physicians and less often from local wise women. Leading gynecologists, like the Serbian Berislav Berić and the Slovenian Franc Novak, wrote with frustration about medically trained illegal abortionists who "performed abortions in private kitchens, bathrooms, living rooms, and basements during the working hours of midnight to midnight!" Berić also complained that illegal abortionists charged "hundreds of thousands of old dinars" and performed abortions "even in the seventh month!"[141] Though the author may have been exaggerating, these comments, published in the Serbian journal for public health, express both the specific frustrations of one physician with others' actions outside of the legal medical system and are indicative of broader issues with the central ministry's ability to regulate physicians in and outside the system.

Soon after the state started medicalizing abortion, it also began to regulate contraception; however, contraception fell under a different banner and was treated as such. The first contraceptive clinics opened in 1955 in Slovenia, and hospitals eventually opened clinics within their gynecologic-obstetrical departments. The Centre for Health Protection of Mothers and Children opened in Zagreb in 1956.[142] The Zagreb center came to be known for the women activists who worked in social work and research and investigated the social implications of contraceptive availability and abortion regulation in Croatia and throughout Yugoslavia. Contraceptive provision became a mandatory activity of the health service in 1958. Unlike abortion, the law on health insurance covered women in the case of pregnancy, childbirth, maternity, and contraception. As contraceptive uptake remained low, general practitioners also started dispensing advice and contraceptives. In 1957, the state established the Demographic Research Centre in Belgrade as part of the Institute for Social Sciences. Demographers went on to research fertility trends and contraceptive and abortion use among the population, and from 1962 the center established its own periodical, *Stanovništvo* (Population). They also published numerous larger studies, based on census, institutional, and statistical data, in both Serbian and English.

Throughout the early 1960s, the state invested more into research on contraceptive use and attitudes to family planning. Dubravka Štampar, the niece of the Croatian public health leader Andrija Štampar, led the work of the Zagreb center, focusing research efforts on understanding how women experienced abortion commissions and what they did after they were rejected. She and her team investigated teen pregnancy rates and the uptake of women's health services among the younger generation, advocating for policy reform. Spurred by Yugoslavia's entry as an associate member of the International Planned Parenthood Federation (IPPF), most of the republics created a Republican Institute for Family Planning in their capital; the most influential of these was in Ljubljana, Slovenia. In an effort to centralize federal influence, the Ministry of Public Health made the Institute for Family Planning in Ljubljana the main research and development facility in Yugoslavia where all products and technologies would have to be approved before they became publicly available.

Conclusion

Driven by dismal population health, inadequate and insufficient medical facilities and staff, and a desire to entrench power across the regions, the state set out to establish a medical infrastructure across the newly socialist country. The state's vision of an integrated and bureaucratized Yugoslav medical system aimed to eradicate community practices and to formalize relationships between physicians and patients in terms of individuals' most private and intimate lives. Over the span of two decades, the state instituted a bureaucratized health service and invested funding and support to burgeoning institutes and promising leading figures in the medical field. Hampered by its own ambition and by conflicts between various interested parties, the state fell short of exacting a comprehensive system across the entire country.

The process of installing such a system saw the demonization of customs that local communities trusted, as patients were coaxed into unfamiliar physical spaces, with unfamiliar, untrusted professionals. In bringing formerly ethnomedical healing processes such as pregnancy, childbirth, and child-rearing under the purview of biomedicine, the state entered the private domestic sphere. The idealized New Yugoslav Woman provided a palatable entry into the family home. In both written testimonials and visual imagery, the figure of the New Yugoslav Woman used biomedical services, advocated for them in her social circles, partook of any health and literacy education available to her from state authorities, and trusted that the state would provide more health care in due course. Through the near absence of reporting on the New Yugoslav Woman's use of abortion and the increasing use of abortion by women across the country, it appears that the state did not deem it necessary to further encourage women to use abortion services. Over the span of two decades, the state was not always effective at convincing people to abandon their old ways in favor of socialist modernity, particularly when it came to birth and contraception, as we see in more detail in chapter 4, especially in rural and remote regions, where they did not have a significant presence.

Though we do not know the extent to which the practices of wise women survived, stereotypes of the old crone persisted into the 1970s and beyond. *Bauk* (Boogeyman), a 1974 short film, centers on an abortion ritual in an unidentified mountainous region where barren land gives way to a dark cave and the mystical and demonic rituals that see a woman killed at the hands of several old women in black.[143] When resources and infrastructure fell short of requirements or legal barriers prevented women from accessing such services as abortion, women and families reverted to what they knew and what their forebears had depended on for centuries. Myths and stereotypes about how those rituals functioned within local communities also persisted beyond the state's early modernization efforts.

Despite manifold campaigns to institute services throughout the countryside and to equip remote regions with medical cadres, some areas, such as Kosovo and Metohija, and Montenegro, remained underresourced throughout the socialist period. In 1968, there was only one full-time permanent physician in Kosovo, who resided in Kosovska Mitrovica.[144] Furthermore, insufficient funding and resources led one social worker to observe that "considering present means and circumstances, it is impossible to even begin required activities in the region."[145]

Owing to the persistence of the state, however, Yugoslav health care, at least as it existed in the urban centers before the Yugoslav wars, came to be seen as state-of-the-art. Research and innovation facilities such as the federal Institute for Family Planning in Ljubljana became world renowned. As we see in the next chapter, its clinical facilities and revolving cast of celebrated gynecologists became integral to the development of new technology and methods in abortion care and contraceptive provision and known for the work it did in the social aspects of abortion and contraceptive provision around the country.

Notes

1. *Svekrvin grijeh* [The mother-in-law's sin], dir. A. Gerasimov (School of Public Health in Zagreb, 1937), 35mm silent film. This excerpt represents the written dialogue at the beginning of the film.

2. Ibid.

3. Throughout this chapter, I use the term *ethno-medical healing practices* to capture the diverse local customs of individuals, families, and communities. I acknowledge that practices were not static. They changed over time and in relation to context and circumstances. They were also not followed by all peasants in the same way. My analysis does not stem from ethnographic fieldwork in local communities. Nevertheless, I offer the reader a glimpse into some of the known practices and attitudes to sex, reproduction, and fertility control, and I deconstruct representations of local customs. Building on the work of the anthropologist Joseph W. Bastient, Paula A. Michaels argues for the utility of the term *ethno-medical* to describe diverse folk healing customs. Michaels, *Curative Powers*; Bastien, *Drum and Stethoscope*.

4. Rusinow, "Some Aspects of Migration," 1.
5. Constitution of the Federal People's Republic of Yugoslavia, January 31, 1946.
6. Breznik, *Population of Yugoslavia*, 49.
7. AJ, 141-9-32/1951, Konsultacije AFŽ-a i lekara po pitanju zaštite žena i dece i iskorenjivanja smrtnosti odojčadi i dece u Beogradu [Consultation between AFŽ and doctors on the issue of protecting women and children and eradicating infant and child mortality in Belgrade], 42.
8. Biomedicine is medicine based on the application of the principles of the natural sciences, especially biology and biochemistry.
9. Bernstein, Burton, and Healey, *Soviet Medicine*, 11.
10. Heitlinger, *Reproduction, Medicine*, 90.
11. Berridge and Loughlin, *Medicine, the Market*.
12. Mukherjee, *Gender, Medicine, and Society*.
13. McMillen and Brimnes "Medical Modernization," 180–209.
14. Kligman, *Politics of Duplicity*, 12.
15. Bernstein, Burton, and Healey, *Soviet Medicine*, 4.
16. Lišková, *Sexual Liberation, Socialist Style*, 3.
17. Headrick, *Tools of Empire*. See also Slezkine, *Arctic Mirrors*.
18. Bernstein, Burton and Healey, *Soviet Medicine*.
19. Slezkine, *Arctic Mirrors*; Slezkine, "USSR," 414–452.
20. Michaels, *Curative Powers*, 9.
21. Bokovoy, *Peasants and Communists*, 29.
22. Petrović, *Banjane*; Petrović, *Rakovica*.
23. Erlich, *Family in Transition*.
24. Halpern, *Serbian Village*; Kerewsky-Halpern, "Trust, Talk and Touch," 319–325; Halpern and Kerewsky-Halpern, *Serbian Village in Historical Perspective*.
25. Bonfiglioli, "Age Fated to Vanish."
26. Erlich, *Families in Transition*, 297.
27. Isić, *Seljanka u Srbiji*, 233.
28. Erlich, *Family in Transition*, 297.
29. Isić, *Seljanka u Srbiji*, 233.
30. Ibid., 296.
31. Ibid.
32. Erlich, *Families in Transition*, 296, 297.
33. AJ, 141-9-32/1951, box 9, "Consultation between AFŽ and doctors," 43.
34. Ibid., 297.
35. Ibid.
36. Isić, *Seljanka u Srbiji*, 234.
37. Ibid., 240.
38. Denisova, *Rural Women*, 181–182.
39. AJ, 141-9-32/1951, "Consultation between AFŽ and doctors," 43.

40. Petrović-Todosijević, "Zdravstveno prosvećivanje," 101–112.
41. Bokovoy, *Peasants and Communists*.
42. Breznik, "Methodology of the Study," 11–12.
43. Milanović, "Materinsko udruženje," 39.
44. Ibid.
45. For scholarship on presocialist birthing services, see Kralj-Brassard and Puljizević, "Clandestine Birth," 37–67. In their study, Kralj-Brassard and Puljizević describe how early lying-in hospitals, particularly for unwed parturients, developed in Dubrovnik, Croatia, from foundling hospitals for the city's abandoned children as early as the end of the eighteenth century. Puljizević has also written a book on Croatian medicalization of birthing from 1815–1915 within the broader context of similar trends occurring across Europe. Puljizević, *U ženskim rukama*. For the Slovenian context regarding the medicalization of childbirth in Slovenia, see Drglin, *Rojstna hiša*.
46. Milanović, "Mother's Society," 38.
47. Istorijski Arhiv Beograda [Historical Archives of Belgrade], Medicinska škola za babice [Medical school for midwives], Korespondencija Ministarstvu javnog zdravlja sa Medicinskog fakulteta za babice [Correspondence to Ministry of Public Health from Medical School for Midwives].
48. Ibid.
49. AJ, 36-27-70/1951, Savet zaštitu majke i dece, materijali delokruga rada saveta za zaštitu majki i dece [Council for the protection of mother and child, materials for the scope of work of the council], 1951, "Rad uprave za zdravstvenu zaštitu matera i dece Saveta za narodno zdravlje i socijalnu politiku NR Srbije od 1945 do 1951" [Work of the administration for the health protection of women and children, Council for Public Health and Social Policy of Serbia from 1945 to 1951], 1.
50. Ibid., 3.
51. Ibid., 1.
52. AJ, 671-12-22/1945-1946, Ministarstvo Narodnog Zdravlja FNRJ [Ministry of Public Health], Odeljenje za Medicinsku Nastavu [Department of Medical Education], Zapisi o postojećim kadrovima i službama, po regionima, 1945–1946 [Records on existing cadres and services, by region, 1945–1946].
53. AJ, 36-27-70/1951, "Rad uprave za zdravstvenu zaštitu," 3.
54. Mila Đorđević, Pronašli su mnogo načina da pomognu majci koja radi [They found many ways to help the working mother], *Žena Danas*, May 1946, 25.
55. AJ, 36-27-70/1951, "Rad uprave za zdravstvenu zaštitu," 3.
56. Breznik, *Population of Yugoslavia*, 77.
57. Ibid.
58. Ibid., 35.
59. Ibid.
60. The census took place in 1953, 1961, 1971, and 1981.

61. The first data collected after war that analyzed regional differences were published in 1949. Across Yugoslavia 58,778 infants died between 1935 and 1939, while in 1949 alone 49,367 infants died across Yugoslavia. "Žena u društvu i privredi Jugoslavije" [Woman in Yugoslav society and industry], *Statistički bilten*, 298 (1964): 87.

62. "Da bi bila mati in njen otrok zaštićena" [So that our women and children are protected], *Naša Žena*, October 1946, 235.

63. AJ, 36-27-70/1951; Mojić, "Zaštita matere."

64. Mojić, "Zaštita matere."

65. Breznik, *Population of Yugoslavia*.

66. Department of Economic and Social Affairs, United Nations, *World Mortality Report 2007* (New York: United Nations, 2011), 18, https://www.un.org/en/development/desa/population/publications/pdf/mortality/worldMortalityReport2007.pdf.

67. "Žena u društvu i privredi Jugoslavije," 87.

68. AJ, 141-33-186/1945-1953, Sekcija za majku i dete [Section for mother and child], 1945, Zapisnik sa I kongresa Savezne AFŽ, Beograd, 19.06.1945 [Minutes from the I Congress of Federal AFŽ, Belgrade, 19 June 1945].

69. For more information regarding the AFŽ's enlightenment activities with particular focus on veil-removing campaigns, see Bonfiglioli, "Revolutionary Networks," 191–193; Simić, *Soviet Influences*.

70. AJ, 36-27-70/1951, "Rad uprave za zdravstvenu zastitu." Heitlinger, *Reproduction, Medicine*, especially the chapter "Socialist Medicine and Reproduction," 75–111; Hrešanová, "Nobody," 961–985.

71. AJ, 141-33-186/1945-1953, "Rad organizacije AFŽ B&H na zdravstvenom prosvećivanju žena" [Work of the B&H AFŽ on health education of women], 1.

72. Ibid., 4.

73. Đorđević, Pronašli su mnogo načina da pomognu majci koja radi, 25.

74. "Žene sela Pejkovca osnovale su porodilište" [Women of Pejkovac village have opened a birthing center], *Zora*, June 1946, 11.

75. Desa Stojiljković, Porodilište na Viču [Maternity home in Vič], *Žena Danas*, March 1946, n.p.

76. Žene Srbije odbacuju zaostalost i neznanje [Women of Serbia reject backwardness and ignorance], *Zora*, February 1947, 8.

77. "Selo-grad" [Village-city], *Zora*, October 1947, 9.

78. AJ, 141-9-32/1951, "Consultation between AFŽ and doctors," 42.

79. "Kako da pomognemo majkama" [How to help mothers], *Žena Danas*, February 1946, 23.

80. Milosava Simić, "U Obrenovcu je otvoreno porodiliste" [In Obrenovac a birthing center has been opened], *Zora*, July–August 1946, 22.

81. "Organizovale smo porodilišta" [We organized the first birth centers], *Žena Danas*, May 1946, 23.

82. Ibid.
83. AJ, 141-9-32/1951, "Consultation between AFŽ and doctors," 41.
84. Stanija Pavlović, "Nega novorodjenčeta" [Care of newborns], *Zora*, July–August 1946, 19.
85. Ibid.
86. Ibid.
87. Grkinić-Vukšin, "Women on Their Rights," 7.
88. Bokovoy, *Peasants and Communists*, 39.
89. Štefanija Grossman, "Dobra i loša njega dojenčadi" [Good and bad care of children], *Svijet*, April 1954, n.p.
90. Ibid.
91. Žene Srbije odbacuju zaostalost i neznanje, 8.
92. Valtchinova, "Between Ordinary Pain," 108.
93. Ibid.
94. Jarska and Ignaciuk, "Marriage, Gender," 161.
95. Simić, *Soviet Influences*, 73.
96. For further reading on peasant collectivization and industrialization, see Bokovoy, *Peasants and Communists*; Unkovski-Korica, *Economic Struggle for Power*.
97. Kligman, *Politics of Duplicity*, 89.
98. AJ, 36-41-94/1952, Biro za statistiku i evidenciju [Bureau for statistics and evidence], Zapisi iz porođajnih centara šire Jugoslavije.
99. Docent F. Bikov, "Principi sovjetske zdravstvene službe" [Principles of the Soviet medical system], *Medicinar* 4 (March 1948): 167.
100. Hrešanová, "Psychoprophylactic Method," 537.
101. Bikov, "Principles," 166.
102. AJ, 141-9-32/1951, "Consultation between AFŽ and doctors," 40.
103. Ibid.
104. Ibid., 41.
105. AJ, 141-33-186/1945-1953, Saveti Ministarstva javnog zdravlja Slovenije AFŽ-u o njihovom radu 1951. godine [Advice from the Ministry of Public Health Slovenia to the AFŽ on their work in 1951], 1.
106. Ibid., 2.
107. AJ, 141-9-32/1951, "Consultation between AFŽ and doctors," 43, 24.
108. Ibid., 2.
109. Ibid., 22.
110. AJ, 141-33-186/1945-1953, "Zaštita majke i djeteta u FNRJ i rad naše organizacije po tom pitanju" [Protection of women and children in Yugoslavia and the work of our organization on that subject], 4.
111. Decentralization refers to a governing system that saw the central state's function reduced and the country's workforce empowered through workers' councils and committees.

112. AJ, 36-22-56/1951-1953, "Zdravstvena služba u Jugoslaviji 1951. Godine Health service in Yugoslavia in 1951," 1.
113. Ibid.
114. Ibid.
115. "Žena u društvu i privredi Jugoslavije," 77.
116. Breznik, *Population of Yugoslavia*, 24.
117. AJ, 141-9-32/1951, "Consultation between AFŽ and doctors," 4.
118. This changed the following year when there were two. "Žena u društvu i privredi Jugoslavije," 77.
119. AJ, 141-9-32/1951, "Consultation between AFŽ and doctors," 3.
120. Ibid.
121. Ibid.
122. Ibid., 40.
123. Ibid.
124. AJ, 141-33-186/1945-1953, Angelina Mojić, "Oboljevanje i smrtnost matera i dece, uzroci u FNRJ" [Morbidity and mortality of mothers and children, causes in FNRJ], 3.
125. Ibid.
126. AJ, 141-33-186/1945-1953, Pismo sa priloženim izvještajem AFŽ Bosne i Hercegovine Saveznim AFŽ, 1952. godine o radu zdravstveno-prosvjetnog tima u Brestovcu [Letter with enclosed report from AFŽ Bosnia and Hercegovina to Federal AFŽ, 1952 regarding the work of the health education team in Brestovac].
127. AJ, 141-33-186/1945-1953, report from traveling teams.
128. AJ, 141-36-234/1947, "Consultation between AFŽ and doctors" 39.
129. AJ, 141-33-186/1945-1953, Pismo sa priloženim izvještajem AFŽ Bosne i Hercegovine Saveznim AFŽ Bosne i Hercegovine Saveznim AFŽ, 2 Jan 1952 o radu zdravstveno-prosvjetnog tima u Jajac.
130. Ibid.
131. Feđa Fischer-Sartorius, "Work of the Center for the Protection of Mothers and Children," *Archive for the Protection of Mothers and Children* 3 (January–February 1959): 2; Feđa Fischer-Sartorius, "On Some Problems in Protecting Women and Children in Croatia," *Bulletin of the Centre for the Protection of Mothers and Children* 4 (March 1957): 5; AJ, 141-36-234/1947, Zapisnik sa sastanka AFŽ Srbije od 1. avgusta 1951. godine [Minutes from 1 August 1951 meeting of AFŽ Serbia]; AJ, 141-36-234/1947, Diskusija o novim akcijama u promociji zdravlja [Discussion about new actions in health promotion]; AJ, 141-9-32/1951, "Consultation between AFŽ and doctors"; Bonfiglioli, "Revolutionary Networks," 191.
132. AJ, 141-36-234/1947, "Minutes," 7.
133. Ibid., 3.
134. Ibid., 6.
135. AJ, 141-36-234/1947, "Discussion about new actions in health promotion."

136. Ibid.

137. Ibid.

138. Schoen, *Abortion after Roe*, 25.

139. Olivera Glisović, "Statistička analiza rezulata ankete o pobačajima u SR Srbiji za 1962 godinu" [Statistical analysis of the result of a survey about abortions in Serbia in 1962], *Glasnik zavoda za zdravstvenu zaštitu SR Srbije* [Journal of the institute for health protection of Serbia] 9 (September 1965): 39.

140. Radivoje Grčić, "Stanje i problem prekida trudnoće i kontracepcije u SR Srbiji" [The state and problems of abortion and contraception in Serbia], *Glasnik zavoda za zdravstvenu zaštitu SR Srbije* 9 (September 1965): 23.

141. B. Berić and S. Milojević, "Abortus kao socijalno-medicinski problem u NAS" [Abortion as a socio-medical problem], *Glasnik zavoda za zdravstvenu zaštitu SR Srbije* 6 (November–December 1969): 89.

142. Fischer-Sartorius, "Tasks and Objectives," 1.

143. *Bauk* [Boogeyman], dir. Živko Nikolić (Belgrade: Dunav Film, 1974).

144. B Čolaković, "Zdravstveni centri—prioritetan problem zdravstvene službe Kosova i Metohije" [Health centres—priority problems of the health service in Kosovo and Metohija], *Glasnik zavoda za zdravstvenu zaštitu SR Srbije* 1–2 (January–April 1968): 9.

145. Ibid.

3

Yugoslavia and Fertility Control Technology, 1960–1974

The boom in the development of abortion and contraceptive technology from the 1960s onward reflects three global phenomena: the global medicalization of reproduction, the gradual legalization of abortion around the world, and the increase in population research, population control policies, and family planning programs. In chapters 1 and 2, I examined Yugoslavia's germinal postwar decade and how the state used laws and institutions to realize its domestic agendas. This chapter explores the evolution of abortion and contraception technology in Yugoslavia. I analyze the long decade of the 1960s as state physicians developed, imported, and produced contraceptives while they innovated vacuum-aspiration technology for the termination of pregnancy. I close in 1974, World Population Year, when Yugoslav physicians took part in large-scale international studies into emerging abortion methods and IUD technology. I draw on firsthand accounts from gynecologists, researchers, and social workers who worked in Yugoslavia from the 1960s to the 1980s, as well as scientific studies and research papers and reports into the development of abortion and contraceptive instruments. I also analyze correspondence between key US and Yugoslav researchers, conference papers, and instructional films and manuals about evolving technologies to create a transnational history of this topic. At home and abroad, how did innovation in reproductive technology serve the state's intent? The state endorsed research that would yield benefits at home while securing Yugoslavia's position as a leader in the international innovation of fertility control technology. The Yugoslav way meant socialist self-sufficiency was complemented by foreign entanglements. The state functioned as a conduit between East and West and between the developed and developing worlds. Yugoslav physicians were integral to the international transference of knowledge and collaboration beyond ideological and geopolitical borders.

Yugoslav gynecologists were central to the testing and development of reproductive technology and techniques to control fertility. Physicians researched barrier methods, including condoms, diaphragms, cervical caps, and sponges; hormonal contraceptives, including several iterations of the oral contraceptive pill; and long-acting reversible contraceptives (LARCs), such as IUDs. Simultaneously, due to high demand for legal medicalized abortion, scientists were preoccupied with developing new, safer techniques for the termination of pregnancy. Attuned to global conversations about population growth and development, Yugoslav researchers recognized that domestic concerns mirrored comparable phenomena abroad. In this chapter, I focus on the development of the IUD for contraception and vacuum-aspiration technology for pregnancy termination. Yugoslav physicians were more actively involved in the development and testing of these technologies than in others, for example, the oral contraceptive pill. They also collaborated with international partner organizations—humanitarian, medical, and scientific—to advance and disseminate these resources. I focus on both contraception and abortion technology in this chapter, as their innovation occurred simultaneously between the 1960s and 1980s in Yugoslavia and globally. Yugoslav physicians were confronted by an increasing demand for legal hospital-based abortions on the one hand and an overwhelming patient disuse of modern hormonal, barrier, and long-lasting contraceptives. Contraception and abortion can be viewed as aspects of a single, global discussion of population control.

Yugoslav gynecologists fit within a longer history of medicalizing reproduction, which saw perceptions of fertility control shifting "from smut to science."[1] In this densely packed historiography, contraceptive technology has loomed larger than abortion technology.[2] Historians have argued that control over contraceptive developments shifted from the hands of local "entrepreneurs" and into the hands of medical and scientific professionals. Through scientifically informed trials and testing, contraception came to be seen as a respectable aspect of scientific research and biomedical health care.[3] All accounts point to a process of medicalization that saw abortifacients and contraceptives shift away from the hands of laity, whose work dominated the clandestine contraceptive market before contraceptives were commercialized. In both the German and US cases, activists and sex reformers wanted to shift birth control from the realm of "quack" products to scientific medicine, and this shift necessitated doctors take the reins.[4] Upper-class women such as the American Margaret Sanger and the British Marie Stopes agitated for such "salespeople" to be replaced by medical doctors, favoring an "alliance with professionals" over those whom they perceived as profit-seeking opportunists.[5] Even though they were reluctant to take on the provision of care for fertility control, physicians were also not willing to lose control of this lucrative endeavor. Andrea Tone argues that the work of such women, entrepreneurs like Clarence James Gamble of the Pathfinder Fund, and a network of dedicated activists "made a once-radical movement middle-class and respectable."[6] Linda Gordon contends that birth control proponents did not view contraception as "part of a process of democratization" but rather as a commodity to be "rationed out by experts."[7] Legal regulation allowed medical authorities to take birth control under their wing at which time they prioritized the study, research, production, and dissemination of physician-controlled contraceptives, such as diaphragms, the pill, and the IUD.[8]

The development, manufacture, testing, and dissemination of contraceptive technologies was an integral aspect of twentieth-century population control globally; nations the world over applied global developments at home. Concerned by what some American representatives termed the "population bomb," which in time could deplete world resources, the US led the charge in battling untamed population growth in the Third World. To this end, Rickie Solinger and Mie Nakachi explain, the US government removed contraception from the impermissible items in foreign aid, allowing the US to have a heavy hand in the distribution of contraceptive devices around the world.[9] Tone argues that US companies and physicians were concerned not only about global population growth but also the excessive family size of poorer families and "financial drain of 'welfare' babies" in the US.[10] Solinger argues that global concerns about the population explosion in the developing world prompted the US to consider its own perceived population problems.[11] In the European context, Grossman explains that "the international context was crucial for German domestic developments" in relation to reproductive and population policies after WWII.[12] Applying international concepts to the domestic stage constituted a global phenomenon in the second half of the twentieth century.

Yugoslav physicians, motivated by ego, the pursuit of scientific discovery, socialist and humanist ideals, state gender equality and population agendas, and international trends, conducted research into international technological developments and offered the women coming through their clinics as test subjects. The New Yugoslav Woman was not simply a potential consumer of birth control technologies but a participant in their development. Women participated as subjects of clinical research, testing methods and innovative technologies, and they participated in surveys of birth control and reproductive practices and knowledge. They were also expected to partake of scientific contraception to better plan and space their pregnancies in pursuit of larger state goals. For example, unplanned pregnancies at times led women to seek abortions, which meant that women's reproductive health would be impacted in both the immediate short term and potentially in the long term as well. The state wanted Yugoslav families to reproduce as the population of the country had been devastated during WWII. However, the state also relied on women as both bearers of children and as a significant portion of the work force. Scientific contraception provided the state with an opportunity to afford women the chance to control their own fertility in a way that suited their family and work life and served its domestic and global population ambitions. The Yugoslav state's idiosyncratic geopolitical position changes the way that we understand the imposition and negotiation of power in a global sense. Yugoslav physicians conducted their own clinical trials in-house. When they worked with international agencies, physicians expanded their studies to capture results over longer periods, across different population groups in multicenter studies, or to test technology that had not been tested extensively anywhere else.

Belgrade IUD: Beospir

Yugoslav women's experiences with IUDs fit within the history of personal fertility control, state reproductive regulation, and international collaboration to influence private behavior for the sake of population control. The history of the IUD traces back to ancient times when the insertion of crude intrauterine objects, such as pebbles, was undertaken to prevent implantation of a fertilized egg or to ease heavy menses. From mid-1800s to the turn of the twentieth century, physicians developed and applied metal and rubber IUDs to treat excessive menstruation or prolapsed or asymmetrical uteruses.[13] Only in the early twentieth century, which saw the expansion of "scientific contraception," did the modern IUD become used for contraceptive purposes.[14] Despite the popularization of the silkworm gut and silver wire Grafenberg ring and its subsequent iterations during the 1930s in Europe and Japan, Americans were late adopting such long-acting devices. Since the ring, IUDs have come in many forms, including plastic, bioactive copper, and hormonal prototypes, each of different shapes and sizes, with their own benefits and drawbacks. In recent decades, the T-shaped IUD has prevailed due to the ease with which it can be inserted and removed, as well as its comparable uterine shape.

Yugoslav scientists and medical professionals became entangled in the evolution of contraceptive technology to control population growth and promote development, improve socioeconomic conditions, and afford women more freedom to plan their fertility. Gamble understood that the best way to proliferate contraceptives to countries other than his own would be to create working relationships with like-minded medical and women's rights leaders of those countries, as well as through established family planning organizations. The Associazione italiana per l'educazione demografica (AIED), the most influential family planning organization in Italy, was associated with the fund and received a start-up donation and one thousand dollars annually along with vaginal diaphragms and jelly, all of which were unavailable in Italy at the time.[15] The Pathfinder Fund's presence in different countries varied in terms of intensity and the amount of work undertaken. In Puerto Rico, Pathfinder was involved with the birth control pill trials during the mid-1950s and with sterilization programs, some of which included forced sterilization of women.[16] During the late 1950s, Gamble sent fieldworkers, including Henry Vaillant who worked in the Population Studies Unit at the Harvard School of Public Health in Boston, all over the world to help set up more such relationships. The fund aimed to use those relationships to disseminate modern contraceptives to women in developing parts of the world and to start local family planning clinics.

Many Yugoslav physicians and women's health professionals were interested in fostering such relationships, welcoming the importation of free contraceptive samples that came as part of their interactions. After his trip, Vaillant supplied Gamble with a list of names, which included Novak, to send contraceptive foam samples. The fund sent some samples of foams to Novak and other family planning advocates all over Yugoslavia at that time. One epidemiologist from Sarajevo, Jakob A. Gaon, wrote to Gamble that "we will use [contraceptive foam] in the villages in the health project for contraception. We will give it to women and after one year, we will be free to inform you about the results."[17] In 1950, the Yugoslav Academic Council sent Novak to the 1950 International Congress of Obstetricians and Gynecologists in Paris, launching a long tradition of a Yugoslav presence at such influential global events.[18] Lidija Andolšek, director of the Institute for Family Planning in Slovenia between 1971 and 1980, took up a fellowship at the Margaret Sanger Research Centre in New York, which ended in 1961, and established a mutually beneficial collegial relationship with the executive director of the Pathfinder Fund, Edith Gates, and its founder, Gamble.[19] Andolšek corresponded with them regularly between 1961 and 1966, exchanging information about the development of contraceptives and the suitability of contraceptive options relative to context. They also exchanged educational pamphlets and product brochures, and they used their letters as networking opportunities. For example, Andolšek connected Gates with NAM colleagues interested in adopting family planning programs in their countries.[20] In one exchange, she refers her to one Miss Benhadji, from Algeria, whom Andolšek met in New York and who expressed interest in opening the first contraceptive clinic in her home country.[21]

Gamble made significant inroads through the fund's collaboration with Andolšek. Another renowned demographer, Marija Lazić Matić, traveled to Ghana in 1961 as an ambassador of the Pathfinder Fund. Seeking to expand her knowledge and experience of demographic study, the Croatian sociologist Dubravka Štampar took up a fellowship at Johns Hopkins in the 1960s. The Yugoslav demographer Miloš Macura worked in Africa during the 1960s and became the director of the World Fertility Survey, a five-year international research program (1972–1977) that documented human fertility trends throughout the developing world, with an aim to increase knowledge of the global population problem. Yugoslav population and family planning experts dove into the global conversation on population, bringing with them their own research, interests, and agendas.

Yugoslav women's first experiences with modern medical contraceptives came by way of such international exchanges. From his travels to the UK and US in the early 1950s, Novak became familiar with contraceptive options available in those countries and brought back samples, the diaphragm being the most effective one. Yugoslavia was fast becoming an industrialized nation, and as such, the country had plenty of factories that could be used to produce contraceptives.[22] Upon his return to Yugoslavia, Novak submitted his specimens to the Slovenian rubber factory Sava and to the Federal and Slovenian Ministry of Industry to spur the production of a comparable model.[23] From 1954, Novak and his colleagues conducted widespread testing and production of diaphragms. Throughout the 1950s, he facilitated the importation of other contraceptives, such as foams, jellies, and pessaries, to test their compatibility with the Yugoslav market. In 1955, the first contraceptive clinic opened in Ljubljana, and from the early 1960s, the pill became available. The pursuit of socialist self-sufficiency meant that consumables, including contraceptives, were primarily produced within Yugoslavia, as was the case in most state-socialist countries.[24] By 1965, the state regularly imported, produced, and circulated contraceptives within Yugoslavia, including Emko contraceptive foam, Anovlar and Lyndiol oral contraceptive pills (fig. 3.1, 3.2, and 3.3), condoms, and diaphragms.[25] However, production was low, importation intermittent, and stocks were largely held in city clinics and hospitals, all of which deterred both practitioners and women and made it nearly impossible for peasant women to

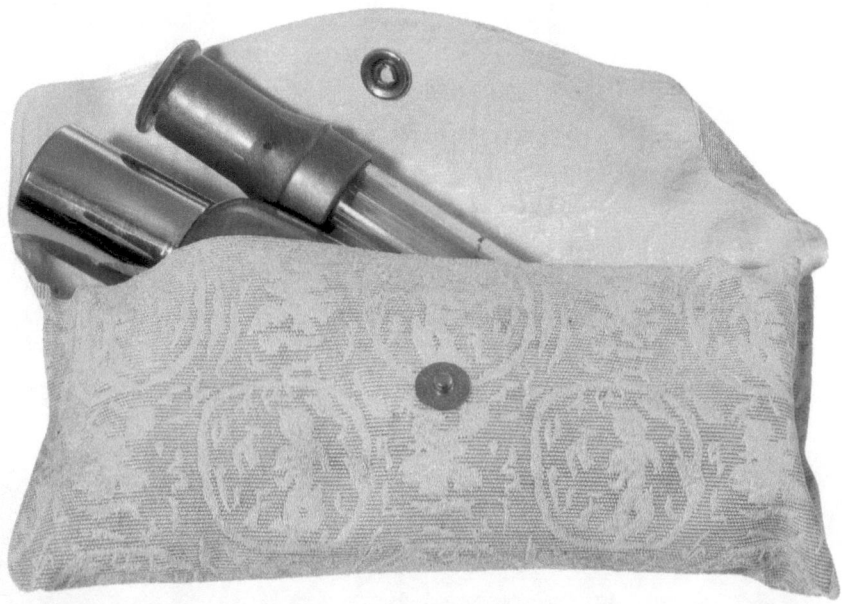

Figure 3.1 Emko Contraceptive Foam, Museum of Contraception and Abortion (MUVS), Vienna, https://muvs.org/en/contraception/barriers/emko-id2563/.

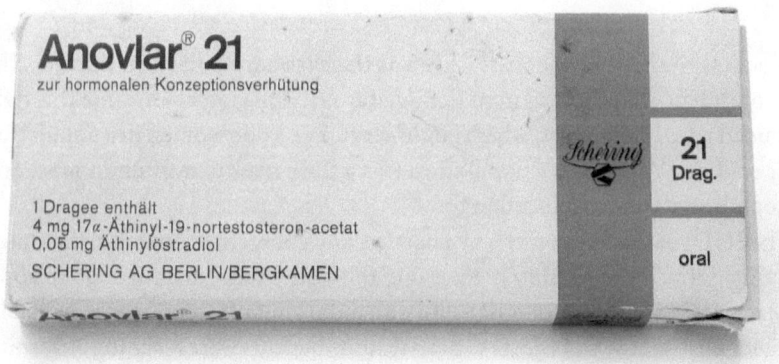

Figure 3.2 Anovlar 21 Oral Contraceptive Pill, Museum of Contraception and Abortion (MUVS), Vienna, https://muvs.org/en/contraception/pills/anovlar-21-id3680/.

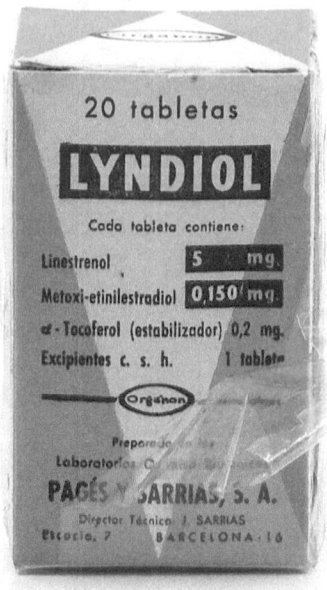

Figure 3.3 Lyndiol Oral Contraceptive Pill, 1964, Museum of Contraception and Abortion (MUVS), Vienna, https://muvs.org/en/contraception/pills/lyndiol-id3223-en/.

gain access to those products.[26] This was the case across Eastern Europe. The peak of Polish pill production of Femigen was in 1974, at which time the state produced 1.7 million boxes, which could service 140,000 women in a population of 34 million. Yugoslavia's population was a little over 19 million in 1965, and 290,000 boxes were produced in total.

The IUD reached Yugoslavia at a particularly energetic moment in the state's evolving narrative of fertility regulation. The state's 1960 liberalization of abortion laws presented gynecologists with a quandary. Contraception was available, albeit inconsistently, and efforts to propagate its benefits were reaching only some communities. Women used contraception irregularly as a result of inconsistent and limited availability, and because they or their partners did not want to.[27] Participants in interviews conducted by the sociologist Mirjana Morokvasić in the 1970s said that being able to get pregnant gave a woman a certain amount of power in a marital relationship and that, even if she did not carry to term, her pregnancy affirmed her husband's virility and her own fecundity.[28] Zrinka Miljan argues that it was resistance to the pill in particular on the part of some Yugoslav physicians during the early 1960s that dissuaded women from taking up any contraceptive options until much later in the decade.[29] Andolšek conducted the first Yugoslav study about women's contraceptive behavior after a legal abortion. The study comprised 725 women who had applied for and received a legal abortion in 1959. Those women were visited by a nurse within a year after their abortion and asked about their contraceptive habits since their abortions. The study concluded that around 40 percent were using coitus interruptus as a contraceptive method, and the other 60 percent used diaphragms and condoms. Even so, respondents reported using these methods irregularly and inconsistently. The two top reasons they gave for low contraceptive use were that they found the contraceptives that were available uncomfortable and because their partners did not want to use contraception. The researchers concluded that women needed to speak with health care professionals they trusted who could guide them through relevant contraceptive information and allow them to make their own decisions about contraceptives. According to the report, men also needed more sex education to give them information about a variety of contraceptive options so that they did not hinder the process for their partners. Finally, they concluded that there was a dire need for simple, easy-to-use, and effective contraceptives. Even so, the women's press urged the women of the new Yugoslavia to take up contraceptives as if contraceptive supply was constant, predictable, and reliable, further demonstrating the gaps in policy and practice, expectation and reality.

When contraception failed or was no longer available, women resorted to what they knew worked: abortion. The state was concerned with women's health and state expenses associated with a high reliance on abortions. Gynecological department heads reported prohibitive abortion costs, which included pregnancy testing, administration costs for applications, and appearances in front of hospital commissions, the procedure itself, and postoperative care.[30] In 1964, an average abortion cost 20,000 dinars, and in that year in Serbia, the state paid 3 million dinars to cover 150,000 cases of abortions.[31] Another key economic motivator constituted women's absenteeism due to abortion-related appointments and convalescence. The state desperately wanted to find a contraceptive option that was long-lasting, inexpensive to produce domestically, effective and easy to use, physician controlled, and safe. Experts wanted it to appeal to "workers, peasant-women, home-makers and their partners, youth in school, soldiers and sportspeople."[32] IUDs fit the bill.

Meanwhile, in the US, physicians led the innovation and production of cheaper and safer IUDs.[33] Physicians began experimenting with new IUD

Figure 3.4 Marguiles Coil, Museum of Contraception and Abortion (MUVS), Vienna, https://muvs.org/en/contraception/spirals/margulies-coil-id1798/.

forms in the 1950s. Two of the most commonly utilized and replicated designs of the IUD were the Margulies Spiral and Lippes Loop (fig. 3.4 and 3.5), developed for the US market in the 1950s and released for use in 1959 and 1962 respectively. Lazar Margulies, of Mount Sinai Hospital in New York, developed a device that was the first nonring plastic IUD; it was inserted via a straight inserter tube with a rigid plastic stalk that protruded from the cervix into the vagina for easy removal. In the early 1960s, the Population Council, which led the way in reproductive health provision across the developing world, commissioned Margulies and his colleague Jack Lippes, of the University of Buffalo in New York, to develop more IUD prototypes and to refine the designs, leading to the innovation of the Gynekoil and Lippes Loop. These forms constituted the most successful and widely used designs up until 1971, when the doomed Dalkon Shield entered the market.[34] American physicians, demographers, and philanthropists had high hopes that the IUD could help tackle the perceived worldwide population explosion problem. Following the council's lead, the US government, having only recently endorsed international birth control aid as vital to national security, began to bankroll efforts at global IUD distribution. The council along with other organizations like the IPPF and the Pathfinder Fund proliferated IUD technology around the world.[35]

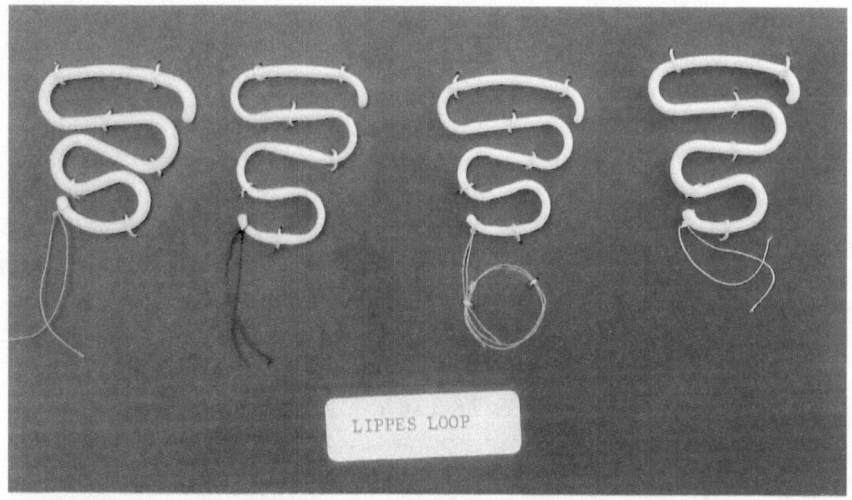

Figure 3.5 Lippes Loop, Museum of Contraception and Abortion (MUVS), Vienna, https://muvs.org/en/contraception/spirals/lippes-loops-id1864/.

Yugoslavia's involvement in research into IUDs occurred at a moment of both robust US innovation in IUD technology and scientific exchange across the Iron Curtain. In 1963, the Yugoslav Federal Institute for Social Insurance decided that "all contraceptives be given to women under the same condition as any other medicine," meaning that in most republics, women could receive contraceptives for free or at a low cost.[36] However, women lacked choice in the contraceptive market, and domestic production was still lacking. From the mid-1960s, a torrent of new research publications revealed that state medical establishment efforts to curb women's reliance on abortion and to encourage them to use contraceptives instead were not having the desired effect. Driven by the situation that those researchers described, the state reacted by energizing institutional efforts to encourage women to use modern contraceptives. In 1967, Yugoslavia became an affiliated member of the European region of the IPPF, intent to apply its strategies to the domestic setting, and in the same year the state endowed the Institute for Family Planning with the responsibility of testing all contraceptives.[37] Also that year, the Federal Assembly established the Federal Council for Family Planning, which, along with the KDAŽ, oversaw family planning work around the country and advocated for a holistic approach to resolving the issue of women's disuse of scientific contraception.[38] The two organizations continually argued that to truly resolve women's overreliance on abortion, the Federal Assembly would need to institute a response that would involve all levels of government and society rather than only relying on interest groups and women's organizations to undertake that work successfully.[39]

Although the state never fully adopted the recommendations made by the council and KDAŽ regarding a holistic state strategy to combat climbing abortion rates, it did begin investing more into the research and production of contraceptive technologies with a view to self-sufficient contraceptive development. Yugoslavia had a developed plastics industry, which meant that procedures for production could be implemented seamlessly.[40] This suited Yugoslavia's domestic self-sufficiency aspirations. Yugoslav and US physicians continued to collaborate as they had been throughout the 1950s and 1960s, and Yugoslavia eventually represented an ideal site for testing and production of contraceptive technologies since physicians had been exchanging insights and developments across the Iron Curtain throughout the preceding decade. Yugoslav physicians offered their country as a site for testing, leading to a vastly different understanding of IUD use and fertility rates regionally.

Yugoslav physicians worked toward the successful development of IUD technology, insertion techniques, and protocol regarding duration of placement and eligibility for insertion. Physicians saw that it was used successfully in the US, and they thought that the adaption of the device to the Yugoslav context would help promote the prevention of unplanned and unwanted pregnancies.[41] The Slovenian Institute for Family Planning had its initial introduction to working with the Lippes Loop and Marguiles Spiral in September 1964. The Pathfinder Fund provided that clinic, along with others all over Yugoslavia, with samples of each prototype.[42] Andolšek led the IUD studies in Yugoslavia, as well as multiclinic studies abroad. Her team investigated how long the IUD could and should stay in the uterus, as well as the overall effects, both contraceptive and otherwise, on the reproductive and overall health of the individual.[43] Of particular interest to the institute was how IUD technology worked when inserted after an abortion.[44] By the early 1980s, the Obstetrical and Gynecological Department in Ljubljana had conducted thirty-one studies and analyses on more than 150,000 women in a fourteen-year period, researching the efficacy and safety of twenty-five different types of IUD.

The fund sent samples of the IUDs to the Gynaecologic-Obstetric Clinic at the University Teaching Hospital in Belgrade in December 1964.[45] Doctors began offering IUDs to Yugoslav women, and the uptake was significant. Bosiljka Milošević of the Belgrade clinic reported that over the course of four years, the clinic's gynecologists had inserted IUDs in 2,030 women, 97 (4.7 percent) of whom became pregnant despite taking this precaution.[46] However, each

Figure 3.6 Beospir, 1965, Museum of Contraception and Abortion (MUVS), Vienna, https://muvs.org/en/contraception/spirals/beospir-d-id1840/.

clinic was only offered a finite number of each IUD, and gynecologists soon ran out of samples. Gynecologists at the Belgrade clinic decided to take the opportunity to produce an IUD themselves and to adjust their design based on feedback and their own observations.[47] They based their design, called Beospir (fig. 3.6), on the Marguiles Spiral, whose looped circular design was thought to reduce the chances of displacement of the device within the uterus as well as its expulsion.[48] The thick stem, however, caused minor cervical irritations and infections. They received approval from Marguiles himself to do so when he was in Belgrade presenting on the device in 1965, with the caveat that the Belgrade model had to be slightly different from the original to avoid issues of patent. The team at the Belgrade clinic saw this as an opportunity and replaced the thick plastic stem with a nylon coil that was just as effective for removal as the Marguiles Spiral and was thought to cause fewer incidents of infection and irritation.[49]

Clinical trials also allowed Yugoslav physicians to investigate the factors that led women to use contraception. Demographers and gynecologists examined such factors as age, education level, employment, and marital status in relation to republic and rural/urban geographies. Researchers consistently found that women living in the "more developed" regions of Yugoslavia—Slovenia, Croatia, Vojvodina, and Serbia proper (which includes all of Serbia apart from Vojvodina and Kosovo Provinces)—and those living in urban centers were more familiar with contraceptive options and were more likely to use contraceptives than their rural compatriots. Scientists claimed that "all contraceptives are effective, however efficacy depends on who prescribes them and who is given them—people should be given a contraceptive that corresponds to their level of health literacy."[50] Additionally, demographers tracked natality across the regions, and throughout the whole of the socialist period, they grew increasingly aware and concerned about the "population explosion" of Kosovo and Metohija. The Center for Demographic Research and Federal Office of Statistics surveys of 1970 and 1976, respectively, found an overall high level of contraceptive knowledge that increased significantly during the period in question. Across the whole of Yugoslavia, contraceptive knowledge increased from 73.9 percent to 86.5 percent, with marked increases in certain regions like Montenegro (55.6 percent to 92.7 percent), Macedonia (60.6 to 85.3 percent), and Croatia (67.6 percent to 98.3 percent), although Kosovo remained low despite an increase (39 percent to 52.5 percent). However, they also found that in the same period, the percentages of women using contraception declined, across Yugoslavia and by region (Yugoslavia 56.2 percent to 52.9 percent).[51] In that cohort only 3 percent of Yugoslav women used intrauterine contraception and 7 percent used hormonal contraceptives, with the vast majority relying on withdrawal (almost 67 percent).[52] In 1984, at the Tenth Gynaecologic-Obstetric Congress in Yugoslavia, Andolšek reported the results of a study into Serbian women's contraceptive use and knowledge, expressing concern at the low levels of contraceptive use and knowledge by Kosovar women, in particular. Of 2,359 Serbian women of reproductive age (15–49) surveyed, only 26 percent used contraception, and a further 26 percent said that they did not know what contraception was. Of the 26 percent who used contraception, the authors write, most were from Vojvodina (31.16 percent) and the least from Kosovo (18.97 percent), confirming demographers' assertions that contraceptive access and use correlated to stage of sociodemographic development of women in society.[53]

Contraceptive uptake varied across Europe, and socialist countries did not necessarily garner higher numbers despite their stance on gender equality. In Poland during the 1960s, female-controlled barrier methods such as diaphragms, cervical caps, and spermicidal jellies were popular; however, as family planning associations lost influence across the country toward the end of the 1960s and owing to the continued influence of Catholicism, the use of all contraceptive products, including IUDs, the pill, and female-controlled barrier methods, declined significantly. For example, between 1967 and 1979 sales of spermicidal jellies and tablets declined from almost a million to a quarter of a million.[54] Mie Nakachi argues that from the 1960s, Russian scientists and medical doctors developed contraceptive pills and IUDs to combat women's reliance on abortion as a birth control method, only to have their efforts thwarted by the state's pronatalist policies that focused on (and failed at) improving the situation for mothers.[55] Such population policies of the 1970s and 1980s increasingly encouraged women to extend maternity leave to focus on childcare responsibilities at home, leading to the "distinctly socialist reproductive practice—young marriage and first births, high reliance on abortion for fertility control, and a very low rate of childlessness."[56]

Regional differences within Yugoslavia made the country a viable site of testing to further enhance global knowledge about contraceptive trends. Throughout the late 1960s and early 1970s, the Pathfinder Fund led international multisite clinical testing studies into various IUDs, of which Yugoslavia was a significant part. Italy was similarly of interest as an ideal site for the global family planning movement because it was "perceived by many ... as situated on the fringes of the Western democratic sphere, post-war Italy was home to the Western world's largest communist party, and marked by poverty and relatively high fertility in the southern regions," and because it had experienced a birth rate boom in the immediate postwar decade, particularly in the country's peripheries.[57] Yugoslavia was chosen "because of the contrasting stages of sociodemographic evolution encountered in the various republics and autonomous provinces."[58] Determination of stages was based on the regions' levels of urbanization and industrialization and residents' education status. These were compared with known demographic factors such as family size, citizens' use of the medical system and of modern contraceptives, and the use of abortion to control fertility.[59] As expected, urbanized and industrialized sites whose residents had higher levels of education and engaged regularly with the medical system, such as Slovenia, were deemed developed, while agricultural regions with a low uptake of biomedical health care and contraception, such as Kosovo and Metohija, were designated developing.

One such study conducted by the Pathfinder Fund investigated clinical activities in Ljubljana (Slovenia), Belgrade (Serbia), Kosovska Mitrovica (Kosovo), and Skopje (Macedonia) and aimed to test IUD insertions and effectiveness of the women involved. The study aimed to understand the efficacy of M-shaped IUDs and what factors, including women's fertility desire combined with regional sociodemographic trends, influenced women's decisions about contraception, parenthood, and abortion. These sites represented a cross-section of densely populated urban areas (Belgrade) and towns whose clinics hosted large peasant populations from the surrounding settlements (Kosovska Mitrovica). These sites also differed vastly in terms of family size (largest in

Kosovska Mitrovica) and abortion use (highest in Belgrade). Ljubljana represented a city whose inhabitants were not only urban dwellers, highly educated and in professional employment; they also habitually accessed doctors' services, used contraceptives with consistency, reported a sound knowledge of contraceptive methods, and had the lowest abortion rates. Conversely, though women in Kosovska Mitrovica had the highest fertility rates, they also had abortions at a comparably similar rate as women in Belgrade, owing in part to each group of women's low contraceptive knowledge and use.

With such sociodemographic variables, researchers wanted to understand women's relationship to contraceptives, to determine what unified women in their low contraceptive use. The International IUD Program oversaw the clinical testing of IUDs using a variety of medical and social scientific tests. It was conducted all over the world, and local family planning advocates contributed to the overall research into IUD efficacy and safety. While the program was concerned with testing different versions of IUDs, including their shapes, sizes, placement in utero, material, and associated procedures, another important research goal was to understand the fertility behavior of certain population groups. In 1968 and 1969, 5,716 Yugoslav women were fitted with IUDs. Alongside expulsion, injury, and ectopic pregnancy rates in that population, the researchers also analyzed women's use of contraceptives in relation to parity.[60]

Apart from a few lines stating that the new M-shaped design, which was the IUD of choice for testing in this study, was less likely to be expelled but more dangerous to women if inserted incorrectly, the report on this particular IUD study in Yugoslavia consists almost entirely of demographic analyses. There is an in-depth examination of the four different clinical sites, listed in the previous paragraph, with a view to understanding why women relied so heavily on abortion, what their fertility desires were, and what motivated them to seek family planning advice and assistance. Researchers found that women in less developed regions had more children not because they desired larger families but because there simply did not exist enough services to support them in their desire to have smaller families. "Fertility desire did not decrease with increasing socioeconomic development. It was as low in South Yugoslavia as it was in the North.... Whatever the socioeconomic level, women wanted to regulate their fertility," a conclusion that led researchers to argue that all people longed "for social progress" in the form of medical provision of contraceptives—a convenient conclusion for people interested in promoting contraception.[61] For Yugoslav communists, such research afforded them the opportunity to address imbalances in population across the country in pursuit of socialist goals and progress. Since women across Yugoslavia, especially in Kosovska Mitrovica and Belgrade, relied heavily on abortion, the study concluded that "the fitting of an IUD must, therefore, be viewed as a welcome brake to the spiraling abortion epidemic at the personal level."[62] The study, and others like it, intended to help local women, who researchers explained suffered not from a lack of desire to keep their families small but rather from a lack of appropriate services to assist them in controlling their preconception fertility. Nevertheless, studies focused on explaining women's private behavior through the relative development of their locales.[63] They often refer to the sites as either developed or not and participants as either knowledgeable and civilized or not. At the same time that physicians developed and tested IUDs, they also innovated technologies to terminate unwanted pregnancies.

Vacuum Aspirator: VE-2

In 2016, Tomaž Tomažević, who worked in the Slovenian Obstetrical and Gynecological Department with Franc Novak, shared with me the international story of the innovation, manufacture, and proliferation of a new, safer, and simpler procedure for terminating pregnancy: vacuum aspiration. Depending on whom you talk to, vacuum aspiration was first developed in either the Soviet Union during the 1920s or China in the 1950s and was then adapted by Soviet physicians and engineers in the 1960s.[64] The Chinese physicians Y. T. Wu, H. C. Wu, and K. T. Tsai published an article presenting their vacuum-aspiration method using a motorized vacuum curette that was applied to eight different locations within the uterus in the English-language edition of the *Chinese Journal of Obstetrics and Gynecology*.[65] The Soviets E. I. Melks and L. V. Roze improved the technology by applying negative pressure using an electrical vacuum pump.[66] Their device, which applied metal crushers, suggested that vacuum aspiration had the potential to work with more advanced pregnancies.[67] The Soviet gynecologist A. V. Zubeev simplified and streamlined earlier versions of the machine, and physicians in Eastern Europe started taking up the technology and modifying it for their purposes almost immediately.[68] Innovators eventually transferred the technology and procedure to the US in the early 1970s, taking a significant and little-known detour through 1960s Yugoslavia. Tomažević further developed the technology with his team in Ljubljana during the early 1960s, the first site in Yugoslavia where the technology was adopted. He eventually became part of the Ljubljana-based research team that, from the early 1960s to the mid-1970s, investigated the advantages of using vacuum aspiration over dilation and curettage to terminate pregnancies.

Prior to the 1970s, gynecologists across the world predominantly used the procedure of dilation and curettage (D&C) to perform abortions. Dilation (widening of the cervix) and curettage (surgical scraping and scooping out the contents of the uterus using a sharp or dull spoon-like tool) was the most commonly used gynecological procedure for the termination of pregnancy.[69] Physicians continued to use D&C after the introduction of vacuum aspiration, especially for terminations after the fourteenth week. Despite its wide use, gynecologists and obstetricians considered D&C a risky procedure that could result in the death of the patient.[70] There were other disadvantages: for example, D&C was not as adaptable to being conducted using local anesthetic as was vacuum aspiration. Even so, during its early development, vacuum aspiration was mostly performed under general anesthetic, not local. Due to the forceful scraping motion employed for D&C, there was the potential to perforate the uterus, which could lead to heavy bleeding, infertility, or even death from sepsis after the operation.[71] The D&C procedure also took more time. Physicians spent ten or more minutes performing the D&C, as opposed to vacuum aspiration, which lasted between thirty seconds and three minutes depending on gestation. The longer time involved in D&C meant that women were usually expected to remain in the hospital for several days after the procedure. As such, D&C required a costly hospital stay.

Excited by the prospect of more efficient, economical, and potentially safer and less painful technology, proponents of vacuum aspiration were very quick to emphasize the relative risks associated with traditional D&C. Novak, one of the main proponents of the new technology, claimed in 1970 that "when the gynecologist who knows only the conventional D&C first sees the apparatus in action, he is impressed by the cleanness, apparent bloodlessness, speed, and simplicity of the operation. While a D&C gives the impression of crude artisan's work, an abortion performed with suction gives the impression of a simple mechanical procedure."[72] Tomažević and Novak aimed to further simplify, automate, and improve the efficiency of their model.

Though Novak and Tomažević aimed to completely replace D&C with vacuum aspiration, the two procedures inherently serve different purposes. According to historical studies and recent research, the vacuum-aspiration procedure has a much lower rate of infection and a lower likelihood of uterine perforation than D&C, because the technique employs suction rather than scraping. For the most part, vacuum aspiration can only be used until ten to twelve weeks' gestation, though sometimes up until fourteen weeks as long as the cervix is dilated enough and the physician uses a sharp, rigid, and wide cannula. The obstetrician Jane Hodgson observes in her book on abortion and sterilization techniques, that "after 14 weeks of pregnancy, vacuum aspiration by necessity becomes a *different* procedure" because of the larger size of the fetus.[73] While it may be the case that vacuum-aspiration technology was actually meant to serve a different purpose from D&C rather than replace D&C entirely, there is no such demarcation in the scientific sources I have consulted.

The vacuum-aspirator unit consists of a handheld metal or glass pipette-shaped cannula the size of which correlates to the gestational stage of the pregnancy. The main compartment of the vacuum aspirator varies in composition. Models from the 1950s were simple units that employed a glass jar that would hold the uterine contents after aspiration and relied on natural pressure for expulsion. Later models included a pressurized vacuum unit. Eventually a motorized vacuum unit was introduced that allowed physicians to control the requisite levels of suction.[74] Connecting the handheld cannula and the motorized extractor unit is a clear tube that allows the physician to monitor the contents of the uterus throughout the entire procedure.[75] One of the most significant improvements that the Ljubljana team made to the unit concerned air pressure. The Zubeev unit, which Novak and Tomaževič first encountered, relied on manually operated negative pressure to remove uterine contents. Given that operators could make a mistake and make the pressure positive, physicians risked killing their patients with a massive air embolism. The new apparatus contained a rotary pump, which produces a vacuum regulated by a valve that enabled continuous adjustment to low pressure, which could be controlled by a foot pedal.[76] At the 1966 IPPF Europe and Near East Region Conference in Copenhagen, Novak spoke about his experiences using this technology in 752 cases of abortions, reporting that "the procedure is quicker, the loss of blood is reduced by more than half, and the number of complications is reduced by more than half," attesting to his belief in the procedure's superiority.[77]

The shift by physicians to using vacuum aspiration over D&C did not happen immediately. In fact, while some contemporary research papers describe it as a stark substitution, D&C remained in use after vacuum aspiration was included as a treatment option. It continues to be used for pregnancy terminations today. D&C was sometimes even used following aspiration to ensure the emptiness of the uterus in terminations after twelve weeks. Despite the perceived and proven negatives of D&C, physicians were proficient in the technique and hesitant to take up something that was new and unfamiliar. In the 1950s especially, vacuum-aspiration technology was underdeveloped, and until 1974 no significant scientific studies had been published to legitimize the move from D&C to vacuum aspiration.[78] As such, the adoption of vacuum aspiration took time and happened haphazardly in isolated hospitals, clinics, and private practices. While versions of the technology had been around for much of the twentieth century, it was not until the 1960s that the technology became normalized, eventually becoming utilized and in some cases favored, along with D&C, across the world.

Other Yugoslav gynecologists and obstetricians soon caught wind of the Ljubljana team's innovations, including Berić, Novak's contemporary and professional rival, who further enhanced vacuum-aspiration technology and protocols. Berić worked on the paracervical block, which was initially unsuccessfully developed to work with D&C, and adapted it to be used with vacuum aspiration.[79] The paracervical block was a cocktail of various drugs that brought on dilation of the cervix and encouraged uterine contractions, which reduced the chances of a patient hemorrhaging due to perforation or uterine bleeding.[80] In 1972, Berić produced an instructional film aimed at gynecologists and obstetricians that demonstrated the process of abortion using vacuum aspiration with the paracervical block.[81] The film follows Berić as he prepares the tools, equipment, and the necessary drugs for a termination within a sterile operating room. A young woman, who has come as an outpatient, enters the operating room. Berić comforts her and asks a few questions about her marital status and if she has any other children, as well as if she is sure that she wants to go through with the termination.[82] After the procedure is performed, Berić escorts the young woman from the operating room so that she can be monitored briefly before heading home the same day.[83] The main message of the film is that using the paracervical block prior to performing an abortion using vacuum aspiration leads to a quicker, safer, and more economical termination.

The changing legal landscape in the 1960s and 1970s promoted innovation in abortion care. The period 1960–1974 represented a dynamic time in the narrative of reproductive regulation in Yugoslavia and globally. Yugoslav abortion laws meant that women could have a termination under safer, medical circumstances, and the demand for hospital-based abortions led Yugoslav physicians to develop technology and techniques and for them to undertake collaborative work within Yugoslavia and internationally. Mara Mlakar, a social worker who worked with Novak and Tomaževič, described this time positively, as there was "a healthy cooperation between politics and the medical profession that did not necessarily exist at other times."[84] As countries globally began decriminalizing abortion, demand increased for legal, hospital-based terminations. Gynecologists had, of course, been performing abortions prior to legalization all over the world. However, these procedures were either completed in a clandestine fashion, to remedy a botched or self-abortion attempt, or out of medical necessity to save a woman's life.

In 1973, *Roe v. Wade* protected the right to access abortion legally all across the United States, which was overturned in 2022. Prior to 1973, the procedure's illegality drove it underground. Women turned to unskilled back-alley abortionists, or they self-aborted, which often led them to the hospital and the completion of their abortions by doctors in emergency settings by way of D&C. After the early 1970s, American physicians were suddenly in need of new technology and methods to serve the women who could now legally seek abortion in designated clinics and hospitals. Schoen argues that "while the systematic persecution of illegal abortionists in the 1950s and 1960s had driven abortion underground and turned it into a risky or even deadly procedure for most women, legalization made abortion into the safest and most widely performed surgical procedure in the United States."[85] The procedure still carried risks, but its legalization meant that physicians were freer to conduct research to reduce those risks.[86]

American gynecologists performed abortions using D&C from 1965 and were not keen to change to vacuum aspiration when it became available, as they were unsure of its dangers.[87] A version of the vacuum aspirator existed in the parts of the US where abortion had been legal prior to 1973, including in California and New York. However, it was a crude machine, and there was little scientific research into its efficacy over other previously used methods.[88] After *Roe v. Wade*, abortion sat openly in the hands of obstetricians and gynecologists who were willing to try new techniques and also had the legal backing to support them.[89] The electrical vacuum aspirator was accepted because it was professionally appealing, adaptable to any clinical setting as it was a standalone machine, and economical.[90] Given their political and financial ties, Yugoslavia represented a convenient ally with whom the US could pair to learn about this work.

The US may have been behind in terms of technological development for abortion, but US physicians quickly learned from their more experienced Eastern European colleagues. Novak made numerous trips to the US to exchange knowledge with American physicians. He presented his new VE-2 unit at the Copenhagen IPPF conference in 1966, where international representatives including those from the US were present. In 1967 at the IPPF congress in Denmark, he presented his first instructional film aimed at physicians that demonstrated the use of the vacuum aspirator in practice. In 1968, Novak traveled to Hot Springs, Virginia, to present his research and clinical experience of vacuum aspiration within the American context, and American adherents to the new technique even traveled to Yugoslavia to observe his technique firsthand.[91] Some who used it in their gynecological departments modified the procedure and conducted studies in their own clinics to determine its efficacy and whether it was a safer method than their previous techniques.[92]

Physicians from the National Institute of Child Health and Human Development (NICHD) joined with representatives from the Slovenian Obstetrical and Gynecological Department and the Institute for Family Planning to conduct the first large-scale study that compared vacuum aspiration with D&C. The Ljubljana Abortion Study, 1971–1973, published in 1974, was financed by the Yugoslavian-American Medical Research Program, organized and coordinated by the institute, headed by Andolšek, and carried out by three institutions: the Obstetrical and Gynecological Department at the University Teaching Hospital, the Family Planning Institute, and the Blood Transfusion Institute of Slovenia.[93] Although Yugoslav gynecologists had suspected that the procedure was indeed safer prior to this study, it was after this study that gynecologists globally became convinced, too. The study population was 4,733 women, admitted to the Obstetrical and Gynecological Department in Ljubljana between January 1971 and December 1972 for abortion on social grounds.[94] The study determined that vacuum aspiration was safer because it showed a reduced likelihood of significant blood loss during the procedure, it led to fewer uterine perforations and to fewer infections, and it was a quicker procedure and more physically comfortable for the patient both during and afterward.[95]

Conclusion

It is no coincidence that innovation should thrive concurrently in the fields of contraception and abortion. On the one hand, as we know from Connelly, Solinger, and Nakachi, population fluctuations and fertility control constituted a global concern. Whether too many births or not enough, an urge to control the population of the world at a national and in some cases ethnic level was prevalent across the world. The IUD was one way to offer the world a sense of control over population growth and, in the case of Yugoslavia, to offer women an alternative to abortion as contraception.

Women of the new Yugoslavia represented an opportunity for the state to enact its modernizing vision for the country. The image of the New Yugoslav Woman in the 1960s and 1970s was a continuation and amplification of that in the immediate postwar decades. In the 1940s and 1950s, she was expected to participate in the development maternity homes and child health clinics and to utilize those services to reduce women's morbidity and infant mortality rates across the country. Yet, despite great efforts to encourage the New Yugoslav Woman to use reproductive health services, the development of those services and personnel to staff them was uneven and inconsistent in different republics and between urban and rural communities. In the 1960s and 1970s, the expectation became that she would become a modern woman who relies on scientific contraception in lieu of abortion to control and space her births. Yet contraceptives were inconsistently available and unreliable for the most part, and cultural attitudes to contraceptives were slow to shift. The New Yugoslav Woman was an idealized form, not a reflection of actual practice or even what was available to women at the time. Even so, New Yugoslav Women participated in the global development of contraception and abortion technologies as physicians, researchers, family planning advocates, and, in vast numbers, as test subjects, health consumers, and patients.

The evolution of the IUD and vacuum aspirator were global events. Each country that partook or opted out of partaking in clinical trials, testing, and development did so for manifold reasons, including economics, human rights, religion, famine, and affluence. Another key aspect of this narrative is Yugoslavia's links with newly independent nations of the Third World. Communist women engaged significantly with development activities in countries of the Global South. This, coupled with scientific exchanges that physicians and researchers nurtured throughout the 1960s and 1970s, constituted Yugoslavia as an ideal conduit for networking with Asian and African countries. In chapter 4, I examine these relationships within the broader context of human rights and how Yugoslavia, yet again, presented itself to a different audience as the developed and modern leader of the developing world.

Notes

1. Tone, *Devices and Desires*, 25.
2. Several historians have analyzed the transfer of abortion technology into the US and its development through that domestic context. This field of inquiry is not nearly as developed as the scholarship on contraception, and no studies deal with the development of contraception and abortion technologies simultaneously. Tunc, "Designs of Devices," 353–376; Heitlinger, *Reproduction, Medicine*; Hodgson, *Abortion and Sterilization*.
3. Grossmann, *Reforming Sex*, 15; Tone, *Devices and Desires*, 13; Löwy, "Sexual Chemistry," 245–274; Dugdale, "Intrauterine Contraceptive Devices," 165–176; Dugdale, "Inserting Grafenberg's IUD," 318–324.
4. Grossman, *Reforming Sex*, 65; Löwy, "Sexual Chemistry," 248; Gordon, *Moral Property of Women*, 117.
5. Löwy, "Sexual Chemistry," 248.
6. Tone, *Designs and Desires*, 117; ibid., 248.
7. Gordon, *Moral Property of Women*, 117, 210.

8. Tone, *Designs and Desires*, 121.
9. Solinger and Nakachi, "Introduction," in *Reproductive States*, 14.
10. Tone, *Devices and Desires*, 50.
11. Solinger, *Pregnancy and Power*.
12. Grossmann, *Reforming Sex*, 190.
13. Tone, *Devices and Desires*, 59.
14. Löwy, "Sexual Chemistry," 248; Williams, *Every Child*, 332.
15. Bracke, "Family Planning, the Pill," 96.
16. Ibid.; López, "Gambling on the Protestants," 345.
17. Folder of correspondence between Gamble and his fieldworkers Henry Vaillant and Sarah Lawrence, box 127, folder 2238, H MS c23, Clarence J. Gamble Papers, Harvard Medical Library Collection, Center for the History of Medicine in the Francis A. Countway Library, Harvard University (hereafter, Henry Vaillant and Sarah Lawrence correspondence).
18. AJ, 55-66-438/1950, Savet Akademija Nauka i Umetnosti SFRJ [Council of the Academy of Sciences and Arts], Kulturna i naučna saradnja s inostranstvom [Cultural and scientific cooperation with foreign countries], correspondence and invitations to attend the International Congress of Obstetricians and Gynecologists in Paris.
19. Henry Vaillant and Sarah Lawrence correspondence.
20. Correspondence between Edith Gates and Andolšek, various dates throughout 1964, box 127, folder 2245, H MS c23, Clarence J. Gamble Papers, Countway Library, Harvard University, Cambridge, MA, Harvard Medical Library Collection, Center for the History of Medicine in the Francis A. Countway Library, Harvard University (hereafter, Edith Gates and Lidija Andolšek correspondence).
21. Ibid.
22. "Letter from Stanka Simoneti to Henry Levin of the Population Council, regarding contraceptive methods," October 14, 1966, Collection FA432 Population Council records, box 195, folder 1855, Rockefeller Archive Centre.
23. Dobrivojević, "Family Planning in Yugoslavia," 124.
24. Ignaciuk, "Clueless about Contraception," 516.
25. Anovlar 197,000; Lyndiol, 93,000; suppositories, 9,0000; jellies, 10,500; condoms, 13 million; diaphragms, 12,000. Population Council, Stanka Simoneti letter. After she describes the plans for production in 1966, she says in a postscript: "We do not use contraceptives because of over-population, but to reduce abortion."
26. Dobrivojević, "For Planned Parenthood," 91.
27. She translated the study into English and sent it to Gamble in 1961. Andolšek, "How Contraception Is Considered by Those Who Have Already Experienced Legal Abortion," box 127, folder 2244, H MS c23, Clarence J. Gamble Papers, Countway Library, Harvard University, Cambridge, MA, Harvard

Medical Library Collection, Center for the History of Medicine in the Francis A. Countway Library, Harvard University.

28. Morokvasić, "Sexuality and Control," 197.

29. Miljan goes on to argue that in the Yugoslav context the sexual revolution was a contraceptive revolution as women started using contraceptives with slightly more regularity by the end of the 1960s. Miljan, "Sexual Revolution," 152.

30. Dubravka Štampar, "Kretanje pobačaja u Hrvatskoj u razdoblju od 1960 do 1970 godine" [Croatian abortion trends between 1960 and 1970], *Arhiv za zaštitu majki i djece* [Archive for the protection of mother and child] 1-2 (1972): 12.

31. In today's currency, 20,000 dinars equated to 228 euros, 363 AUD, 256 USD; 3 million dinars to 34,230 Euro, 38,427 USD, 54,471 AUD. The source for this historical currency conversion came from www.fxtop.com.

32. Radivoje Grčić, "Stanje i problem prekida trudnoće i kontracepcije u SR Srbiji [The state and problems of abortion and contraception in Serbia]," *Glasnik zavoda za zdravstvenu zaštitu SR Srbije* 9 (September 1965): 32.

33. Even though US physicians were hesitant to involve themselves with the development of contraceptive technology, by the 1950s, within the context of the Cold War and global concerns over population growth, US physicians recognized the widespread potential of the IUD.

34. Tone, *Designs and Desires*, 265, 266. The Dalkon Shield was used widely in the early 1970s; however, the porous nature of the string that protruded through the cervix meant that bacteria could thrive and could enter the uterus. This led to a disproportionately high number of septic pregnancies when women fell pregnant using the device, as well as numerous instances of pelvic inflammatory disease and infertility. The A. H. Robins Company, which marketed the shield, was sued in 1975 by over 200,000 women who had experienced these outcomes as a result of wearing the shield.

35. Ibid.

36. Dobrivojević, "For Planned Parenthood," 93.

37. AJ, 142-54-184/1957-1985, Socijalistički Savez Radnog Naroda Jugoslavije [Socialist Association of the Working People of Yugoslavia], Materijali komisije za idejno vaspitni rad saveznog odbora, 1983, "Medjunarodna saradnja" [International collaboration], Belgrade September 1983, 6.

38. Hrvatski Državni Arhiv [Croatian State Archives; hereafter, HDA], 1234-206, Fond Konferencija Društvenih Aktivnosti Žena Hrvatske [Conference for the Social Activity of Croatian Women], reports from Council for Family Planning and the KDAŽ to the Federal Assembly.

39. Ibid.

40. Tone argues that the IUD, unlike the pill, was easy to manufacture in any country with a developed plastics industry. Where there was no such industry, the Population Council advocated for the use of "hand-operated, one-cavity

injection molding machines" in place of factory assembly lines. Tone, *Designs and Desires*, 266.

41. Magazines and academic articles discuss how US women were quick to take it up and found it effective.

42. Correspondence between Clarence J. Gamble and Edith Gates from the Pathfinder Fund and Lidija Andolšek, Collection H MS c23, Clarence J. Gamble Papers, Countway Library, Harvard University; Lidija Andolšek, Z. Ograjenšek, and Slavka Bonta, "Naša Iskustva s Kontraceptivnim Intrauterinim Ulošcima," *Ginekologija i Opstetricija* [Gynaecology and Obstetrics] 4 (1965): 173–174.

43. Ibid.; Alan Guttmacher, "Metode Kontracepcije," *Ginekologija i Opstetricija* [Gynaecology and Obstetrics] 2–3 (1966): 111–116; Lidija Andolšek, "Perspektive Intrauterine Kontracepcije," *Jugoslovenska Ginekologija i Opstetricija* [Yugoslav Gynaecology and Obstetrics] 16 (1976): 265–274.

44. Radoš Germ and Z. Ograjenšek, "Asimptomska Perforacija Materice Kod Artificijalnoga Abortusa i Aplikacije Intrauterinog Kontraceptivnog Uloška," *Ginekologija i Opstetricija* [Gynaecology and Obstetrics] 1 (1968): 25–27.

45. Andolšek, Ograjenšek, and Bonta, "Naša Iskustva," 173–174; B. Milošević, Radmila Mitić, and Aleksandar Radosavljević, "Intrauterina Kontracepcijska Sredstva, Sa Posebnim Osvrtom Na Beogradsku Spiralu (Beospir)," *Ginekologija i Opstetricija* [Gynaecology and Obstetrics] 8 (1968): 335.

46. B. Milošević, Radmila Mitić, and Aleksandar Radosavljević, "Intrauterina Kontracepcijska Sredstva, Sa Posebnim Osvrtom Na Beogradsku Spiralu (Beospir)," *Ginekologija i Opstetricija* [Gynaecology and Obstetrics] 8 (1968): 337. Today, according to the US Centers for Disease Control and Prevention, the failure rates for IUDs are 0.8 percent for copper IUDs based on typical use and 0.1–0.4 percent for the hormonal IUD based on typical use. https://www.cdc.gov/reproductivehealth/contraception/index.htm. Accessed October 25, 2019.

47. Milošević, Mitić, and Radosavljević, "Intrauterina Kontracepcijska Sredstva," 335.

48. Ibid., 336.

49. Ibid., 335.

50. Grčić, "State and Problems," 31.

51. Sentić, "Contraception," 200.

52. Ibid., 204.

53. Andolšek-Jeras, "Demografski aspekti planiranja porodice u SFRJ [Demographic aspects of family planning in Yugoslavia]," *Tenth Congress of Gynecologist-Obstetricians of Yugoslavia* (October 1984): 93.

54. Ignaciuk, "Innovation and Maladjustment," 185.

55. Nakachi, *Beyond Replacing the Dead*, 187.

56. Ibid., 12.

57. Bracke, "Family Planning, the Pill," 91.

58. Bernard, "IUD Testing and the IUD Recipient in Yugoslavia, Inter-Republic Clinical Description of Reproduction in Ljubljana, Beograd, Kos. Mitrovia, and Skopje, with a Reprographic Model of Demographic Transition and Fertility Regulation," July 1972, 2, Emily C Mudd Collection, carton 11, folder 505, Schlesinger Library, Radcliffe Institute for Advanced Study, Harvard University, Cambridge, MA.

59. Ibid.

60. Ibid., 6. The average number of live births (parity) among IUD recipient groups passes from a high 4.4 in rural and less developed Kosovar Mitrovica to a low 1.8 in Beograd, the national capital.

61. Ibid., 44.

62. Ibid., 26.

63. Ibid., 22.

64. Most authors of the primary sources and secondary analyses that I have consulted regarding the development of this technology agree on this loose timeline of development. Jovan Vujić, "Prednosti i Mehanizam Djelovanja Vakuum-Aspiracije Kao Metode Vršenja Artificijalnog Pobačaja," *Arhiv za zaštitu majki i djece* 1–2 (1972): 46; Tunc, "Designs of Devices," 361; Olszynko-Gryn, "Contraceptive Technology."

65. Tunc, "Designs of Devices," 361.

66. Ibid.

67. Ibid.

68. Ibid.

69. Milorad Kovačev, "Metode Veštačkog Prekida Trudnoće," *Druga Ginekološko-Akušerska Nedelja SLD* 27 (1957): 199.

70. Vujić, "Prednosti i Mehanizam"; L. Andolšek and Franc Novak, *The Ljubljana Abortion Study, 1971–1973: Comparison of the Medical Effects of Induced Abortion by Two Methods, Curettage and Vacuum Aspiration; Final Report* (Bethesda, MD: National Institutes of Health, Center for Population Research, 1974).

71. Vujić, "Prednosti i Mehanizam," 45.; Andolšek and Novak, *Ljubljana Abortion Study*.

72. Novak, "Experience with Suction Curettage," 77.

73. Hodgson, *Abortion and Sterilization*, 239.

74. Vujić, "Prednosti i Mehanizam"; Andolšek and Novak, *Ljubljana Abortion Study*; A. Černoch, "Naša Iskustva o Posljedicama Prekida Trudnoće," *Ginekologija i Opstetricija* [Gynaecology and Obstetrics] 1 (1965): 27–31.

75. Vujić, "Prednosti i Mehanizam"; Andolšek and Novak, *Ljubljana Abortion Study*; Černoch, "Naša iskustva," 28.

76. Novak, "Modern Techniques of Controlling Human Reproduction Apparatus for Artificial Abortion with Aspiration," paper presented at the IPPF Europe and Near East Region Fifth Conference, Copenhagen, July 5–8, 1966, 3.

77. Ibid., 2.

78. Gynecologists from most of the clinics that adopted the technology across Yugoslavia, Czechoslovakia, and other parts of Europe had studied its efficacy in their own practice and published based on those findings. However, no long-term comparative controlled studies had been completed until 1974 when the Ljubljana Centre published the Ljubljana abortion study. Andolšek and Novak, *Ljubljana Abortion Study*.

79. Tunc, "Technologies of Choice," 200; Berislav M. Berić and Milan Kupresanin, "Vacuum Aspiration, Using Pericervical Block, for Legal Abortion as an Outpatient Procedure up to the 12th Week of Pregnancy," *The Lancet* 298, no. 7725 (September 1971): 619–621.

80. Tunc, "Technologies of Choice," 200; Berić and Kupresanin, "Vacuum Aspiration."

81. Petar Latinović, *Legalni prekid trudnoće putem vakuum aspiracije pericervikalnog bloka sa ginestezinom* [Legal termination of pregnancy by way of vacuum-aspiration and paracervical block with anaesthesia] (Yugoslavia: Neoplanta Film Novi Sad, 1972).

82. Ibid.

83. Ibid.

84. Mara Mlakar, interview with the author, Ljubljana, September 12, 2016.

85. Schoen, *Abortion after Roe*, 25.

86. Procuring abortions varied (and still does vary) tremendously from state to state in the US—and even within states—as many states did/do not have facilities or sufficient doctors to perform an abortion.

87. Tunc, "Designs of Devices,"; Tunc, "Technologies of Choice."

88. Ljiljana Randić, Verena Kogoj-Bakić, and Tea Stanković, "Intrauterina Kontracepcija i Višekratni Zahtjevi Za Prekid Trudnoće," *Ginekologija i Opstetricija* [Gynaecology and Obstetrics] 6 (1974): 415–20.

89. Tunc, "Designs of Devices," 355.

90. Ibid., 356.

91. Ibid., 1111. Carole E. Joffe also describes this conference. Joffe, *Doctors of Conscience*. The conference was organized by the Association for the Study of Abortion, which was funded by the Rockefeller Fund. John D. Rockefeller III gave a keynote at the opening of the conference endorsing abortion legalization. Forsythe, *Abuse of Discretion*, 61.

92. Vujić, "Prednosti i Mehanizam," 47.

93. Ljubomir Antonovski, "Medical Aspects of Induced Abortion in Yugoslavia," in *Fertility and Family Planning in Yugoslavia* (Belgrade: Institute of Social Sciences, Demographic Research Centre, 1980), 244.

94. Ibid.

95. Andolšek and Novak, *Ljubljana Abortion Study*.

4

Yugoslav Sex Education and Family Planning, 1960s and 1970s

In the 1963 Serbian educational film *Kontracepcija*, the female protagonist is the embodiment of a modern New Yugoslav Woman. Sporting a modern blond bob hairdo, she dresses in fashionable sundresses and high heels. She walks the streets with confidence. Presented as an aspirational figure, our protagonist is a city dweller, a mother to a school-age son, and a wife to a professional. The opening scene, however, is represented as being at odds with the image of the modern woman. The audience first sees the woman as she is wheeled from an ambulance into the hospital on a gurney, seemingly unconscious. Narration reveals that she is there because of heavy uterine bleeding as a result of an abortion, although the narrator does not specify whether the woman had been in the care of a physician or an unlicensed practitioner. We do not see her again until she comes back, sometime later, to attend a contraceptive seminar with other women. Through didactic messages, the film's overall point is that the modern Yugoslav woman needs to match her social status with her sexual and reproductive behavior and that she needs to take personal responsibility to learn about contraceptive options and the fertilization process.

Reading between the lines, it is clear that despite the pretense of socialist gender equality, sexual and reproductive health are solely the domain of women, wherein women are educated by knowledgeable, skilled, and professional men. Produced by the Institute of Healthcare of the Republic of Serbia, with medical advisers from its gynecological-obstetrical department, it represented a social education film that functioned as didactic material: the audience learns about the subject at hand at the same time as the protagonist does. This plot trajectory is typical of Yugoslav sex education media throughout the

1960s. The state-run domestic modernization project was science fueled and medically endorsed. Underlying this narrative is the state's agenda to establish itself internationally as modern and progressive, as part of the developed world that outwardly values and platforms individuals' human rights.

Considering domestic sex education initiatives, how did the state navigate international and domestic dialogues about human rights? Yugoslav physicians and educators viewed family planning as a fresh opportunity to influence reproductive behavior and address what the state perceived as unfavorable demographic trends. Family planning advocates included medical staff (especially gynecologists), social scientists, lawyers, and politicians from across Yugoslavia. Nevertheless, the republics that housed the most prolific proponents of family planning were Slovenia and Croatia. In this chapter, I critically analyze state didactic material to trace the administration's unfolding definition of "normal" reproductive behavior and how national social expectations operated within the broader context of human rights and population control.[1] I follow the historians Lutz Sauerteig and Roger Davidson, who treat "sex education in the broadest sense to incorporate many aspects of the formal and informal shaping of sexual knowledge," addressing not only "officially-sanctioned and regulated sex education delivered within the school system and regulated by the State, but also sex education taking place within the private sphere of the family or obtained through peer-group interactions and through the media such as sex education books, magazines or films."[2]

This chapter opens in the late 1950s, as Yugoslav family planning experts increasingly became involved with US-led international humanitarian and health organizations such as the IPPF. Simultaneously, they created a didactic tradition of informal sex education and eventually began to institute formal school-based sex education programs, aiming to reduce abortion rates, increase contraceptive use, and encourage an upward turn in natality.[3] I demonstrate that throughout the 1950s and 1960s, family planning advocates adapted their language in response to international trends related to human rights. While they had previously encouraged changes to private behavior for the good of the collective and in pursuit of national unity, starting from the mid-1950s, they encouraged women to embrace their individual rights to access reproductive health services and held women personally responsible if they failed to do so. I then examine the state's response to external human rights movements with the passing of the 1969 Family Planning Resolution and examine how the resolution affected Yugoslavia's domestic family planning and demographic landscape throughout the 1970s and 1980s. The state envisioned that standardized sex education programs integrated throughout curricula across the country would eventually "prepare young people for humane, equitable and responsible relations between the sexes" and resolve the need for abortion through contraceptive education.[4] Yugoslav sex education highlights global reformulations of social expectations and the ways that state agendas at times compromised individuals' human rights in favor of national schemes.

Guided by theories of social construction, national histories of sex education commonly analyze how state leaders and medical and educational experts constructed a "close connection between individual sexual conduct and the common weal," via didactic media.[5] These histories have acknowledged that governments used sex education to define deviance and construct the norm, especially among the young. During the 1950s and 1960s, most American and European sex education existed almost exclusively as moral education that shaped social norms and expectations while avoiding detailed anatomical or functional descriptions.[6] In his seminal work on American sex education in the first half of the twentieth century, Julian B. Carter argues that US sex education represented a "desire to restrain vice and inculcate virtue" through media that avoided factual scientific representations.[7] By contrast, Yugoslav sex education combined moral education about being a good, responsible socialist with in-depth anatomical representations and descriptions of the functions of the reproductive system and the process of fertilization. These messages were very similar to the Soviet context, where "sexual enlightenment propaganda implored individuals to eradicate bad habits and overcome personal weaknesses in order to ensure good sexual health."[8] These messages were also exclusively framed within the context of heterosexual romance, if not always marriage.[9] In addition to biomedical representations of conception and contraception, authors of didactic media also promoted a continuing fixation on teaching women about scientific mothercraft. The evolution of Yugoslavia's sex education tradition dovetailed with the state's development of the Yugoslav way. As family planning experts defined expectations in line with state goals, Yugoslav sex educators represented the vanguard in international sex education trends.

Responding to the recent transnational turn in historical scholarship and building on national studies, US and European historians have analyzed sex education from a transnational perspective to demonstrate that domestic agendas were not isolated.[10] Sex education proved transnational in content as material migrated across national borders through translations of didactic publications and the exchange of ideas and information.[11] Sex education became a population control measure at the same time that it became a device for economic development in countries of the Third World.[12] It simultaneously constituted a rallying cry for Western feminists fighting for women's reproductive rights. While international health and family planning organizations utilized sex education to control the population "bomb" in developing countries, the same organizations offered women from Western developed countries "choice" through family planning.[13] Western-inspired feminists adopted previously used population control strategies, such as sex education, to further the cause of individual freedom and women's right to choose: "Activists condemned *both* abusive population control programs *and* efforts to force women to bear unwanted children."[14] Yugoslav family planning advocates constructed sex education campaigns within this charged global domain.

"Conception as Desired": Yugoslav Sex Education Pre-1969

> The majority of our people tend to have smaller families. The only humane way to do that is by way of contraception. When we say "conception as desired," we mean that we want there to be fewer abortions.... We have no intention to reduce the number of births, in fact we intend the very opposite, that birth rates increase.[15]

Novak, *Conception as Desired*, 1962

> When a girl begins to menstruate at age 13 or 14 it is important to teach her about hygiene. That is even more important in our country as the way of life for our women has changed. While before her main responsibility was to be a wife and mother, today she stands equal to men and we find her employed in all branches of industry. For that reason, we have to commit our resources in supporting her to take care of her health, so that she can give birth to healthy and strong offspring.[16]

"Doctor's Advice: Girls in Puberty," 1957

Pre-1969 didactic material suggests that medical experts and educators sympathetic to the state's demographic requirements wanted families to have more children who would be "healthy and strong."[17] The didactic messages that state sympathizers penned illustrate a subtle encouragement toward larger families. This was similar to Germany's approach starting from the 1920s and 1930s. More directly, messages highlight women's personal responsibility to maintain their health, ensuring readiness to conceive, bear, and rear children. The first of the two opening quotations for this section was authored by Novak and appeared in an information pamphlet about conception and contraception, while the second appeared in a popular periodical. Taken together, they are typical of the tone and content of the mid-1950s to mid-1960s in that they reveal a complex negotiation of socialist gender equality and the state's demographic requirements. The first points to the state imperative to decrease abortion numbers as it encourages families to have more children. As he promotes contraceptive use, Novak does not condemn abortions, although he does write that contraception is more "humane." Novak ushers in the new language of family planning as personal responsibility coupled with individual reproductive rights. The unnamed author of the second quote explains that women's obligations begin when they go through puberty. Young girls are instructed to take heed and care for their own bodies while the state merely "commit[s] resources to support" girls in their individual reproductive journeys.[18] Novak skirts the topic of abortion. Legal abortion was a symbol of Yugoslav socialism; without threatening that legal right, Novak emphasizes that women should either choose contraception or have more children. Typical of his writing, the comment is neither blatantly pronatalist nor does it completely condone abortion. Novak concedes gender equality at the same time that he reasserts women's maternal responsibilities by creating a link between young pubescent girls and their biologically and socially predetermined future as mothers.

The amorphous nature of the tone and content of didactic messages was symptomatic of the state's ongoing concerns regarding an asymmetrically declining natality, which suggested continuing national disunity. Gaps in demographic trends kept widening, especially between urban, industrialized regions, such as Slovenia and Croatia, and more rural regions, such as Kosovo and Metohija, Montenegro, and Macedonia. Between the years 1950 and 1954, there were on average 28.8 live births per 1,000 people across Yugoslavia. However, from 1955, the birth rate steadily fell to a low of 17.7 live births per 1,000 people in 1975.[19] Over the course of two decades, the rate of fertility declined from 3.4 births per woman to 2.25 births per woman across Yugoslavia, albeit with regional differences.[20] Kosovo always represented an anomaly in national natality demographics, and this figure became even more pronounced over the course of 1950–1970.[21] In the 1970–1974 band, the Kosovo fertility rate was twice that of other regions. National abortion rates were also increasing. In 1949, over 24,000 abortions were performed in medical institutions across Yugoslavia. This number surpassed 160,000 by 1961, owing significantly to more liberalized access to the medical system for abortion care.[22] The total rate of abortions was likely considerably higher as women continued to pursue abortions outside of the medico-legal system. Though those statistics are incomplete, most available studies concur that as medical system abortions rose so too did abortions outside of medico-legal parameters. While demographers continually highlighted the uneven trends in natality, fertility, and abortion rates, the state did not invoke a particular population policy during the 1960s, perhaps to avoid nationalistic tendencies. Instead of tailoring their education campaigns to suit the specific conditions of each region, family planning campaigns were vague and sweeping: women should control their fertility through contraception while also preparing their bodies for eventual pregnancy and birth.

Despite measures to the contrary, abortions continued to rise across the country and experts had to change tack if they were to stem rising numbers. As is the case today, abortion numbers were difficult to track in Yugoslavia, even after decriminalization. Various collections of demographic statistics show that numbers of abortions completed in health institutions across the country rose consistently starting from 1945 and continued throughout the second half of the twentieth century. One data set shows that abortions completed in health institutions rose by 30 percent between 1963 and 1967.[23] Births, comparatively, only rose by 16 percent in that time frame. Slovenia was the only republic where abortion numbers plateaued and actually reduced by 6 percent during those years.[24] However, statistics were inconsistent, and statisticians admitted that data were only representative of areas where health institutions regularly and routinely declared abortion statistics.[25] Nevertheless, the 28 percent rise in abortions compared to the 16 percent rise in live births over the course of the 1960s implies that the rise in abortions outpaced the rise in live births, a situation that was not what the state desired. Using demographic data, social scientists demonstrated that this overall trend not only put pressure on health institutions and their ill-equipped staff but that they also impacted negatively on women's health, potentially rendering them infertile and unable to return to work for extended periods of time after the procedure.

Even though the international family planning movement presented a logical solution for Yugoslav gynecologists, social workers, and educators, some experts were reluctant to fully endorse the movement's principles. The IPPF was established in 1952, but Yugoslavia did not become an affiliate member until 1963, when the IPPF formally renounced its neo-Malthusian mission and recognized parents' rights to make individual choices about reproduction.[26] Yugoslavia then became a full member in 1972. Some naysayers balked at the IPPF's Western feminist associations at the outset. Despite their hesitation, most experts viewed family planning as a tool that could be applied in the Yugoslav context to serve local demands. Vida Tomšič, one sceptic among many, argued that the American methods could be borrowed to enhance the diffusion of contraception in order to reduce abortions and "liberate women from fear."[27] In terms of contraceptive education measures, Yugoslav medical experts found the language of human and individual rights useful in the Yugoslav context.

Yugoslav family planning advocates asserted that contraceptive education was key to addressing domestic demographic trends, prompting the state to expand the legal framework in support of educational provision. In 1960, with Decree 33, on the "conditions and formalities required for the interruption of pregnancy," legislators responded to the need for an education overhaul among the Yugoslav population.[28] Although the decree elaborated the framework for abortion, it also stressed the need to provide citizens with access to and information about contraceptives. In 1963, the Federal Institute for Social Welfare determined that women would receive contraception at no cost, "like any other drug," along with free contraceptive advice at designated clinics and with general practitioners.[29] In 1969, legislators enacted a new federal General Law that required "social and educational institutions and other organizations which deal with the problems of the health and security of mother and child ... to acquaint women and youth with the harmful consequences of the interruption of pregnancy and with the advantages of the application and means and methods of contraception."[30] The liberalization of contraceptive education was symptomatic of broader societal trends across parts of Western and socialist Europe, where a staggered and uneven liberalization of legislation in support of women's right to sex education and contraception took the place of postwar conservatism. Dagmar Herzog argues that the "turn toward a socialist variant of sexual conservatism in the later 1950s and 1960s (part Stalinist, part ex-Nazi, part petty bourgeois) and the uneven but increasing liberalization from the mid- to late 1960s on and especially in the 1970s are evident in marriage and sex manuals, sexological articles and reference works, popular magazines, and sex education curricula."[31] Lawyers, social scientists, and women's rights leaders viewed legal liberalization as another rung in the ladder leading to the utopian promise of socialist gender equality. Running concurrently alongside those legal developments were experts' efforts to offer some manner of educational material to consumers.

While the state's legal and fiscal endorsements helped nudge educators to conform to the state's agenda, health and education experts asserted medical and pedagogic advancements. Instructional media consisted of brochures and pamphlets as well as films, and the state also proliferated messages within popular magazines. Brochures were usually distributed through state health and educational services. Croatia's capital, Zagreb, had "Schools for Life" and "Schools for Parents," where young people and young married couples voluntarily attended contraceptive information seminars. Through the Red Cross and traveling hygiene and sex education crews, villagers across Croatia also received health education, some of which addressed family life and eventually contraception.[32] Educators also held seminars at community hubs to complement the takeaway media. Specialists from various disciplines—including the Slovenian gynecologists Novak and Berić, the sexologist Marijan Košiček, and the psychologist and pediatrician Grossman—appeared often as authors of state educational material. Such respected party doctors and medical professionals wrote for the popular press, reaching a wide readership and lending the material a sense of medical authority. Over time, the messages and foci changed. Throughout the 1950s and 1960s, sex education materials informed consumers about contraception and fertilization, warning readers of the alleged dangers of abortion. Eventually, by the 1980s, this message had shifted, and family planning experts spent less time moralizing to women about the dangers of abortion and more time informing them of the types of contraceptives that were available to them, how to use them, and where to access them.

Aiming to modernize behavior in line with socialist ideals and party agendas, sex education experts tailored content for mothers in their twenties, the demographic group that represented the highest proportion of women seeking terminations. Each resource's author states at the outset that both men and women, "bračni drugovi [married comrades]," are responsible for family planning.[33] Nevertheless, images and illustrations of women often feature alongside articles about contraception and abortion, inscribing women's bodies as sites of reproductive regulation. Narratives in educational films and articles typically follow an individual woman in her journey to get an abortion, or as her botched abortion is corrected and she attends all-female contraception seminars before the procedure or postrecovery. Sex education material also presents women leaving children or husbands behind to join other similarly aged women to receive contraceptive advice or heading to family planning clinics. The female focus may be a product of the fact that most of the contraceptives promoted, such as diaphragms, pessaries, and pastes, were controlled by women. Even when authors described male condoms, they advised that condoms should be used alongside pessaries or creams that were to be utilized by women. In addition, women were more likely than men to go to contraceptive clinics, places where most of the sex education literature and information was to be found. Furthermore, magazines aimed at a Yugoslav female readership often included sex education in their advice columns.[34]

Magazine content, including advice columns, letters to the editor, and general articles, served a didactic function. The advice columns assumed an authoritative voice that established a hierarchical relationship between reader and writer. The historian Natalia Chernyaeva describes Soviet mothering magazines as "manuals [that] constructed the reader not as a peer, but as, essentially, a student, who needed tutoring and disciplining."[35] Authors imbued advice with the notion of individual responsibility. The columns were presented as conversational and intimate yet placing onus on the reader. Column titles included Vi ste nas pitali (You asked us), Lječnik vam govori (The doctor advises you), Vi ste zabrinuti (You are concerned), Vaš kućni savjetnik (Your home companion).[36] Just as medical experts became household names, women were also invited into the fold; authors invited doctors and female readers into conversation with each other.

Through simulated encounters between medical authorities and female consumers, the state aimed to shape private behavior to conform to state agendas, which included raising natality while also fostering equality within private relationships. The state had high hopes that family planning would help society adopt constitutional gender equality within the private, domestic space. Still, while acknowledging that women unevenly bore the brunt of reproduction, the state and its medical leadership also assumed that women naturally desired to become mothers. Family planning allowed educators to encourage the uptake of contraceptives while also relaying pronatalist sentiment without necessarily embedding that "sentiment within policy." Through family planning, one pamphlet reads, women do not have to limit themselves to having "only 2, 3 or 4 children."[37] Nevertheless, experts did not want those children to be born in quick succession, lest women's health was affected, compromising their future capacities to contribute economically and socially inside and outside the home. By spacing pregnancies, "the modern woman can have more children while remaining young, healthy and in a favorable mood, compared to those women who leave conception to chance and then have abortions or give birth without stopping."[38]

The ideal of modern living existed within advice and education about married life, too, and readers were to understand that they held the power to achieve personal satisfaction in their matrimony. Writers' messages blended individual interests within families with citizens' responsibilities for uplifting socialist society. Readers were taught that to be responsible citizens of a socialist utopia, they had to be responsible in how they chose a partner and careful in maintaining respectful relationships. Marriage became secular, and divorce was permitted in the pursuit of citizens' happiness.[39] Didactic materials affirmed the importance of maintaining happy marriages, especially at a time when divorce rates were on the rise. Herzog argues in the German context that "no sex advice text in the East was complete without reference either to the idea that only socialism provided the context for the most loving and satisfying marriages or to the notion that a couple's commitment to and struggle on behalf of socialism would enhance their romantic relationship."[40] The onus for personal happiness in marriage, prescribed the state, lay on the individual.

By focusing on marital contentment, the state also constructed a frame for acceptable reproductive behavior. While legislation guaranteed that the state would safeguard illegitimate children, responsible parenthood, authors claimed, came via marriage. Columnists, especially the prolific Croatian sexologist Košiček, wrote about how to spice up readers' sex lives and avoid female frigidity and how to encourage loving marriages that would inevitably lead to more responsible parenthood.[41] Authors used marriage advice as a vehicle for instruction about reproductive behavior. Experts like Košiček directed women toward choosing their partners as wisely and carefully "as they would a shoe or a dress" so that married couples would remain married and continue to engage in sexual activity that would lead to procreation.[42] Authors did not want couples to procreate without a plan, however. According to columnists, loving marriages went hand in hand with being responsible citizens who would choose when to have children and would space births responsibly. Love, for the "modern person, who consciously determines the number of pregnancies and births, maintains the will to bring up children."[43] Without deferring to religious morality, authors apprised readers that marriage was the expected precursor to responsible parenthood.[44]

Advice included information aimed at preserving women's mental, emotional, and physical well-being and aimed to make women invest in their own health care, focusing on the individualization of health within a self-management society that was intended as a collective. Specialists wrote about the best diet, how to dress, and what shoes to wear during pregnancy. Articles explained in depth the specific vitamins and minerals required during pregnancy and which foods offered the richest sources of each. Authors cautioned against gaining too much weight, warning women to "eat well, but do not eat for two."[45] They advised pregnant women about what to pack for the birth center and what to prepare at home for when they returned with their baby. Overwhelmingly, writers told mothers that their care of babies and young children should be informed by medical and scientific advice rather than what is often passed down through generations. As Grossman, a regular columnist for *Svijet* from 1953 to the mid-1960s, opined, "without knowledge there cannot be progress."[46] The New Yugoslav Woman needed to know how to properly care for her child in a way that was informed by medical expertise. This exists in stark opposition to what we learned in chapter 2 about women's aversion to planning for the delivery of their babies in the early twentieth century, when the likelihood of their children surviving birth or infancy was low. After only a decade or so of socialism, experts were offering advice expecting that children would survive and thrive.

Readers were also offered instruction about how to educate their children in the same vein. Didactic materials affirmed that parents were responsible for the correct socialist upbringing of their children and that such individual freedoms, represented as unique to Yugoslav socialism, demanded reciprocal responsibility. Educating one's children comprised caring for their health and well-being all the way through to setting a good example as a socialist citizen and preparing them for their responsibilities as future parents. Columns such as Žena's Intimni Razgovori (Intimate conversations) featured guidance from medical professionals about teaching children about sexuality and sexual health within the home. In an effort to assert the modernity of the new Yugoslavia, the overall effect of these columns was to move away from the perception that sexual development was a moral issue. In Intimni Razgovori, Košiček addresses the issue of sex education, emphasizing over several columns that it is not simply a topic that should be addressed during puberty but rather that it can be a point of discussion from the beginning of school.[47] He offers parents tools for answering questions and giving factual answers to their children without embarrassment. Tactics included clarifying their questions, buying time by praising their children's courage to inquire, and offering brief and factual information without overloading them.[48] While it is not often explicitly mentioned, the implication is that religious ideas and morality were considered irrelevant for modern discussions of sexuality and reproduction.

Abortion debates leading up to the 1960 decree further affirm the trend toward apprising women of their responsibilities to care for their own bodies. Although many gynecologists would eventually become abortion-rights advocates, in the 1950s they largely opposed expanding abortion laws for fear that women would come to rely on abortion even more.[49] Reader questions to advice columnists provided a platform for medical professionals to articulate their concerns. The questions' alleged authors express anxiety about the potential side effects of abortion. Rogić, a regular columnist for *Svijet* whom we heard from at the opening of this book, answers one question by detailing a list of short- and long-term consequences of abortion, including issues with fertility, ongoing pain and discomfort, and a changed rhythm of menstruation.[50] He also suggests depression and frigidity as possible consequences. Gynecologists emphasized women's maternal duties outside of the popular press through pamphlets and films that warned women that abortion would lead to certain ill effects in later years. These questions and responses serve primarily as a scaremongering technique, highlighting what women can be exposed to should they consider a termination of pregnancy.

Authors of educational material rendered abortion dangerous, physically and mentally damaging, and irresponsible, even when completed within the legal framework and under medical conditions. To counter the assumption that women would increasingly turn to abortions for fertility control, gynecologists emphasized women's maternal roles and responsibilities, cautioning that abortion could lead to a childless future: "From early on, a girl's reproductive system needs to be prepared for her most important role, that of motherhood."[51] Rogić warns women that they may regret their decision to abort later in their lives when they will "naturally want to have children," equating womanhood with a desire for children.[52] Public rhetoric defended women's rights to partake in employment outside the home and in political activities, though the state all the while expected that women would inevitably choose motherhood.[53] This resonates with the unattainable notion of having it all that was being ushered in alongside second-wave Western feminism and speaks to a universal patriarchal structure that sets women up to be wrong, whatever their choices are. Socialism does not equate to a genuine disruption of gender norms within the household.

Alongside antiabortion messages, gynecologists offered information about fertilization, contraception, and where advice could be solicited so that women would be informed about how to take responsibility for their reproductive health. In-depth information about these topics did not really feature in the popular press until the 1960s. Until then, authors made only vague comments about the availability of contraception around the country, highlighting its modern aspect. Pamphlets of the 1960s feature a similar format: They open with an acknowledgment of the opportunities offered to women in Yugoslavia under socialism, warn against abortion, and then outline the biological aspects of fertilization. After illustrations and descriptions of the fertilization process, they list the various contraceptives available, including pastes, gels, and pessaries, male condoms and diaphragms, and the rhythm method or coitus interruptus. In the second half of the decade, pamphlets describe both the pill and IUDs. Gynecologists highlight the diaphragm above anything else prior to the availability of the pill and IUD, despite the fact that they admit that the only shield from infection is the barrier protection afforded by the male condom. Highlighting the desire to lift the birth rate, women were also informed that a lack of contraception should not dissuade them from intercourse, and gynecologists suggested vaginal douching using a saline solution as a way to expunge sperm from the vagina after intercourse.

During the mid-1960s, authors of the women's press consider the evolution of modern contraceptives and how they have been taken up internationally. In one 1967 article about contraception in *Svijet*, an unnamed author argues that the oral contraceptive pill "will have an impact on the health of millions of yet unborn people comparable to that of Pasteur's discovery about the mechanisms of infection."[54] The title of the article, which translates to "the pill of the century," a nod to US rhetoric on the subject, represents contraceptive use as typical of the modern woman. The unnamed author makes a correlation between American women's sophistication and their high overall quality of life with their rapid and increasing uptake of the contraceptive pill, a state that echoed through the visual imagery. "The IUD is popular in developing countries that have lower socio-economic standards," the article reads, and Yugoslavia needs to increase its acceptance of modern contraceptives if it wants to be considered a modern, progressive state.[55]

While many of the state's medical experts blamed women for not using contraceptives, some gynecologists and leaders of women's organizations expressed disappointment in the state's ability to keep its promises about reproductive health care. In 1965 in *Žena*, Mladen Berghofer, then director of the Centre for Family Planning in Croatia, evaluated the low contraceptive use by women in Yugoslavia. He lays blame largely on the state's lack of financial and political support for family planning institutions and their work. Berghofer argues that increasing women's use of modern contraceptives should not prove as much of a challenge as it had. He claims that women have historically always relied on contraception, be it plant-based home remedies or through coitus interruptus. It is not a matter of "introducing" them to the concept of contraception, he argues, but rather a matter of simply "correcting" their behavior, a task, he reckons, should not be so difficult for state experts.[56] Writers of women's magazines by the late 1960s increasingly criticize the state for its lack of meaningful support in tackling high abortion numbers through an increase in contraceptive use.

Despite multipronged educational strategies, surveys conducted during the 1960s suggest that myths still abounded in the area of sex and relationships. Informed by youth surveys undertaken in the early 1960s by republican women's organizations, sexologists and psychologists argued that youth received misinformation from friends, popular culture, and pornography that shaped unrealistic perceptions of sexual life and relationships, rendering aspects of sexuality taboo.[57] One of the main problems, purportedly, was the fact that there was not enough being done in the area of sex education that was directly and consistently targeted at youth. Throughout the 1960s, surveys of parents, children, and educators suggested that citizens wanted more in the way of formal sex education in schools and across the population.[58] In a 1961 Croatian survey of almost twenty-three hundred women, 95.7 percent endorsed the state to institute formal sex education in schools.⁵⁹ Košiček, a lead proponent of school-based sex education across Yugoslavia, saw sex education curricula complementing home-based parental instruction that would begin in early life. In the early 1960s, school-based sex education advocates suggested that it could easily fit within the regular curriculum to avoid parent protests against separate sex education lessons. Science subjects could easily include aspects of biological reproduction in humans, for example, while humanities subjects could include historical perspectives and instructional information about the family and marital life.⁶⁰ Advocates argued that the state needed to invest in teachers to increase their confidence in instituting a curriculum that included social, cultural, physical, and emotional aspects of sexual life.⁶¹

Formal efforts for implementing sex education curricula across Yugoslavia began in 1963, at the initiative of the federal arm of the KDAŽ, with the formation of the Coordinating Committee for Family Planning in Yugoslavia.⁶² From that year, women's unions in each republic founded a similar agency. Also in 1963, the Coordinating Committee for Family Planning hosted the first conference of educators, psychologists, doctors, and social workers to commence preparations for the entry of sex education curricula into schools. In 1967, the presidency established a federal administrative body, the Council for Family Planning, shoring up the evolving infrastructure that supported the development of nationwide family planning programs and services.⁶³ Encouraged by legal backing, republican women's organizations, education and health ministries, and youth organizations created plans and action programs for developing a curriculum during the mid- to late 1960s. Experts intended to "properly direct the sexual life of youth" by way of formalized school-based sex education.⁶⁴

After four years of discussions, Croatia formed an expert advisory group in 1967 to create curricula for primary and secondary schools.⁶⁵ The group was to oversee the pilot program of curricula while monitoring and documenting results for republic-wide proliferation. The curriculum spanned multiple years, each year building on the previous years' knowledge. Early lessons taught children in age-appropriate language about conception and puberty, while later instruction focused on the biological science of fertilization, conception, and contraception, as well as responsible family life and marriage. Primary schools signed up to test the curriculum between 1968 and 1971, after which the expert advisory group planned to have the curriculum rolled out to all primary schools across Croatia. Secondary schools were more difficult to penetrate because, according to reports, parents worried that sex education would encourage young people to have sex when they otherwise might not have. Feedback was consistently positive on the whole in the experimentation stage; however, education did not seem to have the intended long-term effect. Surveys conducted in family planning clinics in Zagreb, Croatia, in the early 1970s suggested that young people consulted their services "too late," given that many of the young women presenting for advice and treatment were already sexually active without contraceptive knowledge and that many had already had an abortion.[66]

The 1969 Family Planning Resolution

As Yugoslav family planning advocates constructed their own platform of sex education curricula and popular didactic media throughout the 1950s and 1960s, sex education was also a feature of worldwide debate. The UN hosted a series of conferences around the world that addressed issues of women's rights, global population growth and development, and human rights. Together, these global forums ushered in a new zeitgeist, which had been building since the 1948 Universal Declaration of Human Rights. Global forums elaborated the notion of individual human rights for all while they cemented a new worldwide concern about the population explosion. Belgrade hosted the first World Population Conference in 1965, with subsequent conferences in Bucharest in 1974 and Mexico City in 1984. The UN sponsored conferences on the status of women in Mexico City in 1975, Copenhagen in 1980, and Nairobi in 1985.[67] Education featured in discussions as the key to development and raising the social positions of women across the developing world. In the family planning and population control context, that extended to sex education. In ratifying the 1969 Family Planning Resolution, Yugoslavia consolidated such global conversations that outwardly saw responsibility for reproduction and population control shift from the state to individuals as part of their human rights. Though family planning experts had already been touting messages of individual responsibility and reproductive rights, advocates formally reframed family planning under the banner of human rights, for the individual to live freely yet responsibly.

Amid this climate of international deliberations in the area of human rights, women's rights, and population politics, one meeting plaited these threads together. In April and May 1968, representatives from eighty-four UN member states, along with intergovernmental organizations, met in Tehran, Iran, to discuss the twentieth anniversary of the adoption of the Universal Declaration of Human Rights and its progress since 1948. Conference delegates met to monitor international progress in the arena of human rights. Global forums "oftentimes became a Cold War battlefield," where representatives from the Soviet bloc clashed with "newly decolonized countries federated in the Non-Aligned Movement," as well as with Western democratic countries.[68] This deep-seated conflict overshadowed the Tehran agenda as Third World countries' recent entry into the UN had changed the physical landscape of the multilateral organization, definitions of human rights, and topics under discussion. Ronald Burke, a historian of human rights and the UN, argues that the Tehran conference was the "culmination of a shift from the Western-inflicted concept of individual human rights exemplified in the 1948 Universal Declaration to a model that emphasized economic development and the collective rights of the nation."[69] The dominance of Western powers in the UN and the Security Council was threatened by newly independent and emerging Asian and African countries, which pressed their agendas.[70] Western contemporaries considered the Tehran conference a failure because political and ideological clashes stymied progress on the meeting's agenda.

Despite clashes, the conference did recognize the 1966 Declaration on Population signed by twelve heads of state, including Tito, acknowledging individual freedoms in reproductive matters.[71] Individual freedoms, argued the declaration's signatories, could only be harnessed through the provision of education. Signatories committed to integrating population considerations into their national long-term planning while endorsing the notion that "family planning is the enrichment of family life, not its restriction, that family planning by assuring greater opportunity to each person, frees man to attain his individual dignity and reach his full potential."[72] Over the course of the following year, through the efforts of the Population Council's John D. Rockefeller III, eighteen more leaders signed, and this new declaration was presented to UN secretary-general U Thant on December 11, 1967.[73] The UN urged governments to institute educational provisions so that their citizens could make full use of those rights newly defined within the UN framework.

When the UN council passed the Tehran Proclamation, the Yugoslav state followed its recommendations with its 1969 Family Planning Resolution as one step in the state's longer effort to reform reproductive regulation. According to the migration expert and demographer Miloš Macura, the state adopted the resolution "because of humanitarian considerations and on the grounds of safeguarding individual rights."[74] One aspect of the proclamation was its emphasis on individual rights and the state's responsibility for providing not only information and education about family planning but also the means for citizens to be able to exercise their rights fully. As I argued above, this was already an aspect of Yugoslav sex education before 1969, but this legislative tactic offered the state another way to appear modern and progressive domestically and internationally. The resolution extended the 1960 decree's recommendation that the state offer educational provision, and it also permitted abortion on demand up to ten weeks' gestation. The resolution detailed that the provision of contraception was essential to responsible family planning, and it emphasized the need for school-based comprehensive and integrated sex education, especially of youth. While Yugoslav sex education prior to 1969 mainly targeted adult women, most of whom already had children, new legislation aimed to install more formalized sex education curricula within schools and youth programs.[75]

While from the outside, it appears that public officials were responding to external influences in passing such a progressive resolution, the drive for legislative change in terms of abortion laws also came from within the communist ranks. Family planning experts and communist women of the KDAŽ had been advocating for a need to change the laws to make them more permissive since the mid-1960s.[76] They argued that the heavily bureaucratic process that women had to navigate to obtain abortions disadvantaged their most needy populations—uneducated, impoverished women with large families, from remote villages. Since the process was lengthy, women often did not apply for an abortion and, instead, went to their local wise women or performed their own abortions.[77] If they did go through the process of applying for an abortion through the medico-legal system, communist women argued, the trips back and forth to their nearest hospital were long, expensive, and meant that they would abandon their existing children, farmwork, and domestic responsibilities for certain periods. Although the international climate was pivotal to the decision to pass the 1969 resolution, it was the work of communist women activists that set the foundation for such a decision.

If Yugoslavia already enjoyed a wide-ranging education tradition, why was it important for it to incorporate the recommendations of the proclamation? The state's governing administration and its medical and family planning experts wanted to be on the right side of the population control and human rights narrative. It was widely known that population policies varied depending on the region. On one side of this binary were Eastern, Asian countries of the Third World, while on the other were the First World Western democracies. Socialist countries fit somewhere between these two poles, given that, like most European and Western countries, they had no concerns about runaway population growth. They, however, were also not necessarily seen as developed, because the West associated developed countries with capitalism and democracy. With each global encounter on population, development, and family planning, Yugoslav representatives from the Council of Family Planning and the KDAŽ represented the state as the developed anomaly within the socialist realm, what in the language of the Cold War was called the Second World.[78] The 1969 resolution became an aspect of domestic policy that state representatives could tout at global forums.

As it had since the birth of the Yugoslav way, the state presented itself as a temperate, benevolent leader in the world of development and population control. The president of the Council of Family Planning, Nevenka Petrić, reflected in 1983 that Yugoslav laws were easily adopted within developing countries "who follow [Yugoslav] experiences to construct their own development programs, accepting that family planning is a constituent part of the socio-economic development."[79] In many international and domestic settings, she positioned the Yugoslav state between developed and developing worlds, presenting Yugoslavia as more benevolent than the other "developed countries [who] follow their own interests, influenced by Malthusian ideas about population growth, family planning and the limitation of large families, offering family planning as an exchange for development to the less and undeveloped countries."[80] Yugoslav family planning experts, conversely, advocated for state rights to enact national policies for their populations. As they did from the outset, Yugoslav communists utilized reproductive regulation at home and abroad to serve state-formation efforts, continually presenting the Yugoslav way as something to be emulated by the international community.

What did the 1969 Family Planning Resolution do for Yugoslav family planning advocates interested in building on established Yugoslav sex education traditions? It served to catalyze policy changes and offered a chance to review what had already been put in place; it ultimately led to the adoption of parental rights into the 1974 Yugoslav constitution, a version of which survives in the present-day post-Yugoslav states.[81] The resolution and the constitution removed Yugoslavia from the context of other socialist states, whose policies on reproduction were far more outwardly pronatalist. The Yugoslav government wanted to extract itself from associations with such states at the same time that it wanted to be considered a developed leader of the developing world.[82] Family planning as an ideology was already enmeshed within the fabric of the Yugoslav public health system. Leading gynecologists and family planning advocates had been discussing the need for a more formalized approach to teaching young people about sexuality and reproductive health. According to demographers, statistics showed that abortions were still on the rise, that birth rates were still declining, and that contraceptive knowledge was lacking across the country.

The year 1969 represented an important moment for the state's global geo-positioning. Passing the 1969 Family Planning Resolution made Yugoslavia the only socialist state to follow the recommendations of the UN as stipulated by the final point of the 1968 Tehran Proclamation. In ratifying the resolution, the state officially embraced the language of individual human rights by asserting that "parents have the right to freely decide on the number and spacing of their children."[83] In step with global humanitarian mandates, the resolution emphasized the need for contraceptive education as a tool for securing basic human rights for all citizens.[84] Passing the resolution, however, was merely one of many measures in a longer didactic tradition; domestically it represented a reformulated strategy toward fulfilling domestic population goals.[85] The state's formal adoption of the human rights vernacular ostensibly functioned to extend its commitment to gender equality. Yugoslav reproductive rights proponents had been arguing for systemic change that would lead to the actualization of the state's long-standing promise of gender equality. Family planning experts shaped didactic messages aimed at young people to advocate for individual rights and personal responsibility, "preparing youth for understanding and equalizing the relationship between the sexes, for harmonious and responsible relations in marriage and for parental responsibility within the family."[86] Underlying the message of sex equality existed the ongoing pursuit of national unity and a justification of the state's rule. Through Yugoslav representatives' formal international engagements in the area of family planning, state rhetoric changed to include more individual rights together with more responsibilities for citizens. Rather than a divergence, the resolution represented one event on a continuum.

While some gynecologists viewed the 1969 Family Planning Resolution as a failure because it expanded the eligibility criteria under which women could request abortion, other family planning advocates, such as Tomšič, viewed the resolution as a victory for women's rights, and women's health experts agreed. She argued that the resolution and the 1974 constitution extended the original emancipatory and gender equality clauses of the 1946 Yugoslav constitution. Tomšič proclaimed that "the Yugoslav concept of family planning, as a human right, is not as narrow as controlling fertility, as abortion or as contraception, but that it expands to include responsible parenthood as the basis for a happy family and harmonious social development."[87] The resolution offered the opportunity for legal revision in the form of a new abortion law that expanded legal indications for abortions. Tomšič acknowledged that despite the 1946 Yugoslav constitution affording gender equality, women's work in industry was undervalued, and they bore the brunt of domestic burdens. "Sex education is not just about the biology, it is also about teaching young people about social norms and in socialism these norms include equality of the sexes," a factor that

Tomšič had been emphasizing since the early 1950s as she invoked American family planning methods.[88] Contraception, Tomšič argued, allowed couples to be equal in that they could make a decision as responsible adults to have children who were wanted.[89] Ever the vocal and patriotic socialist, she argued that "socialism differs from other social systems because it accepts these social changes, and hastens them, and with conscious social action and education of the people, it continues to fight against discrimination of women."[90]

The state imbued the resolution and the 1974 constitutional amendment with promise; however, it continued to face ongoing challenges at home. After consulting with medical records from the city family planning center in 1971, the Belgrade City Council established that the 1969 resolution had not been implemented meaningfully. The council's report states that "contemporary contraception is the most effective measure in the fight against abortion and offers the only option to safeguard health of women and families. Changes in family and social relations constitute a new aspect of contraceptive measures. It is no longer simply a means to prevent unwanted pregnancy, but an integral part of the holistic efforts for the better and happier lives of man and family."[91] The council rushed to implement the resolution to realize its potential quickly. But the situation did not improve after the constitutional amendment; physicians and town councilors advocated for a more concerted effort in installing better practices to encourage contraceptive uptake. The Serbian Medical Society reviewed family planning in Belgrade between 1976 and 1983, concluding that only 10 percent of the female population reported using any kind of contraception. Furthermore, there were twice as many abortions as live births in Belgrade during that time, and the city suffered "from an ageing population."[92] Toeing the party line, authors concluded that all interested parties must be engaged in educational and propaganda activity to encourage significant numbers of women into contraceptive centers.[93]

An integrated and comprehensive approach to school-based sex education did not eventuate, much to the chagrin of its proponents. Košiček and Aleksandra Novak-Reiss, Croatian sexologists and sex education advocates, lamented the disappointing amount of attention given to sex education and, therefore, to humanizing relations between the sexes: "With great disappointment, we have to emphasize that in the whole of the 8th grade curriculum there only exists 10 lines of text relating to sex education, equal to that of vehicle safety. What do you think is more important: that young people learn about the consequences of abortion or how to register and insure their cars? It seems clear that in this day and age vehicles have become more important than people."[94] Calls for a more focused approach to the calamitous inflation of young and often unwanted parenthood continued throughout the 1970s and 1980s. The Croatians Štampar and Aleksandra Beluhan bemoaned the fact that early parenthood prevented young people from engaging fully in other aspects of life. The 466 students they surveyed in 1976 from all levels at one Zagreb high school regarding sexual activity, contraceptive knowledge and use, and pregnancy reported that teens were indeed having sex frequently. That actuality, in combination with students' self-reported low knowledge of contraception, resulted in high rates of teen pregnancy. Targeted and integrated sex education, the authors charged, was essential to preventing unwanted pregnancy and parenthood.[95]

The changing ideology of family planning gave state demographers a new purpose.[96] Throughout the 1960s and 1970s, demographers like Breznik and others working from the Institute for Social Sciences in Belgrade, claimed that Yugoslav demographic circumstances "developed 'naturally,' with no input from government."[97] Concerned with tracking domestic population trends, demographers argued that their work did not "aim to affect people's decisions, but rather that their research exists purely so that people will get the services they need in the regions where they need them."[98] Nevertheless, gynecologists from the late 1960s advocated for a concerted approach to resolving unfavorable trends in population in some regions. Vojvodina in particular experienced declining birth rates that prompted observers to call for a targeted population policy to increase natality.[99] This trend continued throughout the 1970s. In the same year the 1974 constitutional amendment passed, demographic researchers in Novi Sad, Serbia, submitted an application for the IPPF Founders Research Awards to conduct research into demographic decline in Bačka Topola, a town in Vojvodina of approximately 14,000 inhabitants.[100] The researchers, with approval from the city and republic authorities, applied for the $10,000 award for an eighteen-month project to investigate declining birth rates and the impacts of an aging population so that "future population politics on the territory" could be formed to better align demographic developments.[101] In neighboring Belgrade, the Serbian Medical Society that conducted the Belgrade study analyzed earlier criticized the resolution and 1974 amendment, concluding that "the stance of our society is that children should be born healthy and wanted, meaning that we endorse free decision-making about parenthood. However, this stance and constitution should co-exist with laws that ensure the realization of necessary natality and natural reproduction of the population."[102] The regulation of reproduction and population constituted central aspects of state agendas, both at home and abroad.

In step with technological advances in communication media, Yugoslav family planning experts of the 1980s began collaborating with international agencies on plans for using mass media as a vehicle for sex education around the world. Authors of didactic media began to mirror the language of the IPPF, especially the familiar phrase "every child a wanted child," which featured on pamphlets as an extension of the state's earlier calls for "responsible parenthood." In 1987, given the Council of Yugoslav Family Planning's interest in sex education as a vehicle for state agendas, the council positioned itself as an ideal partner to expand communication and propaganda strategies with the United Nations Educational, Scientific and Cultural Organization (UNESCO), UNICEF, and the World Health Organization (WHO), which had been engaging with broad questions of how to advance and increase the knowledge of the world's population regarding gender equality, responsible parenthood, and demographic development of populations. The authors of the program positioned Yugoslavia within the global conversation on responsible parenthood: "Since we are a part of this world, these questions are also pertinent to us."[103] In the same year, the intermunicipal chapter of the Socialist Union of the Working People of Banja Luka joined with the United Nations Population Fund (UNFPA) to work on a project about mass media and sex education regarding equality of the sexes. Starting in 1985, the UNFPA financed a three-year project, which involved training local and regional mass media outlets by way of a mass media diffusion of scientific and humanitarian messages with the goal that they advance knowledge and incite a positive change to understandings and behaviors in the areas of humanizing relations between the sexes and responsible parenthood.[104]

Conclusion

As the country had with studies into IUDs, the unfolding landscape of reproductive regulation in Yugoslavia became a yardstick for the relationship between family planning and development. At the 1972 UN Seminar on Women in Istanbul, Tomšič argued that the higher a level of social, cultural, and economic development in a country, the more likely the inhabitants of that land would be to accept family planning, even though population control proponents aimed to achieve the inverse. She argued that although there exists a "uniform policy for family planning in the country," the women of its underdeveloped regions (Kosovo and Metohija, Bosnia and Herzegovina, Macedonia, Montenegro) continued to "represent the greatest number of illiterate persons, which largely prevents them from availing themselves of their rights. Illiteracy, combined with their low status in the family, and compounded by an underdeveloped system of health and education institutions, shortage of contraceptives, prevent individuals from realizing their rights."[105] Although multilayered efforts to bring enlightenment—including literacy, health, and political enfranchisement—to the country's underdeveloped regions had fallen short of expectations, Yugoslav family planning leaders nevertheless held high hopes for serving as developmental models to developing countries around the world.

Even though Tomšič and other communist officials believed that the state's developments in family planning expressed socialist gender equality, the fact remained that much of the legwork to bring about legislative and practical change was undertaken by communist women operating within women's organizations and by institutional silos for family planning. While Tomšič continually argued that women would not be left behind in the building of Yugoslav socialism, other family planning advocates attested that the only way to resolve women's reliance on abortion would be to invoke the attention and investment of all state organs and all levels of society.

In ratifying the 1969 resolution, the state helped to represent Yugoslavia as progressive both domestically and on the international stage, even if the resolution was little more than a token gesture. Yugoslav family planning experts had spent the preceding decade establishing a tradition of didactic media with an aim of affecting the private behavior of adult women. The overarching message of state sex education was that women should use contraception to space births but not avoid pregnancy and motherhood altogether, aiming instead to enter into responsible parenthood in which "every child is a wanted child."[106] Women effectively took responsibility for this in practice, despite notional shared parental responsibility. Through sex education, family planning advocates aimed to change women's contraceptive practices, and this sex education framework served as a means of unifying the Yugoslav people through a shared aspiration of modern living. Education material served multiple agendas. Authors of didactic media promoted Yugoslavia's position internationally as progressive, modern, and developed, as they nudged consumers to embody this position through their own individual actions. The resolution helped to reposition Yugoslavia geopolitically; however, it had little impact on domestic events and trends. In passing the 1969 Family Planning Resolution, the state positioned itself as a part of the global trends that seemingly saw responsibility for reproduction and population control shift from the state to individuals. Under the banner of human rights, advocates presented family planning as a tool for the individual to live freely yet responsibly.

Aside from family planning programs falling short of expectations, integrated school-based sex education and demographic trends that continued to concern the state, social attitudes were also slow to change. Scaremongering as a tool to dissuade women from abortion prevailed throughout this period and became more hostile toward women, without acknowledging that they had limited meaningful alternatives. The conservative political atmosphere of the 1970s manifested in the social education films of the latter part of that decade.[107] The producers of two Croatian films, *Abortion* (1977) and *A ljudi ko ljudi* (And people like people [1979]), dutifully acknowledge the 1969 resolution and the 1974 constitutional amendment. However, both films represent abortion as dangerous and irresponsible, utilizing graphic imagery to deter women from accessing the procedure and demonizing those who have resorted to it along the way. Founded in 1946, Jadran Films, Croatia's largest and most prolific production company, produced *A ljudi ko ljudi*, which the Croatian cultural ministry financed. The Croatian production company Zagreb Films, founded in 1953, specialized in animated, documentary, and educational films during the socialist period and produced *Abortion*.

The message of these films is aggressively antiabortion, or at least pronatalist. State film production companies financed by federal or republic state cultural ministries aimed to alter women's behaviors and attitudes toward abortion. In *A ljudi ko ljudi*, the narrator seeks to shame women who have had a termination by showcasing the story of a woman who was desperate for a child whom she adopted in her late thirties and who now brings her overwhelming joy every day by calling her "mama."[108] The woman lives in a humble studio apartment and says that she does not need much to bring up her child, contradicting an oft-cited reason for pregnancy termination. In *Abortion*, an unwed teenager seeks an abortion.[109] After a night of partying with friends and an unseen encounter with a faceless (and seemingly blameless) male presumably leads to an unintended pregnancy, she begs her mother for the last of her pension to pay for the procedure. At the hospital, she joins a long queue of women who are waiting to get terminations that day. She pays her money, explains her situation to the physician who sees her, and receives treatment. State physicians are represented as overworked but professional, while she and other women are depicted as irresponsible for draining the resources of the state and their own families in a selfish pursuit of independence. While outwardly Yugoslavia appeared progressive, internally attitudes were not quick to change.

Yugoslav sex education material from the 1960s captures the evolution of a state that underwent a metamorphosis that was neither linear nor simple. While maintaining its socialist bent, the Yugoslav state proved its responsiveness to international shifts. An examination of Yugoslav sex education offers insights into how the state was at once responsive to the significant global ebbs and flows of evolving social and humanitarian paradigms at the same time as it had a hand in their manufacture. From here, we move to the book's final chapter, where we hear from ordinary women and health care professionals on how these broad formulations of state norms and expectations in the context of global movements to control populations and definitions of human rights manifested in lived experience and how they have lived on into the country's postsocialist legacy.

Notes

1. Sauerteig and Davidson, *Shaping Sexual Knowledge*, 1.
2. Ibid., 4. Other historians have also utilized a similar framework. For example, Angela Y. Davis includes parent education within sex educational analyses in the British context. Davis, *Modern Motherhood*. As Claire Gooder argues in the New Zealand context, there is much that is lost when we only consider sex education as a school-based event: we can learn a lot when we look "beyond the school gates." Gooder, "History of Sex Education," 6.
3. Lišková, "History of Medicine," 183.
4. Nevenka Petrić, "The Human Right to Free Choice on Childbirth in the Socialist Federal Republic of Yugoslavia," Yugoslav Committee for International Women's Year, UN 1975, Belgrade, May 1975, 40.
5. Carter, "Birds, Bees, and Venereal Disease," 216. Other seminal national studies include Moran, *Teaching Sex*; Porter and Hall, *Facts of Life*; Irvine, *Talk about Sex*; Lord, *Condom Nation*.
6. Zimmerman, *Too Hot to Handle*. Zimmerman writes that "family" and "life" education were the terms applied by sex education proponents who wanted to avoid the vulgarity of sex in the title. See also Herzog, *Sex after Fascism*.
7. Carter, "Birds, Bees, and Venereal Disease," 249.
8. Hearne, "Broadcasting Communist Morality."
9. Hilevych and Sato, "Popular Medical Discourses."
10. Zimmerman, *Too Hot to Handle*; Sauerteig and Davidson, *Shaping Sexual Knowledge*; Connelly, *Fatal Misconception*; Solinger and Nakachi, *Reproductive States*.
11. Zimmerman, *Too Hot to Handle*, 80.
12. See Connelly, *Fatal Misconception*; Solinger and Nakachi, "Introduction," 15.
13. Solinger and Nakachi, "Introduction," 11.
14. Connelly, *Fatal Misconceptions*, 369.
15. Novak, *Začeće po želji* [Conception as desired] (Belgrade: Editorial Press RAD, 1962), 10, 12.
16. "Lječnik vam govori" [The doctor advises you], *Žena*, March 1957, 37.

17. Ibid.

18. Ibid.

19. Boško Popović and Milan Škrbić, *Stanovništvo i zdravlje* [Population and health] (Zagreb: *Yugoslavian Medical Journal*, 1987), 26.

20. Ljubomir Antonovski, "Medical Aspects of Induced Abortion in Yugoslavia," in *Fertility and Family Planning in Yugoslavia* (Belgrade: Institute of Social Sciences, Demographic Research Centre, 1980), 69.

21. See the table "Components of natural movement in the Yugoslav population, 1950–1979 (annual average)" in Dušan Breznik. "The functioning of the Yugoslav economy," *Eastern European Economics* 20, no 3/4 (1982), 217.

22. Of course, there are a number of issues with abortion figures. Some institutions, according to the demographers, had not submitted their statistical information, so the numbers were incomplete. It is impossible to know how many women had abortions outside of the medical setting, too, though we do get some hint of how many attempted to self-abort from statistics on abortions completed in hospitals. These, too, are tricky because some of those abortions were actually miscarriages. Breznik et al., *Fertilitet stanovništva u Jugoslaviji*, 312–313.

23. Despite legal medicalized options, women did continue to have abortions outside of the medical system for a variety of reasons, including cost of the procedure, potential travel required to reach regions with hospitals that offered the procedure, and privacy. See chapter 2.

24. Breznik et al., *Fertilitet stanovništva u Jugoslaviji*, 317.

25. Ibid., 319.

26. AJ, 142-54-184/1957-1985, "Medjunarodna saradnja" [International collaboration], 6.

27. Ibid.

28. "Uslovi i formalnosti potrebni za prekid trudnoće" [Conditions and formalities required for interruption of pregnancy], *Službeni list* 9 (1960).

29. Dobrivojević, "Family Planning in Yugoslavia," 125.

30. Resolution on Family Planning adopted by the Federal Assembly on April 25, 1969.

31. Herzog, *Sex after Fascism*, 185.

32. The Red Cross existed throughout the region from the 1800s, and its function changed over time. During the socialist period, each of the republics and autonomous provinces had a Red Cross society within the Red Cross of Yugoslavia.

33. This was a common phrase used throughout didactic media.

34. I have identified no magazines aimed explicitly at a male target audience.

35. Chernyaeva, "Childcare Manuals," 1.

36. These featured in various issues of *Žena danas*, *Svijet*, and *Žena*.

37. Novak, *Začeće po želji*, 3.

38. Ibid.

39. "Zaključci plenarnog sastanka Centralnog odbora Antifašističkog Fronta Žena Jugoslavije" [Conclusions from the plenary meeting of the central organ AFŽJ], *Žena danas*, April 1946, 23.

40. Herzog, *Sex after Fascism*, 194.

41. Marijan Košiček, "Intimni razgovori, još jednom o neugodnim pitanjima" [Intimate conversations, once more about uncomfortable questions], *Žena*, September 1958, 18.

42. Ibid., 26.

43. Ibid.

44. Ibid., 33.

45. "Hrana žene za vrijeme trudnoće" [Women's diet during pregnancy], *Svijet*, April 1953, n.p.

46. Grossman, "Briga za zdrav razvitak naraštaja" [Caring for the healthy development of future generations], *Svijet*, May 1957, n.p.

47. Košiček, "Intimni razgovori," *Žena*, February 1958, 18.

48. Ibid.

49. AJ, 49-39-71/1948-1951, Novak, "Stav ginekologa u pitanju legalnog arteficialnog abortusa" [Position of the gynecologist regarding the question of legal termination of pregnancy], 5.

50. Rogić, "Vi ste nas pitali, Recite mi istinu o pobačaju [You asked us, tell me the truth about abortion]," *Svijet*, August 1958, n.p.

51. "Liječnik Vam Govori" [The doctor advises you], *Svijet*, August 1957, 37.

52. Ibid.

53. While it was not specifically wealthier women who received this choice, by default, it was more likely that women in urban areas, who had the education, time, and resources to access education and services, would have been the more likely beneficiaries of choice.

54. "Pilula stoljeća" [Pill of the century], *Svijet*, February 1967, n.p.

55. Ibid.

56. Mladen Berghofer, "Žene, navodno, odbijaju kontracepciju" [Women are apparently rejecting contraception], *Žena*, March 1965, 13.

57. HDA, 1234–206, "Zapisnici o polnom vaspitanju u školama" [Minutes regarding sex education in schools].

58. Ibid.

59. "Naši razgovori, Planirate li porodicu?" [Our conversations: Are you planning a family?], *Žena*, May 1961, 14.

60. Janja Herak-Szabo, "Seksualno obrazovanje mladih u SR Hrvatskoj i Zagrebu" [Sexual Education of Young People in Socialist Republic of Croatia and in Zagreb], *Gynaecology & obstetrics*, 6 (1966): 267.

61. Ibid., 271–272; HDA, 1234–206. Alojz Cotić, Košiček, Aleksandra Novak-Reiss, and Ante Zadrović, "Rad na uvodjenju odgoja za humane odnose medju

spolovima u škole u SR Hrvatskoj" [Work on the implementation of sex education for humanizing relations between sexes in schools of Croatia].

62. Cotić et al., "Rad na uvodjenju odgoja."

63. Ibid.

64. Herak-Szabo, "Sexual Education," 267.

65. IAB, 1641-5-08-1327/3, Konferencija za Društvenu Aktivnost Žena Beograda [Conference for the Social Activity of Belgrade Women], Novak-Reiss, "Sex education plans for schools."

66. Beluhan and Štampar, "Istraživanje znanja, stavova i prakse planiranja porodice u populaciji žena koje prvi put posećuju kliniku za planiranje porodice" [Survey of knowledge, attitude and practice of family planning in the population of women visiting family planning clinic for the first time], *Arhiv za zaštitu majki i djece* 1–2 (January–February 1972): 76.

67. All these conferences were attended by Tomšič, who led international representation of family planning experts in Yugoslavia. Bonfiglioli, "First UN Conference," 524. On the Mexico City conference and its aftermath, see Olcott, *International Women's Year*. For its fallout in the US, see Spruill, *Divided We Stand*.

68. Bonfiglioli, "First UN Conference," 524.

69. Burke, "Individual Rights," 276.

70. Their concerns, while not monolithic, were seen as at odds with the conception of human rights as set out in the UN Declaration of Human Rights. The issues that new states faced were racism, apartheid, and the fight for national liberation. Taking these factors into account, along with their dismal economies, their definitions of human rights focused less on individual freedoms and civic and political rights and more on lifting the national economy and resolving systemic racism.

71. Other signatories included representatives from the Western countries of New Zealand, Australia, the US, the UK, and the northern European countries of Sweden and Norway, as well as newly decolonized countries, such as Ghana and Morocco, and countries of the Third World, including India and Nepal.

72. Population Council, "World Leaders Declaration," 180–181.

73. Ibid.

74. Miloš Macura, "Population Policies," 370.

75. "General law on abortion," *Službeni list* 20 (March 1969).

76. AJ, 130-587-972/1969-1970, Savezno Izvršno Veće [Federal Executive Council], Zdravstvo [Health], "Advice for the Resolution of Family Planning and Regulating the Conditions for Pregnancy Termination," 4.

77. Ibid.

78. AJ, 130-587-972/1969-1970. "Medjunarodna saradnja," Belgrade, September 1983, 6–12.

79. AJ, 130-587-972/1969-1970, "Summary of the consultation about multilateral collaboration of the Council for Family Planning in front of the Federal Executive Council," Belgrade, November 18, 1982, 2–3.

80. Ibid. Malthusianism is the idea that world resources, including the food supply, would run out in the face of exponential population growth. It derives from the political and economic thought of the Reverend Thomas Robert Malthus from his 1798 writings.

81. In chapter 5, I examine the ways that the 1974 constitutional amendment was remembered by Yugoslav physicians, especially those physicians who still practice. Each post-Yugoslav successor state currently retains some version of the 1974 amendment; however, due to aggressive lobbying by special-interest groups, such as Catholic groups in Croatia, some governments are considering repealing reproductive rights in favor of more conservative legislation.

82. Macura, "Population Policies," 67.

83. In resolution 2542, passed in 1969, the UN General Assembly Declaration on Social Progress and Development affirmed the Teheran Proclamation and urged governments to provide parents not only the "education" but also the "means necessary to enable them to exercise their right to determine freely and responsibly the number and spacing of their children." General Assembly Resolution 2542, U.N. Doc. A/7630, accessed May 6, 2019, https://www.unfpa.org/events/international-conference-human-rights.

84. Thompson, "Tehran 1968," 84–100; Whelan, *Indivisible Human Rights*; Burke, *Decolonization*; Mazower, *No Enchanted Palace*; Lauren, *Evolution*.

85. As I outlined in chapter 2, the tradition of sex education began in the interwar period with hygiene campaigns that encouraged peasants into the medical system and science-based practices.

86. Resolution on Family Planning adopted by the Federal Assembly on April 25, 1969.

87. Tomšič, "Planiranje porodice u Jugoslaviji," *Medjunarodna politika* [International politics] 545 (1972): 3.

88. Ibid.

89. SDA, 1413–4, Slovenski Državni Arhiv [Slovenian State Archives], Vida Tomšič, "Speech on sex education," 1971, 7–8.

90. Ibid., 4.

91. IAB, 865-5-A-7/1944-1972, Fond Savez Komunista Srbije, Organizacija SK Beograda, Gradski Komitet—Beograd [Coucil of Communists Serbia], Belgrade City Council, "Conclusions on measures to advance the work of family planning in Belgrade and health and education of children and young people in primary schools and high schools," May 31, 1971, 2.

92. Marta Husar, "Regulation of fertility in Belgrade," *Srpski Arhiv za celokupno lekarstvo* [Serbian archive for general practice] 113 (1985): 608.

93. Ibid.

94. HDA, KDAŽH-1234, Košiček and Novak-Reiss, "Primjedbe na program 'Sata razredne zajednice" [Remarks on school curricula], December 6, 1971, 3.

95. Beluhan and Štampar, "Evaluacija nastave iz planiranja obitelji u srednjim školama" [Evaluation of sex education in high schools], *Arhiv za zaštitu majki i djece* 22 (January 1978): 113, 119.

96. "While this type of extreme neo-Malthusian, racist, ideas could find their way to a party publication at the level of republics there was no political will within the Communist party at the federal level to implement any kind of population policies. Both pronatalism and even more anti-natalism (or neo-Malthusianism) were considered potentially disruptive for the policy of 'brotherhood and unity' of the Yugoslav nations." Drezgić, "Policies and Practices," 197.

97. Breznik, *Fertility of Yugoslav Population*, 24.

98. Ibid.

99. Draga Belopavlović and Vladimir Vilićev, "Preliminarni sumarni prikaz totalnog biološkog bilanca stanovništva Vojvodine i Jugoslavije" [Preliminary summary of the total biological balance of the population of Vojvodina and Yugoslavia], *Jugoslovenska pedijatrija* [Yugoslav paediatrics] 11 (1968): 3.

100. AJ, 130–489, "Lady Rama Rau, IPPF Awards 1974, correspondence and project proposal."

101. Ibid.

102. Husar, "Regulation," 601.

103. AJ, 130–489, "Uloga sredstava javnog informisanja na razvijanju i svesti o slobodnom i odgovornom roditeljstvu" [Role of mass media in developing an understanding about free and responsible parenthood], Belgrade, November 1987.

104. AJ, 130–489, Ć Rakić, J Savić, and S Šiljegović, "One approach for using mass media in humanizing relations between the sexes," November 1987, 2, 15.

105. AJ, AJ, 142-54-184/1957-1985, UN Seminar on the Status of Women and Family Planning in Istanbul, Turkey, July 11–24, 1972, 3.

106. Ibid., 15.

107. Yugoslav cinema of the 1970s experienced a conservative turn. In Croatia, the federal government squashed the mass social movement known as the Croatian Spring, which agitated for more self-governing rights and autonomy within Croatia throughout the 1960s and 1970s. The film industry was not immune to the conservative turn, and many filmmakers associated with the Croatian Spring were censored and blacklisted. They pursued safer films, such as animated children's films and documentaries. Škrabalo, *101 godina filma*, 541.

108. *A ljudi ko ljudi* [And people like people], dir. Petar Trinajstić (Zagreb: Jadran Film, 1979).

109. *Abortion*, dir. Ljubica Janković (Zagreb: Zagreb Film, 1977).

5

Deconstructing Yugoslav Women's Recollections of Reproductive Regulation

Mirjana Jelinić, a Belgrade woman in her sixties at the time of our interview in 2016, graphically described her experience when she miscarried and doctors had to evacuate her uterus surgically in 1978. Mirjana had been admitted to hospital after a miscarriage ten weeks into her pregnancy. She found herself left alone in a cold and dark hallway, naked on a surgical gurney. "They forgot me," she said, "and that's when I really thought I would die."[1] She remembered how she started to bleed vaginally, shivering from loss of blood and the frigid temperature of the hospital corridor. Eventually, she was able to call to someone who helped her. She was taken to an operating theater, injected with a local anesthetic, and surgeons performed a curettage evacuation of her uterus. Despite the anesthetic, the pressure from the surgeons opening her vagina and cervix and completing her miscarriage felt like "everything was collapsing inside" her. She said of the procedure that it felt like the surgeon was "literally ripping" the contents of her uterus. Afterward, she gradually recovered, but the memory of the event haunted her through her two subsequent pregnancies and live births.

I asked her to tell me what she remembered about Belgrade's birthing clinics and women's health services. She listed how facilities were very comfortable and clean, a far cry from "when cats used to wander the halls" in the buildings of the hospital. She said that staff were friendly, and she emphasized that "we [women] had everything then." The discord between the dominant narrative of socialist care for women, as captured in Mirjana's description of women's access to health services and her own memory of her personal experience of these services, is ubiquitous. This "internal paradox," as the Soviet historian and anthropologist Alexei Yurchak calls it, lies at the heart of women's memories of their reproductive pasts under socialism and the way that women's lives, roles, and experiences were and are represented in popular media and academic scholarship.[2] This chapter uncovers women's memories of their experiences and examines what factors shape their retelling.

What do these women's personal narratives of their experiences of reproductive regulation tell us about the Yugoslav past and its postsocialist legacy? While in no way a representative sample, it does capture the experience of women of urban middle-class backgrounds.[3] One might expect my cohort to have had the most positive encounter with the Yugoslav medical system given their relative privilege. The interviews suggest that even comparatively elite women, as teenagers and adults, experienced obstacles to exercising reproductive decisions. Yugoslav women and their doctors experimented with whatever contraceptives were available; they balanced work responsibilities and life in the home; they made decisions about their families and about their bodies; and despite legal enfranchisement, they experienced coercion, trauma, pain, and fear when navigating a medical system designed ostensibly to help them. Yugoslav physicians also worked within the parameters of public policies and laws, hospital regulations, their personal communities and professional networks, and their own beliefs.

Below, I plumb the intersubjectivity of the interview process. I explore how factors that may otherwise be explained by nostalgia for the recent socialist past were shaped by our common and contrasting experiences and how women responded to my presence as an interviewer.[4] Through our shared authority over the interview process, I examine how much we can and cannot attribute to a peculiar socialist experience. Then, I focus on interviewees' recollections of contraception and abortion. I analyze the ways that Yugoslav women drew on dominant narratives of the past and shared cultural memories to fill the gaps in their own recollections to make sense of their past experiences and to make them relevant today. This type of remembering is not unique to Yugoslav women, but the testimonies reveal the influence of historical and present-day factors on the process of remembering and the ways oral history enables researchers to understand the past through the perspective of the present.

The oral histories demonstrate that women's recollections of their experiences as patients in the socialist health care system show continuity with the past rather than a dichotomy between the socialist and postsocialist world. Furthermore, the women in my study expressed a longing for the way that things used to be that was shaped by a combination of factors peculiar to their experiences of life in socialist Yugoslavia and many more factors that had nothing to do with socialism or Yugoslavia. Malgorzata Fidelis argues, "In 1989, the world looked on at revolutions across the Eastern bloc with surprise. But when analyzed through the stories of those behind the Iron Curtain, the collapse of communism may be seen less as a breakthrough moment and more as a continuation, expansion, and modification of previous trends."[5] Romanian women shaped their memories of socialist consumption through their experiences of relative consumerist abundance in the 1960s, even as reproductive rights were brutally revoked and despite the material difficulties that families faced during the 1980s. Jill Massino argues that, regardless, the "socialist period is still remembered fondly by some people. This is especially the case for those who have struggled financially since the collapse of communism."[6] And this was not exclusive to socialist society. Jennifer Helgren, writing about young women and safety in the UK, argued that her subjects "did not simply misrepresent the past, but rather their nostalgic reflections critique the present, especially with regard to the perceived loss of institutions and communities that made positive differences in their lives, and may anchor their current identities in gendered and class-based descriptions of middle-class girlhoods where protection and shelter signify status."[7] Post-Yugoslav women shared commonalities with other women in crafting their narratives to suit the autobiographical needs of their present circumstances.

Memory studies in Yugoslavia have tended to focus on collective or social memory, heightening nostalgia for the communist past. Oral history research and methodology hold the potential to bring the past into dialogue with the present and to interrogate the "relationship between individual and collective memory."[8] Scholarly analyses of examples of collective memory—such as commemorations, events, and cultural products—emphasize the distinctive phenomenon of Yugo-nostalgia, the "projection of a utopian past into the future of post-socialist societies that have emerged from Yugoslavia."[9] The turn of the twenty-first century ushered in "the umbrella concept of 'postcommunist nostalgia,'" a commodification and glorification of the recent unified past.[10] The phenomenon of Yugo-nostalgia, unlike its Eastern European equivalents, is compounded by the brutal Yugoslav wars that saw the end of the country. Nostalgia is not a phenomenon peculiar to the socialist and postsocialist world. Sean Field, writing about memory in postapartheid Cape Town and how respondents in his study imagined the communities from which they were displaced, describes how "narrators' mental images of the past yield clues about their conscious and unconscious struggles with forms of loss. Nostalgia is an imaginative process of finding words to make sense of memories laden with uncomfortable images and feelings evoked in the present but linked to what has been lost from the past."[11] The pervasiveness of contemporary state-socialist mythmaking through all manner of media, along with the "distinctively brutal dissolution" of Yugoslavia in the early 1990s, created a longing for the unified socialist past.[12] Following the idea that Yugoslavia was exceptional, with a focus on the postsocialist construction of a shared cultural memory of the Yugoslav past, Aleksandar Bošković argues that Yugoslavia's brutal end "plays a significant, if not a critical role in framing and filling postwar Yugonostalgia and its representations."[13]

Perhaps because nearly three decades have passed since the fall of Yugoslavia, scholarly analyses of remembering in the postsocialist world have started to examine critically the enduring power of the dissolution and the effects of Yugo-nostalgia. In the last decade especially, scholars have utilized oral history as primary source material to recount nondeterminist historical narratives, as well as to attempt to disentangle analyses from the pervasive powers of Yugo-nostalgia.[14] The historian Sabina Mihelj argues that rather than "focusing solely on the power of the present to remake the past, future research on post-state socialist memory should pay attention to the ability of the socialist past to outlive the end of the cold war."[15] Maja Maksimović describes Yugo-nostalgia as a "bittersweet craving for the past—passive, static, and restricted," negating complex analyses of recollections of Yugoslavia's past and opportunities in the present.[16] In analyzing oral history interviews with workers from a cable factory that never underwent a formal privatization process during the postsocialist democratic transition, Tanja Petrović critiques the concept of nostalgia because it amplifies a division between East and West (as something that only happens in Eastern European countries), and socialism and postsocialism (countering the idea that socialism completely ended in 1989).[17] The Jasenovac cable factory retained the old socialist self-management structure, as the new government forgot to remove it in the transition process. She argues that in their habitual invocation of socialist rhetoric and the party line, Jasenovac cable workers demonstrate the ways that the communist legacy persists despite the fall of European communism, the end of Yugoslavia, and the protracted process of democratization. While powerful, Yugo-nostalgia is not the only factor shaping individuals' recollections.

Women's testimonies of their reproductive pasts emphasize how socialist remnants live on in individuals beyond the institutional level. Women interwove socialist ideas with their present-day politics and personal agendas and negotiated historical and enduring stigmas having to do with reproduction. As Jill Massino and Shana Penn argue of Eastern European society generally, "socialism decisively shaped, and continues to shape, how individuals think about government, the economy, society, and their lives more generally."[18]

In constructing narratives of their reproductive pasts, women's stories, body language, and mannerisms revealed that they were not accustomed to discussing their lives as individuals or sharing their private experiences; they deferred to the dominant narrative of legality and ease of access. Cultural theorists and oral historians have demonstrated how individuals intermingle personal memories with collective shared narratives when recalling the past, especially in instances when our memories fail us.[19] Some respondents had discussed their private lives with friends and family; however, they were unaccustomed to discussing aspects of their private lives publicly, and this was the first time they had spoken with the intention of bringing their experiences to a larger audience. My respondents drew on collective and shared narratives of the past, a phenomenon that oral historians identify as occurring frequently regardless of location or ideology.[20]

Intersubjectivity

The use of oral history offers an opportunity to look at Yugo-nostalgia through the idea of intersubjectivity. On the one hand, the women may have felt comfortable speaking with me because of our shared cultural background, but on the other hand, my subjectivity as a Western feminist created distance. Specifically, these women may never have thought to discuss their private stories of abortion, and many attested that it was the first time they had spoken about these experiences openly with strangers. Yet when they heard from a researcher who was born and raised in their country, they felt a duty to our shared origins. My position as a younger person returned from overseas to their homeland might have elicited more nostalgic recollections of the way things were, and they were perhaps interested in passing on positive stories of Yugoslavia to the next generation. At the same time, however, my position as a Western feminist then living in Australia may have stymied some discussions about the limitations of the socialist health system in which they underwent their terminations. Women who otherwise may not have thought about the Yugoslav past in relation to their experiences of contraceptive and abortion services felt compelled to defend that past as better for women when faced with a Western feminist. This was especially the case when their hunch about my feminist leanings led them to believe that my political affiliations would stand at odds with socialism and that I inherently opposed the system. In discussing Canadian working-class women's narratives, Joan Sangster observes that age, class, ethnicity, and "the ideological similarity/distance that women felt in relation" to her resonated with her subjects, allowing her interviewees to "recast their own history by recovering and revaluing" their own personal histories, in a way that my subjects did with me.[21]

The atmosphere of the interviews was informal and intimate, perhaps qualities that were necessary in light of the potentially sensitive topics under discussion. When I met my respondents, I was greeted with cups of tea and coffee, nourished with home baking, and taken on strolls through city neighborhoods, offices, and clinics. Women invited me into their homes, their workplaces, and their social spaces, such as the *kafana* (tavern) across from their apartment building or the park where they walk their dog. Beyond the formal and detailed responses my queries elicited, I have had many casual, often fleeting interactions with women in the region. I draw on such casual interactions rarely as anecdotal evidence. Taken together with more in-depth and systematic interviews, these tidbits help to establish a clearer, broader pattern of evidence that highlights women's intimate experiences of reproductive health. Interlaced with casual conversations about women's families, some of whom I knew, I asked questions about their experiences of sex education, their knowledge and use of contraception, and their experiences during pregnancy, childbirth, and abortion.[22] I also asked them to reflect on their memories of the Yugoslav medical system, on their family dynamics, and on the Yugoslav political system, especially in comparison to their present circumstances. I consulted physicians about their experience of medical training and education, working within the socialist system and interacting with international colleagues, and what they remembered about the process of birth and abortion service provision.

My local connections helped to establish a foundation of trust that allowed me to broach intimate topics. I was collected from train and bus stations and dropped off at my rented apartment with strict instructions to send regards to my parents (who were strangers to my hosts) and to call when I had my first baby. I was gifted precious research materials whose authors said, "It is more useful in your hands, now."[23] Given their professional interest and sense of authority, unsurprisingly, physicians tended to be more direct and spoke for sometimes twice as long as patients.[24] The health care consumers who agreed to speak to me were eager to talk about reproductive health during the interviews, even if they might have initially been timid when first hearing about my project. Some women were willing to speak to me face-to-face, while others preferred to submit written answers to a questionnaire. Many conversations continued, both related to my research and beyond, over instant messaging applications. Information flowed in both directions. I learned more about their lives in Yugoslavia, its successor states, and beyond, while offering a window into the lives of their friends and family in Australia and New Zealand. Mirjana, whose words opened this chapter, asked about her son and daughter-in-law who live in Australia, with whom she Skyped every morning but had not seen in person in four years. Our conversations perhaps gave her a fuller and comforting picture of their faraway world.

Despite the relatively uniform demographic distribution of my interviewees, they were far from of one mind in their views about the past, the present, and the relationship between the two. I met ardent unionists and anticapitalists, one of whom asked why my questionnaire referred to socialism as a "regime."[25] One woman, who asked for anonymity, came highly recommended as someone I had to speak to for her activism against abortion restrictions since the 1970s. However, the current religious backlash in Croatia had left her emotionally exhausted, and after a brief chat with her by phone, she cut our conversation short and asked me not to call again because she was "unable to speak on the topic any further."[26]

While some women balked at my feminist ideology, several women and physicians saw me as an ally to their causes as they gleaned my own personal feminist beliefs. Sensing correctly my ethos and knowing that I grew up in the West, my respondents drew comparisons between Yugoslav socialism and Western capitalism, and with Western feminism. Health professionals' motivations to participate in interviews at times stemmed from their activism to retain and enlarge women's reproductive freedoms. Since the break-up of Yugoslavia, women's rights advocates have embraced feminism, invoking its principles in their advocacy work fighting for women's reproductive and sexual rights.[27] Physicians still working in Slovenia and Croatia lamented the present situation that threatens legal abortions on demand. The Croatian gynecologist Jelena Grubič's main area of activism in 2016 was to abolish doctor's rights to claim conscientious objection as an excuse to refuse to perform abortions.[28] She said that religious doctors could and did claim conscientious objection and were then rewarded, promoted, and celebrated as a result of their commitment to their Catholic faith.[29] Others followed suit. Conscientious objection and its impact on the provision of services was the case not only in Croatia but in other former Yugoslav republics and other European nations since the fall of European socialism.[30] Nostalgia crept into Grubič's narratives frequently, but she did not point to specifically Yugoslav aspects of the past that she imagined were somehow better. Her memories of different aspects of the socialist system were punctuated with comments like, "We all pitched in then. No one loved doing it [performing abortions], but it was important, and we all stood together."

My interviewees had their own reasons for granting me their time and attention. At times, these reasons included actively correcting the dominant narrative and dispelling the myth of a socialist utopia. My position as a researcher created a platform for interviewees to challenge such myths and to assert how such depictions omitted and potentially silenced their own experiences. Female medical professionals all pointed to persisting, "smoldering" patriarchal attitudes about women's sexualities and gender roles that stemmed from the socialist past.[31] The Slovenian social worker Mlakar used our interaction to redress the assumption that legality equated to acceptability and nonjudgmental care.[32] Mlakar described her male gynecologist colleagues as "all the same," regarding the negative views they held of women's overreliance on abortion, and remembered the ways in which some physicians shamed women and undermined their decisions to undergo abortions. Of the 1974 constitution, she said, "It was just paper."[33] Some physicians and women were so keen to share their emotional experiences that they often did not let me finish asking a question; they wanted to guide the narrative. Reclaiming past narratives and rectifying dominant narratives were experienced perhaps as a cathartic process for these professionals. The physician and literary scholar Rita Charon describes the process of narrating the past in the context of what she calls "narrative medicine": "By telling stories to ourselves and others—in dreams, in diaries, in friendships, in marriages, in therapy sessions—we grow slowly not only to know who we are but also to become who we are."[34]

Some women wanted to correct assumptions that I might have had about them in relation to their own knowledge and relationships with their partners and children. One common recollection was that even though they said they did not have any sex education growing up, they often stated that they redressed this in their own relationships with their daughters and sons. They shaped their narratives to allow a comparison between their own experiences of youth and their remedial actions today. Most respondents said that, unlike their relationships with their parents, they speak to their children openly about sex, reproduction and health, attesting that their "children can always come to" them. Sangster explains of her cohort that women's understanding of social norms gained from lifelong interpersonal experiences led women "to explain or excuse their wage work, since it was viewed critically by society. If we presume that 'subjectivity is not a romantic fiction of the self prior to socialization, but rather bears marks of the person's interaction with the world,' then the powerful influence of social context can never be ignored."[35] Influenced more by reflections of their personal experiences as children and as parents, women did not solely reflect nostalgia in their narratives of the past.

Dominant Narratives and Personal Recollections: Contraception and Abortion

Contraception

Through their interviews, one can see how participants have internalized popular representations of their Yugoslav past, drawing on shared memories of their past to retract their own experiences. Scholars have demonstrated how individuals' retelling of their past experiences construct an identity. Their personal narrative sits within a broader, collective narrative: a subjective memory that functions in relation to and in negotiation with a collective memory.[36] One historian of Yugoslavia, Sabrina Ramet, has described how "the 'collective memory' of a nation consists not of the sum of the individual memories of its members, but rather of the product of a diversity of sources, including history textbooks, media, and the photos and images which become part of the common heritage."[37] Interviewees perceived and relayed events or experiences that punctuated their lives as either in line with expectations or outside of the expected. Drawing simultaneously from socialist propaganda and contemporary public medico-legal knowledge, my interviewees used cultural memories to fill in the gaps in their own recollections, to make up for something they lacked in their historical knowledge, and to address larger narratives.

The narrative generated through collective memory constructs a past in which the New Yugoslav Woman enjoyed all the perks of Western consumerism in combination with socialist security and a uniquely Yugoslav brand of gender equality. Women's reproductive rights contributed to Yugoslav communists' avowed commitment to parity. During the socialist period and since, Yugoslav laws from that era have been hailed as some of the most consistently progressive around the world, leaving women's everyday lived experiences of those political circumstances largely without critical analysis.[38] While legal guarantees certainly made the medical procedure more accessible, at least to middle-class urban women, the lived reality of accessing terminations was far more complex.

Women carried popular sentiments into their post-1989 world. The story of the modern New Yugoslav Woman is pervasive across all forms of state media in the socialist period.[39] Women also echo this version of Yugoslav gender history in their recollections of socialism, often by repeating the phrase "those were beautiful times" and insisting that "we had everything then." Erasure is evident in an oft-repeated quip I heard from some interviewees: "There isn't much to say about that [abortion in Yugoslavia]." The socialist propaganda machine reduced women's personal experiences to aberrant anecdotes. In light of the political, economic, and social crises that have unfolded since Yugoslavia's break-up, women had further incentives to shunt their less positive recollections to bolster the image of a Yugoslav socialist paradise.

During the 1970s and 1980s, the dominant narrative held that contraception was available and accessible for all. Yet not all could easily access contraceptive services and products. Stigmas continued to surround women's sexual activity outside of wedlock, leaving unmarried women unwilling to seek advice about birth control options, for fear of shaming.[40] Nevertheless, my respondents knew about contraceptives, felt comfortable in using medical language to discuss the clinical aspects of contraception, and reported having had some personal experience with several different types—predominantly the pill, IUDs, and diaphragms. Many women asserted that their gynecologists provided them with most of their knowledge. The urban-dwelling middle-class women I interviewed reported a sound understanding of contraceptive methods and knew how to access services and whom to approach for prescriptions and information. The oral historian Alessandro Portelli argues that individuals commonly adopt formal—in this case, medical—language when calling on aspects from dominant or collective memories, in part to demonstrate their participation in that larger structure.[41] The women in my study used medical language to evidence their understanding of the system and to assert their authoritative voice.

Despite women's technical common sense, they often used contraception for short periods and usually only once they were married. This may be because of generational factors, as these women were young during the 1960s. Most women said that their disuse of contraception as married adults was due to personal preference and being open to starting a family. Most did not use contraception before marriage, and statistics demonstrate that teenagers had little knowledge about contraception and therefore did not use it.[42] It is likely that my respondents could not easily access contraceptives because of their age or marital status or because contraception was not consistently available through their doctors. Moreover, women did not gain their detailed knowledge as part of their school curriculum. My respondents only developed their technical intelligence about contraception through visits to gynecologists after they were married. Ultimately, their knowledge of contraceptive methods, brands, and types, along with their reported trust in medical professionals, did not translate completely to their private practice since they had not gained that knowledge while growing up.

Women's accounts of where and from whom they learned about matters of contraception and sex reveal disjuncture between their experiences as teenagers and as adults. All the women said that as teenagers they read books, watched educational films that explained conception and contraception, and read about pregnancy and birth control in magazines. Remembering her student years in Belgrade in the 1970s, Sanja Dobrivojević said that "there were brochures about contraception everywhere and women could please themselves," as to whether they would partake of that education.[43] Collectively, their introduction to matters of sex, sexuality, and reproduction were ad hoc and unguided. Though educational material was widespread, the state relied on teenagers to locate and utilize instruction without offering an integrated educational system to ensure that students felt sufficiently informed.

Generational and geographic factors affected whether and how women experienced sex education through schools or with their parents. When it came to school-based sex education, there was no consensus. A few women said they attended "regular, weekly seminars" at school, and others said there was the occasional "throwaway" or "makeshift" lesson as part of a broader biology or health-and-hygiene curriculum.[44] When describing the latter, women said that teachers looked "embarrassed and we [students and teachers] all wanted to get it over and done with quickly."[45] Regardless of the quantity or quality of sex education, women rejected any suggestion that they felt inadequately informed and explained that "it was very different then" and "you wouldn't find that today."[46] Through body language—a shrug, for example—women dismissed what they perceived as my disbelief in any part of the socialist health or education system constituting a positive or modern experience for young people. For others, descriptions of fertilization and contraception did not exist in their high school education. In my sample, women from Vojvodina, Belgrade, Zagreb, and Ljubljana were more likely to have received regular instruction than women from smaller towns. Younger respondents also reported more curriculum-based learning than the older generation: "We learned about all of that from biology class."[47] This finding could indicate that, at least for women of urban middle-class backgrounds, there was an increasing availability of information about contraception at school over time. A similar pattern emerged when women remembered discussing sex and contraception with their parents. Younger, city-born subjects were more likely to have discussed contraception and pregnancy with their mothers, though none had spoken to their fathers about contraception.

Even though women cited school-based educational seminars, women's contraceptive knowledge did not come from there or from conversations with their parents but rather through their experiences and relationships in adulthood, implying that the social climate viewed contraception as an aspect of marital sexual relationships.[48] Only as adults did women receive their first formal contraceptive advice, which they sought out from their gynecologists. This new patient-physician relationship led to their personal introduction to contraception. Women said that as teenagers, they absorbed fragmented information from the deluge of printed and audiovisual sources that existed; however, they found they received the most practical information from their gynecologists, whom they began to consult in adulthood. Women mostly used contraception during marriage, explaining that their grasp of the intricacies of contraception was limited as a teenager, and describing their knowledge as "poor" or "terrible."[49]

Yet, largely unprompted, they provided detailed biological accounts of sperm and ovum cells joining, traveling through the fallopian tube, and eventually embedding within the uterine wall. They matter-of-factly reported that the pill had to be taken once at the same time each day and that diaphragms had to be fitted by a gynecologist to work correctly. When they spoke about contraception, they often reported back as if they were being examined on the subject and had dutifully studied about conception and contraception in their youth. Though confident in their recall, they often stuttered as they struggled to remember particularly technical details. For some, for example, the names of contraceptive products came easily. For others, they searched with looks of concentration written on their faces as they pierced the corners of the room with their eyeline, willing the walls to produce the correct answers. Sociologists who studied teenage pregnancies during the 1970s and 1980s reported high rates of teenage pregnancy across Yugoslavia and conducted surveys to understand the root of the problem.[50] Student responses revealed that they were sexually active during their high school years but knew next to nothing about how to prevent unwanted pregnancies, leading researchers to conclude that without sound contraceptive knowledge, teenagers were left vulnerable.[51] Given that my respondents were teenagers during the 1970s and 1980s, it seems likely that they had shared experiences with the teenagers from those studies, gaining their technical knowledge not during their high school years but as adults.

Heteronormative instructions divided the sexes, girls advised to take care of themselves and boys told to take care of their girlfriends, in what Dobrivojević described as "patriarchal messages regarding expectations of young women's sexual lives," that taken together "would never leave you feeling as if you'd learned anything."[52] Young women in the 1970s and 1980s appear to have felt inadequately prepared to navigate their reproductive health options and the medical system. For the most part, respondents asserted that during contraceptive seminars at school or community centers, they were vaguely told to "take care of themselves." While Dobrivojević and others pointed to a patriarchal system of oppression that disempowered teenage girls by refusing them access to pragmatic knowledge and skills to take advantage of safe medical provisions, others simply said that "people just didn't talk about such things."[53] Women recalled hearing the same advice—"look after yourself"—from their mothers, as if the phrase was a stand-in for any practical contraceptive advice. Women sometimes said that there were still taboos around publicly discussing one's personal situation—"we never really even talked to our friends about contraception or sex"—implying that general discussions of the medical aspects of contraception were acceptable, while personal experiences were not.

Official state discourse asserted that contraceptives were widely and readily available, yet women's recollections attest to the unreliability and inaccessibility of contraceptive products. While all of them used contraception at times throughout their adult years, none of them used contraception consistently or for long periods. Magda Langdan abandoned the contraceptive pill due to its side effects.[54] She and others said that they experienced headaches and gained weight, which they perceived as undesirable side effects, and the pill's prophylactic potential did not outweigh those significant drawbacks. Some women decided to try the IUD option in the early 1970s; one woman got pregnant while she had an IUD in place, leaving her distrustful of other contraceptives.[55] Many women said they stopped using contraceptives after an abortion or after they had a child. Since they did not gain a thorough, factual, and judgment-free introduction to contraception from their teachers, parents, or other adults during their formative years, women also did not have a personal history of using contraceptives that would see them include new resources in their birth control routine.

Health professionals reasoned that women's distrust of contraceptives was perpetuated by physicians' ignorance about and mistrust of contraceptives. Grubič said that many male physicians would not prescribe the pill because they were unfamiliar with the drugs and methods.[56] The Croatian midwife Kata Kovačić explained that since doctors did not understand hormones in contraceptive pills or how the IUD functioned in preventing pregnancy, women distrusted those modern methods.[57] Doctors who did prescribe contraception only had one or two to choose from, which did not suit all women, so even if doctors had benevolent intentions, they were limited by circumstances. At times, women would return to refill their prescription, and the brand that they had been using would no longer be available, leaving them discouraged. Some professionals also claimed that physicians would not even tell women about contraceptives or would intentionally dissuade them from using contraceptives, for the financial benefits. Social insurance would pay doctors for abortions, not for contraceptive consultations and prescriptions. As was common elsewhere, respondents concurred that women's lack of trust in modern contraceptives made them turn to things they knew or learned about from their peers or elders—tracking ovulation days and coitus interruptus—relying on abortion if those methods failed.[58]

Abortion

Contrary to contemporary studies and to enduring stereotypes that women relied on abortion as their primary means of fertility control, my sample suggests that educated middle-class women used a combination of abortion and contraception to space their births rather than relying on abortion alone. Demographers reported that abortion rates were high and contraceptive knowledge and consumption low (as was outlined in chapter 3) and presumed that the two seemingly disparate populations were almost mutually exclusive. However, that does not appear to be the case, though many factors, including social stigmas having to do with accessing contraceptives, deterred women from using them consistently throughout their lives. Their decisions had more to do with the long historical use of abortion in Yugoslavia than the legalization and the ongoing improvements to services and accessibility for women. My subjects did not directly state that the established practice of resorting to abortion as birth control influenced their decision-making. Nevertheless, the ways they described abortions as nothing out of the ordinary and as fitting unproblematically within the narrative of their lives speak to the abiding and established practice of abortion alongside contraception.

As was the case with contraception, the common narrative among my interviewees was that in Yugoslavia it was simple and easy to terminate an unwanted pregnancy. Most of my interlocutors pointed out that present conservative circumstances threatened to take away what the socialist state built. Their stories all started in the same way: the woman fell pregnant and went to her gynecologist to seek an abortion. If a woman wanted an abortion, she would "just go and get one."[59] She got the abortion, and "that was that." The relative ease that women recall in this common retelling can be attributed to the fact that the women I interviewed lived their reproductive years after the 1969 General Law that permitted abortions on demand before ten weeks' gestation. Once I pressed my respondents to elaborate on their experiences beyond "that was that," the pat narrative collapsed.

The process of decision-making, accessing abortions, and the emotional weight of those decisions lay with women. Given that my respondents were older women, some retired and many with grandchildren of their own, their memories of teenage and young adulthood years were likely tempered by political, cultural, and social shifts, time, and personal experiences. Vladislava Andrić said that the only reason she aborted was because her boyfriend at the time wanted her to; though she did not regret it, she did not feel like it was her decision. For others, the decision was theirs alone. For many respondents, men did not feature in their narratives at all, and such omissions spoke volumes considering the broader context of their stories. In a way, their partners feature through their absences. Their partners had left them, or their pregnancies were the product of casual sex. Several respondents recalled busy and crowded hospital wards where they awaited their procedure surrounded by other women in the same position all talking about their families, jobs, and sometimes the circumstances that led them to those appointments yet extracted temporarily from those lives to terminate a pregnancy on their own.

My respondents did not present their decisions as having been made out of desperate circumstances, though a critical reading of their constructed narratives suggests that lack of material support from state institutions in combination with women's personal circumstances led them to make the decision to terminate. Most of the women in my study said they felt nothing about their experiences of terminating a pregnancy: "It was the right decision and I rarely think about it" was a common summative comment on their experiences. Despite their relatively high socioeconomic status, women still said that finances, accommodation, and their employment status affected the way they viewed their pregnancies. Jovana Djoković, a Sombor-based lawyer, had an abortion one year after she gave birth to her oldest child.[60] She said it was the best course of action for her, even though she was a "fearful person who was afraid of needles."[61] She pointed to "environmental factors," such as money, work, and living in a small apartment, as reasons for her decision. She shrugged, signaling to me that she did not carry guilt over her choice, and said, "It was not an easy decision, but the reality of the situation compels you to make that choice."[62] This collection of reasons—money, job, and accommodation—was so prevalent among my respondents that I almost expected it during each interview. None of the women whom I spoke to claimed that medical circumstances influenced their decisions, which unseats the illusion that socialist utopia equated to a context where social circumstances would not be a factor for women in making decisions about their pregnancies.

While abortion was not a negative experience for all women who experienced it, in Yugoslavia or anywhere else for that matter, deciding to have an abortion conveys agency while it raises questions about the limitations of exercising agency under compromising and restrictive circumstances. Based on ethnographic research, Michelle Rivkin-Fish asserts that Russian women did not understand their access to abortion through the lens of a right to choose—the dominant discourse for framing the Western, especially American, debate on abortion rights. Instead, they understood abortion access as a reflection of the "dire lack of choices that plagued daily life."[63] Citing such discourse and other factors, Teodora Babić, a Sombor-based administrator, recalled her decision to abort a twin pregnancy because her mother was on her deathbed, she did not have a partner at that time, and she did not have an apartment of her own or a job.[64] She told me that she still often thinks about how old her twins would be and how she wished she could have continued the pregnancy but that material circumstances made that option impossible. Even though this may very well have been true, women also may have clung to that reason because it was much more socially and legally acceptable than their not wanting to keep the baby irrespective of material circumstances. Either way, dominant narratives of abortion legality overshadowed women's personal narratives.

Women, for the most part, were satisfied that they had made the right choice for themselves. Their experiences of isolation speak to persistent stigmas surrounding abortion, despite its legality, and single parenthood, despite state measures to protect children born out of wedlock. I sometimes spoke to women in cafés, at their request. When talking about laws and services, they would speak at a normal volume, but when the conversation came to be more personal or individual, they would lean in and lower their voice. Aleksandra Vladić, a Belgrade-based botanist, said that women did not talk about their personal experiences of abortion. She declared that a woman either went and got an abortion quickly and quietly, "sweeping it under the rug," or she had a "very quick wedding."[65] Branka Kostić pointed to religious doctrine denouncing abortion as a sin, but if it had to be done, "people looked the other way."[66] Aleksandra, along with many other respondents, said that she did not talk about her experiences often with friends or family. Teodora did not tell her close friends about her abortion at the time because she did not want to be dissuaded. She only told them later, "after," and it was not something she ever discussed again with friends or family.

Women's recollections of arranging a termination echo socialist medical propaganda that coaxed women into the biomedical health care system. All my respondents gushed that clinics were "clean, orderly, and organized" and that medical staff were informed and well equipped. Women routinely juxtaposed their memories of the Yugoslav health system with present-day health care shortcomings. "It may not have been perfect," said Aleksandra of the socialist structure, "but at least we were all equal and all of our health care was covered by insurance."[67] In recounting the clean and orderly nature of the clinical space, women had also perhaps been reacting to a fairly odd question that asked them to think beyond their own experiences—the decision-making path, the procedure and its aftereffects—to describe the environment and setting of their terminations.

Collectively, women conveyed a sense of respect for medical institutions and for medical staff, especially their specialists, even if their experiences of the medical system did not meet their expectations. Vladislava said that she trusted her gynecologist completely and that her termination went "smoothly and according to plan."[68] For most women, consulting their gynecologists was a central step in carrying out their decisions to terminate, not only because that was necessary to prompt the process but because they felt that their physicians were the ones they could speak to openly.

Women said that physicians working illegally outside of the medical system offered respite when women sought discretion. This was especially clear in the case of young women who fell outside legal protections. When recalling their own or their friends' experiences as teenagers, women's stories took a more reticent tone. Teenage girls needed one parent's permission to abort, and my respondents explained that no one they knew had a close enough relationship with their parents to ask them for their consent. Recalling their teenage years, women described seeking physicians who would run a pregnancy test privately, outside of the medical system and in secret, because their parents "would kill them." None of my respondents reported that they or their friends actually had a termination outside of the medical system, though they did recall that the prospect of entering the medico-legal system for reproductive health services was a source of considerable anxiety. Some women remembered that their families were very "traditional," "patriarchal," or "religious," all of which seemed to mean that teenage pregnancy was not something that was tolerated within families and was taboo in wider society, turning women toward potentially unskilled or unlicensed practitioners. When talking about this aspect of their and their friends' lives, women were less forthcoming and kept details to a minimum: "There was a doctor like that here, too."[69] They referred to "their acquaintances" or to a "friend of a friend" who needed help from such practitioners. Perhaps they never experienced such a need themselves, or if they did, they may have not wanted to admit to it even decades later to someone outside their social circles, which would suggest that such taboos were so powerful as to cross generations and life stages. Some women, like Vladislava, spoke about the notoriety of such physicians: "All of Sombor knew him."[70] Adult women also sought private care offered by physicians who wanted to earn extra money. If underage girls did not have their parents' support, they sought assistance outside regular channels.

Sexual behaviors among adolescents posed a considerable concern for population health and family planning experts. As I discussed in chapter four, teenagers did not appear to have the level of information about contraception and safer sex practices to enable them to prevent unwanted pregnancies from occurring. In the 1980s, sociologists Dubravka Štampar and Aleksandra Beluhan conducted research into the sexual behaviors of teenagers, and particularly around the use of contraception and abortion.[71] Štampar and Beluhan consistently supported legalization of abortion as they understood that women would seek assistance through illegal channels if they were denied abortions through the committees, which was sometimes the case if girls did not have the required parental permission.[72] One set of data from 1976 surveys of women concluded that being married tended to decrease women's use of abortion, especially when they were under the age of 25. Researchers draw a correlation between women's desire to have children once they were married with their low use of abortion, compared to their unmarried counterparts. Between 1966 and 1971, abortions requested by married women increased by 16 per cent, while, during the same period, the abortions by unmarried women increased by almost 44 per cent, signaling a considerable difference in birth control behaviors between married and unmarried women.[73] The increasing anxiety over teenage pregnancy was symptomatic of conservative and religious attitudes about sex outside marriage that did not disappear after WWII. Another significant factor is that the birth rate continued to decrease per woman and across the entire country. Gynecologists believed that abortion, especially abortions performed on childless young women, would cause infertility in later years, explaining the increasing anxiety over the sexual and contraceptive behaviors of young women.

Despite women's general fondness for their gynecologists, their experiences and opinions diverged based on their own circumstances. Even as women explained that they trusted their gynecologists, they also reported that these doctors frequently attempted to dissuade them from having a termination. These testimonies complicate ideas that terminations were easily accessible; instead women often found themselves pressured by gynecologists to continue with pregnancies. Mirjana, who we heard from at the beginning of the chapter, said that she terminated a pregnancy when she was 18. She went to her gynecologist to schedule a termination who left her "completely disheartened," advising her not to abort, to get married and have the baby.[74] Teodora recalled a similar scenario. Her gynecologist begged her to reconsider terminating her pregnancy, especially since there were two embryos, but she held fast with her decision, as did Mirjana.[75]

The testimonies indicate that some gynecologists tried to delay an abortion until the woman had passed ten weeks gestation, by which time it would be too late to proceed with the procedure. Indeed, Mirjana and Teodora, along with several other women said that their physicians asked them to leave and come back the following week. Had they agreed to do so that might have meant that their pregnancies were too far along for an abortion. Delay tactics were common, and have been common all over the world. Though she did not elaborate how far along the woman was exactly, two outcomes are possible. It was possible that she had gone past 10 weeks at which point she would have had to apply to the commission for approval. She may have found this a daunting prospect because she would require proof that supported her application. For example, if she claimed on medical grounds she would need a psychiatrist or physician referral. If she was claiming on social grounds, she would need something in writing from community services. The other outcome would be that she was over 20 or 24 weeks pregnant. When the state expanded abortion laws in 1969, authorities advised that healthcare professionals do all they can to educate people in preventing unwanted pregnancies. If women experienced unwanted pregnancy, they were to "help parents to give up on the idea of getting an abortion, by showing them that even medical system abortions were harmful."[76] Mlakar, who attended many procedures and worked in Ljubljana in the early 1970s as a social worker, corroborated that physicians used this tactic frequently. She recalled a time when a termination was about to happen and the patient was undressed on the operating table with her legs in stirrups. The male gynecologist leant on the patient's knees and said to her "madam, do you realize how beautiful this baby would be, look at how beautiful you are."[77] She went on to say that this exchange led the woman to go home to rethink her previous decision. When she got home, according to Mlakar, she "faced the same financial situation, she lived in the same inadequate apartment, she had the same marital problems," and she came back to terminate. By then, exactly as the physician had presumably hoped, it was too late because the pregnancy had advanced too far.[78]

Although women rarely recalled instances where they were shamed by their health care workers, the few instances that they shared with me were illuminating for the grounds on which they castigated them. Male health care professionals admonished women about being sexually active, blaming them for the circumstances they found themselves in. Mlakar recalled another incident where her patient was in the surgery and was asked to take off her clothes and put on a robe. The patient asked if that included her underwear to which the doctors replied, "Well, did you have them on when you got into this mess?" referring to her unwanted pregnancy. Another woman, who did not abort her pregnancy but miscarried late in her second trimester, delivered the baby vaginally, and as she screamed in pain, nurses chided her saying that she must have been making the same noise when she got pregnant. These recollections were tinged with discomfort. The abortion itself was not necessarily a traumatic event, but for respondents, these rude comments continued to rankle. They were eager to set the record straight, to talk back to health care workers—albeit indirectly—in a way that they were unable to at the time when they were initially stung by these harsh words. This is especially true for Mlakar. She was emphatic in wanting to set the record straight about how male doctors conducted themselves during her time as a social worker. She said that while the legal situation may have been better and more secure during socialism, the doctors still held patriarchal and misogynistic attitudes about women. Mlakar asserted that attitudes were widely held by health professionals who resented the time, energy, and resources that went into something that they "did not really like doing."[79]

An extensive medical infrastructure had evolved in response to women's increasing use of abortion.[80] Sally Sheldon, writing on the legalization of abortion in the United Kingdom, characterized "the shift from illegal to legal abortion in her country as a move from criminalization to medicalization which, while making abortion more easily and safely available, replaced one set of constraints with another."[81] On average, across the socialist period, women were having as many abortions as they were delivering live babies, and at times and in some regions, such as Belgrade and Kosovo, abortions surpassed births. Each hospital or clinic had a dedicated reception area for abortions attached to birthing centers, where women would report to and pay. The Ministry of Public Health charged health care workers to take turns serving on abortion commissions, developing new practices and technologies and training new specialist cadres. Abortions were costly and women occupied patient beds before surgery and in recovery. Stretched beyond capacity, hospital staff felt compelled to make the best of difficult situations. Kovačić remembered that midwives were not trained to perform abortions and were not meant to be involved in abortion care; however, because resources were stretched thin, they assisted physicians by sterilizing instruments and laundering sheets between procedures. The Belgrade-based gynecologist-obstetrician Edvard Kobrić said that although social insurance covered hospitals for twenty-four hours of care for each woman who got an abortion, women were often released two hours after the procedure.⁸² According to all the physicians I spoke to and some of the women, financial incentives for gynecologists and the promise of discretion for women led physicians to perform abortions outside the clinical space.

Though many physicians resented the material demands of providing terminations, they supported its legality, even as they admitted that there were manifold ways in which legality did not align with the demands of real life. The women's health specialists I spoke to echo what Barbara Baird argues about the complex nature of "the contemporary relations of power that shape the practice of abortion . . . [which] are more complex than suggested by the opposition between 'pro-choice' and 'anti-abortion'" ideologies in the Australian context. They all expressed concern at the current conservative turn that threatens legal guarantees for women. Physicians held the same mantra: "Once a woman had decided to abort, there was very little she wouldn't do to achieve her goal." Medical personnel pointed to a single moment that affirmed their views that abortion should remain legal and that women should be apprised of that legality and availability. Belgrade-based Kobrić and Kovačić, who worked primarily in Zagreb, both recalled their days in residency, tending to young women who had self-aborted. Bowing her head, speaking softly and saying that she felt sick thinking about it, Kovačić did not go into detail about the outcome in her experience but said that she never wanted to see anyone suffer like that again.⁸³ Kobrić listed ways that women tried to perform a self-abortion—"in Vojvodina they did it with goose feathers"—and he said that he could not believe that women could do that to themselves.⁸⁴ Živa Novak, a gynecologist and daughter of Franc Novak and Vida Tomšič, and Tomaž Tomaževič, Novak's colleague, both said of Franc Novak that his early experience working at a birthing center in Belgrade in the 1950s, where conditions for women were much harder, left him convinced that abortion needed to be legal, free, and accessible.⁸⁵

Conclusion

By critically analyzing subjective recollections of the past, I challenge the dominant narrative of ease, accessibility, and acceptance of abortion and contraception within socialist Yugoslav society. Women's testimonies shed light on not only their experiences of the past, through the present, but also their perceptions of present circumstances. Narratives attest to the abiding inequalities in the sphere of reproductive matters, too.

Another thread is the role that nostalgia played in women's recollections of their reproductive experiences. Yugoslavia's violent destruction and the chaos wreaked on its population have collectively left their impression on women.

While undeniably significant for how women viewed themselves in relation to me, to their peers, and to their shared and collective history, it also represents a dominating force over how scholars interpret the complex processes of women's remembering of personal experience. At times, women recalled the way things were with nostalgia, although they overwhelmingly did this not in relation to anything specifically or uniquely Yugoslav or socialist. They related to their own experiences, relationships, and motivations for agreeing to be interviewed. Nostalgia formed one aspect of their narrative construction, but to claim it was the driving force behind the formation of their stories would be to deny that they understood their experiences as individuals, as women, as mothers, as sisters and daughters, and as survivors.

Notes

1. Mirjana Jelinić, interview by author, Belgrade, October 1, 2016. Like Mirjana, most of the participants have been given pseudonyms to protect their identity. Where they have not, I indicate that in the note. Throughout the chapter, I introduce the full name or pseudonym of each respondent the first time that I refer to them. In subsequent references, I differentiate between physicians and patients by using the last name only for the former, first name only for the latter.

2. Yurchak, *Everything Was Forever*, 8.

3. My sample does not include rural, poor, or less educated women, Muslim women, or women who are disadvantaged or discriminated against in other ways. Several other studies exist that analyze socialist Yugoslav women's experiences of reproduction, and each one's cohort is similar to mine demographically. The sociologist Mirjana Morokvasić interviewed women who had migrated from Yugoslavia in the 1970s to Western European countries. Her respondents had enough resources to be able to move to a different country and work there. Morokvasić, "Sexuality and Control." Ethnographers at the Centre for Women's Studies in Zagreb conducted interviews with women about all aspects of their lives—childhood, family relationships, working history and education, and reproductive lives—and the center published a volume consisting of transcriptions of the interviews. Dijanić et al., *Ženski biografski leksikon*.

4. Lynn Abrams describes intersubjectivity in the oral history interview: "The oral history interview is a conversation between a researcher and a narrator. Usually the narrator is responding to questions posed by the interviewer, and hence the story told is a product of communication between two individuals, both of whom bring something of themselves to the process. Oral history theory is now founded on this idea of there being two subjectivities at an interview, interacting to produce an effect called intersubjectivity which is apparent in the narrator's

words." Abrams, *Oral History Theory*, 54. I focus on intersubjectivity here because the relationship that my interviewees and I had lent weight to how they shaped their narratives. For seminal and relevant work on the theories of subjectivity and intersubjectivity in oral history, see Yow, "Do I Like Them," 55–79; Summerfield, *Reconstructing Women's Wartime Lives*.

5. Fidelis, "Conclusion," 202.

6. Massino and Penn, *Gender Politics*, 244.

7. Helgren, "'Very Innocent Time,'" 52.

8. Perks and Thompson, "Introduction," 5–6.

9. Luthar and Pušnik, *Remembering Utopia*, 18; Bošković, "Yugonostalgia," 54–78.

10. Todorova, "Introduction," 2.

11. Field, "Imagining Communities," 114.

12. Bošković, "Yugonostalgia," 65.

13. Ibid., 54.

14. Ljubica Spaskovska achieves this in her 2017 book. Although she demonstrates knowledge of the latest oral history techniques and methodologies, she deliberately avoids analyzing aspects of remembering and instead uses her interviews to retract an account of the last decade of Yugoslavia. She does so not to understand the decline of Yugoslavia but to elaborate different ways that interest group—in her case, the Youth League—wanted to reshape or redefine, not destroy, the socialist framework during the 1980s. Spaskovska, *Last Yugoslav Generation*, 14–16.

15. Mihelj, "Persistence of the Past," 467.

16. Maksimović, "Unattainable Past, Unsatisfying Present," 1066.

17. Petrović, "When We Were Europe," 128–129. Also see Petrović, "Towards an Affective History," 504–520.

18. Massino and Penn, "Introduction," 1.

19. Alistair Thompson's article about Anzac histories and "putting popular memory into practice" is a well-cited example of individuals drawing on dominant depictions of their experiences. Thompson, "Anzac Memories," 343–353. Portelli also writes about individuals' memories of the past being entwined with their "fantasies." "While the perception of an account as 'true' is relevant as much to legend as to personal experience and historical memory, there are no formal oral genres specifically destined to transmit historical information; historical, poetical, and legendary narratives often become inextricably mixed up. The result is narratives in which the boundary between what takes place outside the narrator and what happens inside, between what concerns the individual and what concerns the group, may become more elusive than in established written genres, so that personal 'truth' may coincide with shared 'imagination.'" Portelli, "What Makes Oral History," 51.

20. Figes, "Private Life," 359.

21. Sangster, "Politics and Praxis," 61.

22. I circulated translated versions of the questionnaire to respondents in their language.

23. Tomaž Tomaževič, interview with author, Ljubljana, September 18, 2016. Tomaževič told me this as he handed me his hard-copy report of the Ljubljana Abortion Study, the transnational story I tell in another chapter. His name has remained the same.

24. Physicians also had clear agendas, which I elaborate on in subsequent pages. Interviews with physicians lasted one and a half to two hours versus twenty to sixty minutes with private individuals.

25. Sanja Dobrivojević, interview with the author, Belgrade, October 20, 2016. She seemed antagonized by this phrasing at the outset, but I responded that she had a point, we discussed the word and its West-centric implications, and I crossed it out on her questionnaire. Once we had overcome that obstacle, she warmed to my presence, and we talked for almost two hours.

26. Anonymous, in conversation with author, Zagreb, September 14, 2016.

27. Some Belgrade and Zagreb based women also publicly identified as feminists and used the ideology to fight for women's equality during the 1970s and 1980s. Many were academics and used their identities as feminists to expand their academic analyses into Yugoslav politics and society. Žarana Papić's (1949–2002) sociological and anthropological work focused on women's rights and women's emancipation. Influenced by Western second-wave feminism, she helped to organize the first international feminist conference in Eastern Europe, in 1978: Drug/ca žensko pitanje, novi pristup? (Comrade woman: The women's question; A new approach?). Lydia Sklevicky (1952–1990), a sociologist and anthropologist, was a feminist academic whose work dealt with women's history and the integration of women's stories into broader histories of Yugoslavia. Recently, feminist groups have formed in all the major centers, advocating for women's rights and fighting against the conservative backlash threatening women's social positions and reproductive rights.

28. Grubič, interview.

29. Croatia is 90 percent Catholic, and there is widespread support for doctors claiming conscientious objection to refuse to perform abortions. Women are often left in bureaucratic limbo as doctors have no obligation to refer women to another gynecologist who would be willing to perform the termination.

30. Milosavljević et al., "Serbian Gynecologists' Views," 141–148; Kristan, "Freedom of Choice," 603–610; Tongue, "On Conscientious Objection," 349–371.

31. Grubič, interview.

32. Mlakar, interview.

33. Ibid.

34. Charon, *Narrative Medicine*, vii.
35. Sangster, "Politics and Praxis," 67. Therein she quotes Rosenwald and Ochberg, "Introduction," 8.
36. Brison, *Aftermath*; Kokanović, Michaels, and Johnston-Ataata, *Paths to Parenthood*.
37. Ramet, "Memory and Identity," 872.
38. See the introduction and chapter 1 for an analysis of these legal changes.
39. I explore these trends in more detail in chapters 1 and 2.
40. Morokvasić, "Sexuality and Control," 195; Simić, *Soviet Influences*, 40.
41. Portelli, "What Makes Oral History," 52.
42. Repeated surveys confirmed this. In one survey of women workers in the factories of Josip Kraš and Astra about family planning and motherhood, researchers determined that 72 percent used coitus interruptus, and 15 percent used the pill. They also found that women learned more from the press, their friends, and their husbands than from their doctors (22 percent). HDA, 1234–207.
43. Dobrivojević, interview.
44. Magda Langdan, interview with the author, Sombor, October 27, 2016.
45. Jovana Djoković, interview with the author, Sombor, October 27, 2016
46. Ibid.
47. Živa Novak, interview with the author, Ljubljana, September 9, 2016. Novak's name has been left unaltered.
48. Morokvasić, 196.
49. Dobrivojević, interview.
50. Ibid.
51. I analyze these studies in more depth in chapters 2 and 3.
52. Dobrivojević, interview.
53. Ibid.
54. Langdan, interview.
55. Vladislava Andrić, interview with the author, Sombor, October 28, 2016.
56. Grubič, interview.
57. Kata Kovačić, interview with author, Zagreb, September 15, 2016.
58. Morokvaić's respondents explained that this was the case for their continued use of abortion instead of turning to modern contraceptives.
59. Dobrivojević, interview.
60. Djoković, interview.
61. Ibid.
62. Ibid.
63. Rivkin-Fish, "Change Yourself," 287.
64. Teodora Babić, interview with the author, Sombor, October 25, 2016.
65. Aleksandra Vladić, interview with the author, Belgrade, October 19, 2016.
66. Branka Kostić, interview with the author, Belgrade, October 20, 2016.

67. Vladić, interview.
68. Andrić, interview.
69. Jelinić, interview.
70. Andrić, interview.
71. Štampar, "Poznavanje i primjena kontracepcije"; Štampar and Beluhan, "Fertilitet i ponašanje," 93–101.
72. Štampar, "Croatia," 267.
73. Lalović, "Birth Control," 220, 218.
74. Jelinić, interview.
75. Babić, interview.
76. AJ, 130-587-972/1969-1970, "Advice for the Resolution of Family Planning and Regulating the Conditions for Pregnancy Termination," 4.
77. Mlakar, interview.
78. Although she did not elaborate, I assume that this means that the woman had gone past twenty-four weeks' gestation, though it may have been as early as twenty weeks. The cutoff for terminations is determined by medical professionals with multiple factors in mind: whether the fetus could survive outside the uterus if delivered at that point in the pregnancy, the risk of hemorrhage if the fetus were to be extracted at that stage.
79. Mlakar, interview.
80. I discuss this at more length in chapter 2.
81. Baird, "Happy Abortionists," 422.
82. Edvard Kobrić, interview with the author, Belgrade, October 20, 2016. It should be noted that Kobrić said most women wanted to be released early, too, so this practice was not necessarily unsympathetic to women's needs. It does illustrate that hospitals did what they could to stretch resources.
83. Kovačić, interview.
84. Kobrić, interview.
85. Novak, interview; Tomaževič, interview.

Conclusion

Regulating Reproduction in Yugoslavia during Socialism and Beyond

The debate about who regulates reproduction in the region extends into the postsocialist period. Since 2016, coordinators of the Walk for Life initiative have held annual antiabortion marches in Croatia's cities, attracting thousands of sympathizers each year.[1] Similar protests and walks, initiated by domestic organizations like Walk for Life in Croatia or international organizations of the same ilk, have been conducted throughout major cities across Serbia, too, and tied to the Orthodox Christian traditions of that country. Zagreb, Rijeka, and Split since 2016, and in 2019 Zadar and Osijek joined as well. This is just one of the many groups associated with conservative messages that threaten the rights of women, homosexual men and women, transgender people, and other marginalized communities. The group and its supporters work mainly to raise awareness of the widespread use of abortion across Croatia and fight for the unborn fetus's right to life. Members also advocate for restricting Croatia's abortion laws and for doctors' rights to conscientious objection.[2] In 2019, protesters planned marches to be held in Zagreb and Split on May 25, Electoral Silence Day, held one day before European parliament elections. The State Election Commission determined that the event did not violate the day's electioneering ban but cautioned participants who were election candidates to respect the law. Several conservative political candidates joined the march in support of the initiative's platform. Each year, in opposition to the march and the broader platform it speaks to, Croatian feminists have rallied to protect women's rights to safer medical abortions. This year, protesters wore red clothes or white garments splattered with red paint to symbolize women's battle for legal abortion and the lives lost due to botched back-alley abortions. The

Zagreb-based Platform for Reproductive Rights and other feminist prochoice groups organized countermarches, called Walks for Freedom, to coincide with antiabortion demonstrations.

This book's central interventions speak to this political brawl. It elucidates the dynamic interplay between ordinary citizens, state leaders, experts, and interest groups and highlights how groups and individuals have consumed and deployed mass media. I break down constructions of the socialist period and what came after, especially with respect to women's access to safe, medical, and hygienic reproductive health services. Throughout the book, the central theme of the New Yugoslav Woman persists as an idealized representation of the state's vision of female citizenship and Yugoslav womanhood. Through legislation, institutions, and the concept of the New Yugoslav Woman, many Yugoslav communists claimed to have resolved what the Croatian feminist anthropologist Lydia Sklevicky called the "sacred monster of the 'woman question,'" a perennial stand-in for the problem of persisting inequalities between the sexes at home and in the public sphere.[3] The slew of clashes over women's reproductive autonomy—in the Yugoslav successor states and globally—suggests otherwise. Given that the Walk for Life initiative was inspired by similar marches the world over and that it has recently sprouted in other postsocialist European states, reproductive regulation in the region continues to be an internationally enmeshed phenomenon that plays out on the domestic stage.

Discord between women's private practices of fertility control, the concerns of interest groups and opinionated experts, and the agendas of states is not peculiar to socialist Yugoslavia. As the state did throughout the socialist period, each organization draws on scientific authority to lend weight to its arguments, though each disagrees on the relevance of religious dogma to women's right to make reproductive choices. The impassioned clashes also highlight the role of women in the unfolding narrative of reproductive regulation—as subjects of political altercations, as active participants in the formulation of social expectations and norms, and as agents of change. Men's roles pepper the book, if only through their marginalization and absence. It is women's practices that are probed, criticized, or rendered taboo and their roles within society that are put to public debate.

Each group's campaigns speak to a national "Croatian" identity and how this identity feeds into the broader historical and political context of the country within present-day Europe. Distancing Croatia from its socialist past, Walk for Life coordinators argue that to not revise communist-era laws would be to return to Yugoslavia's totalitarian regime.[4] Ultranationalist conservative anthems, sung live alongside religious hymns, have set the tone for the protests aimed at guarding the future population of Croatia.

Leftist journalists and feminist activists are vehemently defending Yugoslav-era abortion laws, which they view as the "bright moment" in the region's history of reproductive rights. While laws have remained in place through Yugoslavia's dissolution, fewer and fewer gynecologists in Croatia are willing to perform the procedure on moral grounds, claiming conscientious objection based on their religious beliefs, something they could not do during socialism. In Serbia, abortion is provided by private clinics; regional differences abound. In the prochoice camp, activists have asserted that Croatia must continue to be the progressive leader of the Yugoslav successor states. Croatia is one of two Yugoslav successor states in the European Union, and prochoice advocates have rejected Croatia's conservative turn, arguing that it should be leading the way for other ex-Yugoslav countries vying for EU membership. Each Yugoslav successor state has constructed its own path regarding women's health and policy in the wake of the Yugoslav wars.

***

This book has traced the evolution of state formation through its legislative and structural foundations, its foreign entanglements, and its postsocialist legacy. Chapters 1 and 2 established that the Yugoslav state had stronger pronatalist intentions in both laws and propaganda than has previously been acknowledged. In chapter 1, I focused on the early Cold War era, analyzing the state's legislative measures to legitimize its rule and consolidate power across the diffuse country. Chapter 2 was concerned with the ways those legislative moves translated into practice through the establishment of an interconnected medical infrastructure designed to coax the peasantry into the biomedical health care system and, by implication, into the purview of the state. Chapters 3 and 4 examined Yugoslavia's international entanglements and its interests in the Global South in shaping self-management socialism. In chapter 3, I traced the development of fertility control technologies—the IUD and vacuum aspiration—and the collaborative role that Yugoslav physicians played in the proliferation and normalization of those technologies around the world. Chapter 4 examined sex education and the evolution of a didactic tradition within Yugoslavia, which saw family planning advocates incorporate the international language of human rights into existing educational material, emphasizing the responsiveness and involvement of the state within international reformulations of definitions of human rights. In chapter 5, I analyzed memory and the role that nostalgia for the socialist past does and does not play in the present-day construction of memory.

Women's reproductive health and rights were a central tenet of Yugoslav state formation and played a central role in the shaping of a distinctive Yugoslav way. The New Yugoslav Woman provides a window onto how Yugoslav communists engineered the Yugoslav way in response to several key factors. The demographic calamity left in the wake of World War II propelled state authorities to act in pronatalist ways. They aimed to rehabilitate the Yugoslav population, revitalize the economy and agricultural production, and ultimately transform society through a social revolution. Party officials also responded to shifts in global politics. It was through gender and reproductive policies, reproductive health services, and consumables that the state connected to a previously dispersed population: Yugoslav women. Women were pivotal for rehabilitating the nation and decreasing infant mortality, which the state held as one of the most significant issues throughout the early Cold War period. Yugoslav women also held the potential to access the peasantry and to connect to larger areas of the far-flung country. Potentially more so than other domestic political strategies, targeting women's health allowed the state to engage with peasants and urban dwellers, to enter the private homes and lives of its citizens, and to disrupt long-held beliefs, including religion and custom.

The Yugoslav socialist state was always interested in the unfolding narrative of population, both at home and abroad, even before the CPY took power. Domestic reproductive policies and agendas intermingled with international trends in very specific ways. The state cherry-picked from a vast array of world events and global movements to construct an image of the country as a progressive and modern leader of the developing world. The image of the modern, worldly, educated, and self-sufficient New Yugoslav Woman represented the national ideal. Self-management came to be, at least partially, defined by the state's foreign engagements, and this manifested clearly in the unfolding narrative of reproductive regulation within the state. Beyond its well-established position as a conduit between East and West, the state's international entanglements, in relation to population, situate Yugoslavia as a bridge between the Global North and South.

The New Yugoslav Woman represented the agendas of the state. However, closer examination of her evolution reveals the vast discrepancies between policy and reality, state expectations of women and families and everyday practices, and the heavy responsibilities women bore, both within the home and outside of it, to meet the demands of constructing a new state. Although the context changed—whether it was maternity care, contraceptive use, or sex education—Yugoslav women were expected to not only partake of new biomedical offerings and services but to essentially create them in their own communities, all the while maintaining the image that the communist leadership would eventually deliver on wartime promises.

This book presents a Yugoslav history of reproductive regulation, situated transnationally, during its socialist years and beyond. Memory and the process of remembering have been enmeshed throughout the process of my research, analysis, and writing, through my own reflections, those of other scholars, and my informants'. Influenced by a desire to view the past in a positive light, by the traumatic events of the 1990s Yugoslav wars, as well as their own personal experiences, motivations, and memories, ex-Yugoslavs consistently told me that there is not much to the story of reproductive regulation in Yugoslavia. In many ways, the story was, indeed, obscured by the dominant narrative of Yugoslav progress and modernity. In other ways, the complex narrative was ever present. After extended conversations with those same ex-Yugoslavs, many of them changed their tune somewhat. They recalled a traumatic experience, a hurtful or shaming comment, prompting them to reflect more deeply on their feelings about socialist-era reproductive laws. I followed their lead. Over time, I examined different angles, sources, and perspectives, and I unpicked, layer by layer, one rendition of the tale of Yugoslav reproductive regulation. Yugoslav women, their doctors, and public officials were each interested in the complex development of reproductive rights and health care access for women. Each party exercised power and influence in different ways: the state through legislation and institutional change, galvanized through state propaganda; medical experts by way of scientific research and development and with their own experience working with women in clinics; and women by negotiating, welcoming, and resisting medicalizing processes. This narrative is not solely a historical account. Its relevance extends into the present day and into the purview of future generations, who continue to fashion national and social identities and lay claim to political legitimacy by wielding authority over women's health, reproduction, and population.

Notes

1. See the initiative's website: https://www.hodzazivot.hr/.
2. The group's platform is fairly broad and vague. In chapter 5, I discussed the views of the Croatian gynecologist Jelena Grubič, whose activism focuses almost entirely on removing doctors' rights to conscientious objection.

3. Sklevicky, "More Horses than Women," 72.

4. The main basis of this argument is that under socialism, religion was not to be publicly practiced; therefore; doctors were not allowed to conscientiously object based on their religious beliefs. In present-day Croatia, where 90 percent of the population identifies as Catholic, most doctors refuse to perform abortions based on this clause.

GLOSSARY

Abortifacients are substances, of a drug, chemical, or herbal variety, used to bring on abortion.

Biomedicine captures various types of medicine, justified on the basis of and in accordance with the norms of modern science.

Cannulas are thin tubes that can be inserted into the body (via vein or through a body cavity) to administer medication or insert a surgical instrument. Cannulas come in different sizes, appropriate to the task at hand, and while they used to be metal, they are often made of plastic now. They are sometimes rigid and sometimes not. In the context of pregnancy termination, the gynecologist would use a cannula the size of which would be relative to the size of the pregnancy. They would insert the cannula through the cervix and suction or scrape out the contents of the uterus.

Cervix is the narrow passage at the lower end of the uterus, which separates the vagina from the uterus. While it is usually nearly closed, during a termination, it is opened slightly to allow for a cannula to be inserted

Coitus interruptus is a method of birth control in which a man, during sexual intercourse, withdraws his penis from a woman's vagina prior to ejaculation, to avoid insemination.

Dilation and curettage is a surgical procedure, first used in the late nineteenth century, used to diagnose and/or treat conditions that affect the uterus. Dilation (widening of the cervix) and curettage (surgical scraping and scooping out the contents of the uterus using a sharp or dull spoon-like tool) was the most used gynecological procedure for the termination of pregnancy before the invention of vacuum-aspiration technology. It remains in common use alongside vacuum aspiration.

Ethno-medical healing captures diverse healing practices grounded in nonbiomedical belief systems often with religious, spiritual, or customary overtones.

Fertility control technology encompasses four categories of abstinence, contraception, sterilization, and induced abortion.

Gestation pertains to the process of the development of an embryo and fetus within the uterus from conception to birth.

Gynecology is a branch of medicine concerned with women's reproductive health and breast health.

International Planned Parenthood Federation is a global nongovernmental organization that promotes sexual and reproductive health.

Intrauterine devices come in many different shapes and materials. Today, they are typically either made of copper or plastic. The copper IUD does not contain hormones and can be used both as a contraceptive device and as emergency contraception if inserted 120 hours after unprotected sex. The hormonal IUD, usually made of plastic, emits low levels of hormones within the uterus. Both types serve as a spermicide but do not prevent ovulation, as does the pill. The hormonal IUD also thickens the mucus lining of the uterus, inhibiting the ability of a fertilized egg to implant itself in the uterine wall.

Multiparas have given birth more than once.

Obstetrics is a branch of medicine and surgery that is concerned with childbirth.

Oral contraceptive pill, commonly known as the pill, is a hormonal contraceptive taken orally once per day that stops the release of an egg from the ovaries.

Paracervical block is an anesthetic procedure used to numb the cervix in preparation for obstetric and gynecological procedures.

Parity is defined as the number of times that a woman has given birth.

Parturient pertains to women who are in labor and about to give birth.

Primiparas have given birth once.

Self-management was the system of socialism that evolved in Yugoslavia from 1953 that was typified by a decentralization of federal power and the forging of an economic and governing system that would see the central state's function reduced and the country's workforce empowered through workers' councils and committees.

Sexually transmissible infections are bacterial or viral infections transmitted through sexual contact.

Vacuum aspiration, in common use since the late 1950s, uses gentle suction instead of scraping to remove the contents of the uterus for the termination of earlier gestation pregnancies (typically three to twelve weeks' gestation). Like dilation and curettage, it is used to diagnose adverse uterine conditions.

Vračare translates to "fortune teller" and is a word used for folk healers or wise women.

Yugo-nostalgia is a cultural phenomenon in postsocialist Yugoslav successor states whereby citizens express a shared nostalgia for the socialist past.

BIBLIOGRAPHY

Primary Sources

Archives and Libraries

Arhiv Republike Slovenije [Archives of the Republic of Slovenia], Ljubljana, Slovenia
    AS 1413 Collection of Vida Tomšić
Arhiv Srbije [Serbian archives], Belgrade, Serbia
    G-218 Council for National Health and Social Policy, Serbia
    Đ-123 Serbian Medical Council
Arhiv Jugoslavije [Archives of Yugoslavia], Belgrade, Serbia
    25 Ministry of Labour of the Socialist Federal Republic of Yugoslavia
    36 Council for National Health and Social Policy
    49 Ministry of Justice of the Federal People's Republic of Yugoslavia
    55 Council for the Arts and Sciences
    319 Federal Council for Education and Culture
    141 AFŽ
    142 Federal Assembly
    671 Ministry of Public Health
Hrvatski Državni Arhiv [Croatian state archives], Zagreb, Croatia
    HR-HDA 1234 KDAŽ Hrvatske [Conference for social activity of Croatian women]
    HR-HDA 2046 Republican Committee for Health and Social Protection
    HR-HDA 287 Ministry of Public Health
    HR-HDA 1228 Socijalistički savez radnog naroda Hrvatske (SSRN)

Hrvatska Kinoteka [Croatian film archives], Zagreb, Croatia
Istorijski Arhiv Grada Beograda [Historical archives of the city of Belgrade], Belgrade, Serbia
  1641 KDAŽ Beograda [Conference for social activity of Belgrade women]
  234 Medical School for Midwives in Belgrade
  865 A-7 Council for Education, Culture and Social Health
Jugoslovenska Kinoteka [Yugoslav film archives], Belgrade, Serbia
Schlesinger Library, Radcliffe Institute for Advanced Study, Harvard University, Cambridge, MA
  73-143-90-M103 Papers of Emily Hartshorne Mudd, 1873–1990
  82-M129 Papers of Mary Steichen Calderone
Harvard Medical Library Collection, Center for the History of Medicine in the Francis A. Countway Library, Harvard University.
  H MS c23 Papers of Clarence J. Gamble, 1920–1966
Rockefeller Archive Centre, New York, NY
  FA432 and FA210 Population Council records

Interviews Conducted by the Author

All names pseudonyms except for Živa Novak, Bojana Pinter, and Tomaž Tomaževič.

Andrić, Vladislava, Sombor, October 28, 2016.
Arsenijević, Katarina, Celje, November 1, 2016.
Babić, Teodora, Sombor, October 25, 2016.
Bošković, Maksina, Sombor, October 25, 2016.
Dimitrijević, Isidora, Celje, November 2, 2016.
Djoković, Jovana, questionnaire returned.
Djordjević, Andrea, Belgrade, October 22, 2016.
Dobrivojević, Sanja, Belgrade, October 20, 2016.
Grubič, Jelena, Zagreb, September 17, 2016.
Ilić, Maja, Sombor, October 26, 2016.
Jelinić, Mirjana, Belgrade, October 21, 2016.
Jovanović, Malina, questionnaire returned.
Kobrić, Edvard, Belgrade, October 20, 2016.
Kostić, Branka, Sombor, October 26, 2016.
Kovačić, Kata, Zagreb, September 15, 2016.
Langdan, Magda, Sombor, October 27, 2016.
Marković, Anja, questionnaire returned.
Milošević, Silvija, questionnaire returned.
Mlakar, Mara, Ljubljana, September 12, 2016.
Nikolić, Petra, Belgrade, October 21, 2016.

Novak, Živa, Ljubljana, September 9, 2016.
Petrović, Ema, Questionnaire returned.
Pinter, Bojana, Belgrade, October 19, 2016.
Popović, Vesna, Belgrade, October 20, 2016.
Tomašević, Eva, Belgrade, October 18, 2016.
Tomaževič, Tomaž, Ljubljana, September 18, 2016
Veselinović, Jana, questionnaire returned.
Vladić, Aleksandra, Belgrade, October 19, 2016.
Zečević, Kaja, Belgrade, October 17, 2016.

Published Primary Sources

Andolšek, L., and Franc Novak. *The Ljubljana Abortion Study, 1971–1973: Comparison of the Medical Effects of Induced Abortion by Two Methods, Curettage and Vacuum Aspiration; Final Report*. Bethesda, MD: National Institute of Health, Center for Population Research, 1974.

Breznik, Dušan. *The Population of Yugoslavia*. Belgrade: Institute for Social Sciences, Demographic Research Centre, 1974.

———. "Methodology of the Study." In *Fertility and Family Planning in Yugoslavia*. Belgrade: Institute of Social Science Research, Demographic Research Centre, 1980.

Breznik, Dušan, Angelina Mojić, Miroslav Rašević, and Miroljub Rančić. *Fertilitet stanovništva u Jugoslaviji* [Fertility of the Yugoslav population]. Belgrade: Institute for Social Sciences, Demographic Research Centre, 1972.

Novak, Franc. *Surgical Gynecologic Techniques*. Translated by Wilfrido Cameron Curry. Padua, Italy: Piccin Medical Books, 1978.

Petrović, Aleksandar. *Banjane: socijalno-zdravstvene i higijenske prilike* [Banjane: Socio-medical and hygiene circumstances]. Belgrade: Biblioteka Centralnog higijenskog zavoda, 1932.

———. *Rakovica: socijalno-zdravstvene i higijenske prilike* [Rakovica: Socio-medical and hygiene circumstances]. Belgrade: Biblioteka Centralnog higijenskog zavoda, 1939.

Periodicals

Arhiv sa zaštitu majki i djece [Archive for the protection of mothers and children]
Ginekologija i opstetricija: časopis udruženja ginekologa-opstetričara Jugoslavije [Gynecology and obstetrics: Journal of the society of gynecologist-obstetricians of Yugoslavia]
Glasnik zavoda za zdravstvenu zaštitu Srbije [Journal of the Council for Health Protection of Serbia]
Liječnički Vjesnik [Medical journal]
Medicinar [Physician]

Naša Žena [Our woman]
Nova Žena [New woman]
Praktična Žena [Practical woman]
Primaljski Vjesnik [Midwifery journal]
Službeni list [Official gazette]
Srpska Lekarska Nedelja [Serbian medical journal]
Stanovništvo [Population]
Statistički bilten [Statistical journal]
Svijet [World]
Zdravstvena Zaštita [Health protection]
Zora [Dawn]
Žena [Woman]
Žena danas [Woman today]
Žena i dom [Woman and the home]
Žena u borbi [Woman in battle]
Ženski list [Women's newspaper]

Audiovisual Sources

Čalić, Zoran, dir. *Lude godine* [Foolish years]. Belgrade: Zvezda Film, 1977.

———. *Lude godine 2: Došlo doba da se ljubav proba* [Foolish years: The time has come to try love]. Belgrade: Zvezda Film, 1980.

Gerasimov, A, dir. *Svekrvin Grijeh* [The mother-in-law's sin]. Zagreb: School of Public Health in Zagreb, 1937. 35mm silent film.

Janković, Ljubica, dir. *Abortion*. Zagreb: Zagreb Film, 1977.

Latinović, Petar, dir. *Legalni prekid trudnoće putem vakuum aspiracije pericervikalnog bloka sa ginestezinom* [Legal termination of pregnancy by way of vacuum aspiration and paracervical block with anesthesia]. Novi Sad, Serbia: Neoplanta Film Novi Sad, 1972.

Matanović, Jovan, dir. *Kontracepcija* [Contraception]. Belgrade: Institute of Healthcare of the Republic of Serbia Photo-Film Section, 1963.

Nikolić, Živko, dir. *Bauk* [Boogeyman]. Belgrade: Dunav Film, 1974.

Pogačić, Vladimir, dir. *Pukotina raja* [Cracked paradise]. Belgrade: Jadran Film, 1959.

Radovanović, Vlastimir, dir. *Groznica Ljubavi* [Fever of love]. Belgrade: Avala Film, 1984.

Trinajstić, Petar, dir. *A ljudi ko ljudi* [And people like people]. Zagreb: Jadran Film, 1979.

Secondary Sources

Aariä-Kundaliä Broza, Elisabeth Fritz, Christoph Dobeš, and Johannes Saukel. "Traditional Medicine in the Pristine Village of Prokoško Lake on Vranica

Mountain, Bosnia and Herzegovina." *Scientia Pharmaceutica* 78, no. 2 (April–June 2010): 275–290.

Abrams, Lynn. *Oral History Theory*. London: Routledge, 2010.

———. "Liberating the Female Self: Epiphanies, Conflict and Coherence in the Life Stories of Post-War British Women." *Social History* 39, no. 1 (February 2014): 14–35.

Albanese, Patrizia. "Abortion and Reproductive Rights under Nationalist Regimes in Twentieth Century Europe." *Women's Health and Urban Life: An International and Interdisciplinary Journal* 3, no. 1 (November 2004): 8–33.

———. *Mothers of the Nation: Women, Families, and Nationalism in Twentieth-Century Europe*. Toronto: University of Toronto Press, 2006.

Allen, Beverly. *Rape Warfare: The Hidden Genocide in Bosnia-Herzegovina and Croatia*. Minneapolis: University of Minnesota Press, 1996.

Alpern Engel, Barbara. "New Directions in Russian and Soviet Women's History." In *Making Women's Histories beyond National Perspectives*, edited by Kate Haulman and Pamela Susan Nadell, 38–60. New York: New York University Press, 2013.

Alsop, R., and J. Hockey. "Women's Reproductive Lives as a Symbolic Resource in Central and Eastern Europe." *European Journal of Women's Studies* 8, no. 4 (November 2001): 454–471.

Antić, Ana. "Heroes and Hysterics: 'Partisan Hysteria' and Communist State-Building in Yugoslavia after 1945." *Social History of Medicine* 27, no. 2 (May 2014): 349–371.

———. "The Pedagogy of Workers' Self-Management: Terror, Therapy, and Reform Communism in Yugoslavia after the Tito-Stalin Split." *Journal of Social History* 50, no. 1 (September 2016): 179–203.

———. *Therapeutic Fascism: Experiencing the Violence of the Nazi New Order*. Oxford: Oxford University Press, 2016.

———. "Therapeutic Fascism: Re-educating Communists in Nazi-Occupied Serbia, 1942–44." *History of Psychiatry* 25, no. 1 (March 2014): 35–56.

Antić, Milica G. "Democracy between Tyranny and Liberty: Women in Post-Socialist Slovenia." *Feminist Review* 39, no. 1 (October 1991): 149–154.

Anton, Lorena. "On Memory Work in Post-Communist Europe: A Case Study on Romania's Ways of Remembering Its Pronatalist Past." *Anthropological Journal of European Cultures* 18, no. 2 (September 2009): 106–122.

Apple, Rima D. *Perfect Motherhood: Science and Childrearing in America*. New Brunswick, NJ: Rutgers University Press, 2006.

———. "Seeking Perfect Motherhood: Women, Medicine, and Libraries." *Library Trends* 60, no. 4 (Spring 2012): 694–705.

———. *Women, Health, and Medicine in America: A Historical Handbook*. New York: Garland, 1990.

Arsenijević, Jelena, Milena Pavlova, and Wim Groot. "Shortcomings of Maternity Care in Serbia." *BIRTH* 41, no. 1 (March 2014): 14–25.

Attwood, Lynne. *Creating the New Soviet Woman: Women's Magazines as Engineers of Female Identity, 1922–53*. New York: St. Martin's Press in association with the Centre for Russian and East European Studies, University of Birmingham, 1999.

———. *Gender and Housing in Soviet Russia: Private Life in a Public Space*. Manchester: Manchester University Press, 2010.

———. "Men, Machine Guns, and the Mafia: Post-Soviet Cinema as a Discourse on Gender." *Women's Studies International Forum* 18, no. 5 (September–December 1995): 513–521.

———. "Privatisation of Housing in Post-Soviet Russia: A New Understanding of Home?" *Europe-Asia Studies* 64, no. 5 (June 2012): 903–928.

———. *Red Women on the Silver Screen: Soviet Women and Cinema from the Beginning to the End of the Communist Era*. London: Pandora, 1993.

Baird, Barbara. "'Happy Abortionists': Considering the Place of Doctors in the Practice of Abortion in Australia since the Early 1990s." *Australian Feminist Studies* 29, no. 82 (2014): 419–434.

Baloutzova, Svetla. *Demography and Nation: Social Legislation and Population Policy in Bulgaria*. Budapest: Central European University, 2011.

Banac, Ivo. *With Stalin against Tito: Cominformist Splits in Yugoslav Communism*. Ithaca, NY: Cornell University Press, 1988.

Bastien, Joseph W. *Drum and Stethoscope: Integrating Ethnomedicine and Biomedicine in Bolivia*. Salt Lake City: University of Utah Press, 1998.

Batinić, Jelena. "Feminism, Nationalism, and War: The 'Yugoslav Case' in Feminist Texts." *Journal of International Women's Studies* 3, no. 1 (November 2001): 1–23.

———. "Motherhood and the Yugoslav Communist State in the Revolutionary Era, 1943–1953." In *Parenting and the State in Britain and Europe, c. 1870–1950*, edited by H. Barron and C. Siebrecht, 255–276. Cham, Switzerland: Palgrave Macmillan, 2017.

———. "Voices of the Other from the 'Other Europe': Recovering East-Central European Women's Literary Heritage." *Journal of Women's History* 15, no. 2 (Summer 2003): 207–213.

———. *Women and Yugoslav Partisans: A History of World War II Resistance*. Cambridge: Cambridge University Press, 2015.

Bayly, C. A., Sven Beckert, Matthew Connelly, Isabel Hofmeyr, Wendy Kozol, and Patricia Seed. "AHR Conversation: On Transnational History." *American Historical Review* 111, no. 5 (December 2006): 1441–1464.

Bekić, Darko. *Jugoslavija u hladnom ratu: Odnosi s velikim silama 1949–1955* [Yugoslavia in the Cold War: Relations between superpowers]. Zagreb: Plava Biblioteka, 1988.

Bell, John D. "Giving Birth to the New Soviet Man: Politics and Obstetrics in the USSR." *Slavic Review* 40 no. 1 (Spring 1981): 1–16.
Benoit, Cecilia, and Alena Heitlinger. "Women's Healthcare Work in Comparative Perspective: Canada, Sweden and Czechoslovakia / Czech Republic as Case Examples." *Social Science and Medicine* 47, no. 8 (October 1998): 1101–1111.
Bernard, R. P. "International IUD Programme: The Pathfinder Fund." In *Population Control: Implications, Trends, and Prospects (Proceedings of the Pakistan International family planning conference, Dacca, January 28–February 4, 1969)*, edited by Sadik Nafis, 163–177. Boston: Pathfinder Fund, 1969.
Bernstein, Frances Lee, Chris Burton, and Dan Healey, eds. *Soviet Medicine: Culture, Practice, and Science*. DeKalb: Northern Illinois University Press, 2010.
Bijelić, Nataša. "Sex Education in Croatia: Tensions between Secular and Religious Discourses." *European Journal of Women's Studies* 15, no. 4 (November 2008): 32–343.
Bjelica, Artur. "Socio-demographic Factors Influence Contraception Use among Female Students of the University of Novi Sad Serbia." *European Journal of Contraception and Reproductive Healthcare* 13, no. 4 (January 2008): 422–430.
Bokovoy, Melissa K. *Peasants and Communists: Politics and Ideology in the Yugoslav Countryside, 1941–1953*. Pittsburgh, PA: University of Pittsburgh Press, 1998.
Bokovoy, Melissa K., Jill A. Irvine, and Carol S. Lilly, eds. *State-Society Relations in Yugoslavia, 1945–1992*. 1st ed. New York: St. Martin's, 1997.
Bonfiglioli, Chiara. "Belgrade, 1978: Remembering the Conference. Comrade Woman. The Women's Question: A New Approach? Thirty Years After." Master's thesis, Utrecht University, 2008.
———. "Revolutionary Networks: Women's Political and Social Activism in Cold War Italy and Yugoslavia (1945–1957)." PhD diss., Utrecht University, 2012.
———. "The First UN Conference on Women (1975) as a Cold War Encounter: Recovering Anti-Imperialist, Non-Aligned and Socialist Genealogies." *Philosophy and Society* 17, no. 2 (January 2016): 521–541.
Bonnell, Victoria E., and Lynn Avery Hunt, eds. *Beyond the Cultural Turn: New Directions in the Study of Society and Culture*. Berkeley: University of California Press, 1999.
Bošković, Aleksandar. "Yugonostalgia and Yugoslav Cultural Memory: Lexicon of Yu Mythology." *Slavic Review* 72, no. 1 (Spring 2013): 54–78.
Boxer, Marilyn J. "Rethinking the Socialist Construction and International Career of the Concept 'Bourgeois Feminism.'" *American Historical Review* 112, no. 1 (February 2007): 131–158.
Bracewell, Wendy. "Orijentalizam, okcidentalizam i kosmopolitizam: Balkanski putopisi o Evropi" [Orientalism, occidentalism and cosmopolitanism: Balkan travel writing about Europe]. *Sarajevo Notebook* 6–7 (2004): 179–193.

———. "Women, Motherhood, and Contemporary Serbian Nationalism." *Women's Studies International Forum* 19, no. 1–2 (January–April 1996): 25–33.

Bracke, Maud Anne. "Family Planning, the Pill, and Reproductive Agency in Italy." *European Review of History* 29, no. 1 (2022): 88–108.

Bradley, Mark. "Decolonization, the Global South, and the Cold War, 1919–1962." In *The Cambridge History of the Cold War*, edited by Melvyn P. Leffler and Odd Arne Westad, 464–85. Cambridge: Cambridge University Press, 2010.

Braidotti, Rosi, and Gabriele Griffin, eds. *Thinking Differently: A Reader in European Women's Studies*. London: Zed Books, 2002.

Bren, Paulina, and Mary Neuburger, eds. *Communism Unwrapped: Consumption in Cold War Eastern Europe*. Oxford: Oxford University Press, 2012.

Brison, Susan J. *Aftermath: Violence and the Remaking of a Self*. Princeton, NJ: Princeton University Press, 2002.

Brookes, Barbara. *Abortion in England 1900–1967*. Abingdon: Taylor & Francis, 2013.

Brunnbauer, Ulf. "'The Most Natural Function of Women': Ambiguous Party Policies and Female Experiences in Socialist Bulgaria." In *Gender Politics and Everyday Life in State Socialist East and Central Europe Magazines*, edited by Jill Massino and Shana Penn, 77–96. New York: Palgrave Macmillan, 2009.

Brunnbauer, Ulf, and Karin Taylor. "Creating a Socialist Way of Life: Family and Reproduction Policies in Bulgaria, 1944–1989." *Continuity and Change* 19, no. 2 (August 2004): 283–312.

Bryceson, Deborah Fahy, and Ulla Vuorela, eds. *The Transnational Family: New European Frontiers and Global Networks*. Oxford: Berghahn Books, 2002.

Bucur, Maria. "An Archipelago of Stories: Gender History in Eastern Europe." *American Historical Review* 113, no. 5 (December 2008): 1375–1389.

———. *Eugenics and Modernization in Interwar Romania*. Pittsburgh, PA: University of Pittsburgh Press, 2002.

———. "Gender and Religiosity among Orthodox Christians in Romania: Continuity and Change, 1945–1989." *Aspasia* 5 (January 2011): 28–45.

Burke, Ronald. "From Individual Rights to National Development: The First UN International Conference on Human Rights, Tehran, 1968." *Journal of World History* 19, no. 3 (September 2008): 275–296.

———. *Decolonization and the Evolution of International Human Rights*. Philadelphia: University of Pennsylvania Press, 2010.

Burton, Chris. "Minzdrav, Soviet Doctors, and the Policing of Reproduction in the Late Stalinist Years." *Russian History* 27, no. 2 (Summer 2000): 197–221.

Butler, Judith. *Gender Trouble: Feminism and the Subversion of Identity*. New York: Routledge, 1990.

Byford, Jovan. "'Shortly afterwards, We Heard the Sound of the Gas Van': Survivor Testimony and the Writing of History in Socialist Yugoslavia." *History and Memory: Studies in Representation of the Past* 22, no. 1 (March 2010): 5–47.

Caiazza, Amy B. *Mothers and Soldiers: Gender, Citizenship, and Civil Society in Contemporary Russia*. New York: Routledge, 2002.

Canaday, Margot. "Thinking Sex in the Transnational Turn: An Introduction." *American Historical Review* 114, no. 5 (December 2009): 1250–1257.

Carter, Julian B. "Birds, Bees, and Venereal Disease: Toward an Intellectual History of Sex Education." *Journal of the History of Sexuality* 10, no. 2 (April 2001): 213–249.

Cerwonka, Allaine. "Traveling Feminist Thought: Difference and Transculturation in Central and Eastern European Feminism." *Signs* 33, no. 4 (June 2008): 809–832.

Charon, Rita. *Narrative Medicine: Honoring the Stories of Illness*. Oxford: Oxford University Press, 2006.

Chernyaeva, Natalia. "Childcare Manuals and Construction of Motherhood in Russia, 1890–1990." PhD diss., University of Iowa, 2009.

Clark, Anna, ed. *The History of Sexuality in Europe: A Sourcebook and Reader*. London: Routledge, 2011.

Clements, Barbara Evans. "The Birth of the New Soviet Woman." Paper presented at the Conference on the Origins of Soviet Culture, Kennan Institute for Advanced Russian Studies, the Wilson Centre, May 18–19, 1981. https://www.wilsoncenter.org/sites/default/files/op140_new_soviet_woman_Clements_1981.pdf.

Cockburn, Cynthia. "A Women's Political Party for Yugoslavia: Introduction to the Serbian Feminist Manifesto." *Feminist Review* 39, no. 1 (October 1991): 155–160.

Connelly, Matthew. *Fatal Misconception: The Struggle to Control World Population*. Cambridge: Cambridge University Press, 2008.

Constantinescu, Sorana-Alexandra. "How Women Made the News: A Case-Study of *Femeia* Magazine in Communist Romania under Ceaușescu." *Journal of Media Research* 10, no. 1 (2017): 32–41.

Daskalova, Krassimira. "How Should We Name the 'Woman-Friendly' Actions of State Socialism." *Aspasia* 1 (January 2007): 214–219.

David, H. P. "Abortion in Europe, 1920–91: A Public Health Perspective." *Studies in Family Planning* 23, no. 1 (January 1992): 1–22.

David, H. P., and J. Skilogianis. *From Abortion to Contraception: A Resource to Public Policies and Reproductive Behavior in Central and Eastern Europe from 1917 to the Present*. Westport, CT: Greenwood, 1999.

Davis, Angela Y. *Modern Motherhood: Women and Family in England, 1945–2000*. Manchester: Manchester University Press, 2012.

———. "A Revolution in Maternity Care? Women and the Maternity Services, Oxfordshire c. 1948–1974." *Social History of Medicine* 24, no. 2 (August 2011): 389–406.

———. "Wartime Women Giving Birth: Narratives of Pregnancy and Childbirth, Britain c. 1939–1960." *Studies in History and Philosophy of Biological and Biomedical Sciences* 47 (September 2014): 257–266.

de Haan, Francisca. "Continuing Cold War Paradigms in Western Historiography of Transnational Women's Organisations: The Case of the Women's International Democratic Federation (WIDF)." *Women's History Review* 19, no. 4 (September 2010): 547–573.

———. *Women's Activism: Global Perspectives from the 1890s to the Present.* New York: Routledge, 2013.

de Haan, Francisca, Krassimira Daskalova, and Anna Loutfi, eds. *A Biographical Dictionary of Women's Movements and Feminisms: Central, Eastern, and South Eastern Europe, 19th and 20th Centuries.* Budapest: Central European University Press, 2006.

Denisova, Liubov. *Rural Women in the Soviet Union and Post-Soviet Russia.* Hoboken, NJ: Taylor & Francis, 2010.

Dijanić, Dijana, Mirka Merunka-Golubić, Iva Niemčić, and Dijana Stanić. *Ženski biografski leksikon: Sjećanje žena na život u socijalizmu* [Women's biographical lexicon: Women's memories of socialism]. Zagreb: Centre for Women's Studies, 2004.

Dimić, Ljubodrag. *Agitprop kultura: agitpropovska faza kulturne politike u Srbiji 1945–1952* [Agitprop culture: The agitprop phase of cultural politics in Serbia]. Belgrade: RAD, 1988.

———. "Historiography on the Cold War in Yugoslavia: From Ideology to Science." *Cold War History* 8, no. 2 (June 2008): 285–297.

Djokić, Dejan, and James Ker-Lindsay, eds. *New Perspectives on Yugoslavia: Key Issues and Controversies.* London: Routledge, 2011.

Doboš, Manuela. "The Women's Movement in Yugoslavia: The Case of the Conference for the Social Activity of Women in Croatia, 1965–1974." *Frontiers: A Journal of Women's Studies* 7, no. 2 (January 1983): 47–55.

Dobrivojević, Ivana. "Planiranje porodice u Jugoslaviji, 1945–1974" [Family planning in Yugoslavia, 1945–1974]. *Istorija 20. veka* [History of the 20th century] 34, no. 2 (August 2016): 83–98.

———. "Za željeno roditeljstvo. Državna politika Jugoslavije u oblasti planiranja porodice 1945–1974" [For planned parenthood: Yugoslav national politics in the area of family planning, 1945–1974]. *Istorija 20. veka* [History of the 20th century] 36, no. 1 (February 2018): 119–132.

Dockrill, Saki, and Geraint Hughes, eds. *Palgrave Advances in Cold War History.* Basingstoke, UK: Palgrave Macmillan, 2006.

Dowbiggin, Ian Robert. "Medical Mission to Moscow: Women's Work, Day Care, and Early Cold War Politics in Twentieth-Century America." *Journal of Policy History* 23, no. 2 (April 2011): 177–203.

Drakić, Gordana. "Termination of Pregnancy under the Criminal Code of the Kingdom of Yugoslavia and the Projects that Preceded It." *Collection of Works of the Legal Studies University of Novi Sad* 3 (January 2011): 533–542.

Drapac, Vesna. *Constructing Yugoslavia: A Transnational History*. Basingstoke, UK: Palgrave Macmillan, 2010.

———. "Women, Resistance and the Politics of Daily Life in Hitler's Europe: The Case of Yugoslavia in a Comparative Perspective." *Aspasia* 3 (January 2009): 55–78.

Drezgić, Rada. "Policies and Practices of Fertility Control under the State Socialism." *History of the Family* 15 no. 2 (June 2010): 191–205.

———. "The Politics of Abortion and Contraception." *Sociologija* 46, no. 2 (December 2004): 97–114.

———. "Religion, Politics and Gender in the Context of Nation-State Formation: The Case of Serbia." *Third World Quarterly* 31, no. 6 (September 2010): 955–970.

Drglin, Zalka. *Rojstna hiša: Kulturna anatomija poroda* [Maternity home: Cultural anatomy of childbirth]. Ljubljana: Delta, 2003.

Duda, Igor. "Uvod: od nazadnosti do svemira, od projekta do zbornika." In *Stvaranje socijalističkoga čovjeka Hrvatsko društvo i ideologija jugoslavenskoga socijalizma*, edited by Igor Duda. Zagreb: HRZZ, 2017.

Dugac, Željko. "Popular Health Education and Venereal Diseases in Croatia between Two World Wars." *Croatian Medical Journal* 45, no. 4 (August 2004): 490–498.

Dugandžić, Andreja, and Tijana Okić, eds. *The Lost Revolution: Women's Antifascist Front between Myth and Forgetting*. Sarajevo: CRVENA, 2018.

Dugdale, Anni. "Inserting Grafenberg's IUD into the Sex Reform Movement." In *The Social Shaping of Technology*, edited by Donald MacKenzie and Judy Wajcman. Buckingham, UK: Open University Press, 1999.

———. "Intrauterine Contraceptive Devices, Situated Knowledges, and the Making of Women's Bodies." *Australian Feminist Studies* 15 (June 2000): 165–176.

Eckart, Wolfgang Uwe. *Man, Medicine, and the State: The Human Body as an Object of Government Sponsored Medical Research in the 20th Century*. Stuttgart: Steiner, 2006.

Edvinsson, Sören, and Sofia Kling. "The Practice of Birth Control and Historical Fertility Change: Introduction." *History of the Family* 15, no. 2 (June 2010): 117–124.

Einhorn, Barbara. *Cinderella Goes to Market: Citizenship, Gender and Women's Movements in East Central Europe*. London: Verso, 1993.

Engel, Barbara Alpern. "Engendering Russia's History: Women in Post-Emancipation Russia and the Soviet Union." *Slavic Review* 51, no. 2 (Summer 1992): 309–321.

———. *Women in Russia, 1700–2000*. Cambridge: Cambridge University Press, 2003.

Erlich, Vera Stein. *Family in Transition: A Study of 300 Yugoslav Villages*. Princeton, NJ: Princeton University Press, 1966.

Evans, Janet. "The Communist Party of the Soviet Union and the Women's Question: The Case of the 1936 Decree 'in Defense of Mother and Child.'" *Journal of Contemporary History* 16, no. 4 (October 1981): 757–775.

Ewing, E. Thomas. "Maternity and Modernity: Soviet Women Teachers and the Contradictions of Stalinism." *Women's History Review* 19, no. 3 (July 2010): 451–477.

Farmerie, Samuel. "Education in Yugoslavia." *The Clearing House* 47, no. 3 (1972): 145–49.

Ferber, Marianne A. and Phyllis Hutton Raabe. "Women in the Czech Republic: Feminism, Czech Style." *International Journal of Politics, Culture and Society* 16 no. 3 (Spring 2003): 407–430.

Ferree, Myra Marx. "The Rise and Fall of 'Mommy Politics': Feminism and Unification in (East) Germany." *Feminist Studies* 19, no. 1 (April 1993): 89–115.

Field, D. A. *Private Life and Communist Morality in Khrushchev's Russia*. New York: Peter Lang, 2007.

Field, Sean. "Imagining Communities: Memory, Loss, and Resilience in Post-Apartheid Cape Town." In *Oral History and Public Memories*, edited by Paula Hamilton and Linda Shopes, 107–124. Philadelphia: Temple University Press, 2008.

Fisher, Pamela. "Abortion in Post-Communist Germany: The End of Muttipolitik and a Still Birth for Feminism." *Women's Studies International Forum* 28, no. 1 (January–February 2005): 21–36.

Fleming, K. E. "Orientalism, the Balkans, and Balkan Historiography." *American Historical Review* 105, no. 4 (October 2000): 1218–1233.

Fodor, Eva, Christy Glass, Janette Kawachi, and Livia Popescu. "Family Policies and Gender in Hungary, Poland, and Romania." *Communist and Post-Communist Studies: Gender and the Experience of Poverty in Eastern Europe and Russia after 1989* 35, no. 4 (2002): 475–490.

Forsythe, Clarke D. *Abuse of Discretion: The Inside Story of Roe v. Wade*. New York: Encounter Books, 2013.

Foucault, Michel. *The History of Sexuality, Vol. 1: An Introduction*. New York: Pantheon Books, 1978.

Frejka, Tomas. "Determinants of Family Formation and Childbearing during the Societal Transition in Central and Eastern Europe." *Demographic Research* 19 (July 2008): 139–170.

———. "Induced Abortion and Fertility: A Quarter Century of Experience in Eastern Europe." *Population and Development Review* 9, no. 3 (September 1983): 494–520.

Funk, Nanette. "A Very Tangled Knot: Official State Socialist Women's Organizations, Women's Agency and Feminism in Eastern European State

Socialism." *European Journal of Women's Studies* 21, no. 4 (November 2014): 344–360.

———. "Feminist Critiques of Liberalism: Can They Travel East? Their Relevance in Eastern and Central Europe and the Former Soviet Union." *Signs* 29, no. 3 (March 2004): 695–726.

———. "Fifteen Years of the East-West Women's Dialogue." In *Living Gender after Communism*, edited by Janet Elise Johnson and Jean C. Robinson, 203–226. Bloomington: Indiana University Press, 2007.

Funk, Nanette, and Magda Mueller, eds. *Gender Politics and Post-Communism: Reflections from Eastern Europe and the Former Soviet Union*. New York: Routledge, 1993.

Gal, Susan. "Gender in the Post-Socialist Transition—the Abortion Debate in Hungary." *East European Politics and Societies* 8, no. 2 (Spring 1994): 256–286.

Gal, Susan, and Gail Kligman. *The Politics of Gender after Socialism: A Comparative-Historical Essay*. Princeton, NJ: Princeton University Press, 2000.

———, eds. *Reproducing Gender: Politics, Publics, and Everyday Life after Socialism*. Princeton, NJ: Princeton University Press, 2000.

Ghodsee, Kristen. "Feminism-by-Design: Emerging Capitalisms, Cultural Feminism, and Women's Nongovernmental Organizations in Postsocialist Eastern Europe." *Signs* 29, no. 3 (March 2004): 727–753.

Gooder, Claire. "A History of Sex Education in New Zealand, 1939–1985." PhD diss., University of Auckland, 2010.

Gordon, Linda. *The Moral Property of Women: A History of Birth Control Politics in America*. Champaign: University of Illinois Press, 2002.

Goscilo, Helena. *Dehexing Sex: Russian Womanhood during and after Glasnost*. Ann Arbor: Michigan University Press, 1996.

———. *Fruits of Her Plume: Essays on Contemporary Russian Woman's Culture*. Armonk, NY: M. E. Sharpe, 1993.

Goscilo, Helena, and Beth Holmgren, eds. *Russia—Women—Culture*. Bloomington: Indiana University Press, 1996.

Goscilo, Helena, and Andrea Lanoux, eds. *Gender and National Identity in Twentieth-Century Russian Culture*. DeKalb: Northern Illinois University Press, 2006.

Goulding, Daniel J. *Liberated Cinema: The Yugoslav Experience, 1945–2001*. Bloomington: Indiana University Press, 2002.

Graff, Agnieszka. "Lost between the Waves: The Paradoxes of Feminist Chronology and Activism in Contemporary Poland." *Journal of International Women's Studies* 4, no. 2 (April 2003): 100–116.

Grandits, Hannes, and Karin Taylor, eds. *Yugoslavia's Sunny Side: A History of Tourism in Socialism (1950s–1980s)*. Budapest: Central European University Press, 2010.

Grossmann, Atina. *Reforming Sex: The German Movement for Birth Control and Abortion Reform, 1920–1950.* Oxford: Oxford University Press, 1995.

Gudac-Dodić, Vera. "Brak i porodični odnosi u Srbiji u drugoj polovini 20. Veka" [Marriage and family relations in Serbia in the second half of the 20th century]. *Tokovi istorije* [Currents of history] 3–4 (September 2003): 39–52.

———. "Under the Aegis of the Family: Women in Serbia." *Journal of International Social Research* 3, no. 13 (September 2010): 110–119.

———. "Zdravstvena zaštita žena u Srbiji (1945–2000)" [Women's healthcare in Serbia (1945–2000)]. *Tokovi istorije* [Currents of history] 1, no. 2 (September 2003): 55–72.

Hall, Stuart, ed., *Culture, Media, Language: Working Papers in Cultural Studies, 1972–79.* Birmingham, UK: Centre for Contemporary Cultural Studies and University of Birmingham, 1980.

———, ed. *Representation: Cultural Representations and Signifying Practices, Culture, Media, and Identities.* London: Sage, 1997.

Halpern, Joel Martin. *A Serbian Village.* New York: Columbia University Press, 1958.

Halpern, Joel M., Karl Kaser, and Richard A. Wagner. "Patriarchy in the Balkans: Temporal and Cross-Cultural Approaches." *History of the Family* 1, no. 4 (January 1996): 425–442.

Halpern, Joel M., and Barbara Kerewsky-Halpern. *A Serbian Village in Historical Perspective.* Long Grove, IL: Waveland, 1972.

Haney, Lynne. "Familial Welfare: Building the Hungarian Welfare Society, 1948–1968." *Social Politics* 7, no. 1 (April 2000): 101–122.

Harsch, Donna. "Eroticism, Love and Sexuality in the Two Postwar Germanys." *German Studies Review* 35, no. 3 (October 2012): 627–636.

———. *Revenge of the Domestic: Women, the Family, and Communism in the German Democratic Republic.* Princeton, NJ: Princeton University Press, 2007.

———. "Society, the State, and Abortion in East Germany, 1950–1972." *American Historical Review* 102, no. 1 (February 1997): 53–84.

Hatzopoulos, Pavlos. "'All that Is, Is Nationalist': Western Imaginings of the Balkans since the Yugoslav Wars." *Journal of Balkan and Near Eastern Studies* 5, no. 1 (April 2003): 25–38.

Hau, Michael. *The Cult of Health and Beauty in Germany: A Social History, 1890–1930.* Chicago: University of Chicago Press, 2003.

Headrick, Daniel. *The Tools of Empire: Technology and European Imperialism in the Nineteenth Century.* Oxford: Oxford University Press, 1981.

Heineman, Elizabeth D. "Single Motherhood and Maternal Employment in Divided Germany: Ideology, Policy, and Social Pressures in the 1950s." *Journal of Women's History* 12, no. 3 (Fall 2000): 146–172.

———. *What Difference Does a Husband Make? Women and Marital Status in Nazi and Postwar Germany*. Berkeley: University of California Press, 1999.

———. "Whose Mothers? Generational Difference, War, and the Nazi Cult of Motherhood." *Journal of Women's History* 12, no. 4 (Winter 2001): 139–164.

Heitlinger, Alena. "Framing Feminism in Post-Communist Czech Republic." *Communist and Post-Communist Studies* 29 no. 1 (March 1996): 77–93.

———. *Reproduction, Medicine, and the Socialist State*. Hampshire, UK: Macmillan, 1987.

———. *Women's Equality, Demography and Public Policies: A Comparative Perspective*. London: Palgrave Macmillan, 1993.

Helms, Elissa. "East and West Kiss: Gender, Orientalism, and Balkanism in Muslim-Majority Bosnia-Herzegovina." *Slavic Review* 67, no. 1 (Spring 2008): 68–119.

———. *Innocence and Victimhood: Gender, Nation, and Women's Activism in Postwar Bosnia-Herzegovina*. Madison: University of Wisconsin Press, 2013.

Helmut, Gruber. *Women and Socialism, Socialism and Women: Europe between the Two World Wars*. New York: Berghahn Books, 1998.

Herzog, Dagmar. *Sex after Fascism: Memory and Morality in Twentieth-Century Germany*. Princeton, NJ: Princeton University Press, 2005.

———. *Sexuality in Europe: A Twentieth-Century History*. Cambridge: Cambridge University Press, 2011.

———. "Syncopated Sex: Transforming European Sexual Cultures." *American Historical Review* 114 no. 5 (December 2009): 1287–1308.

Hitchcock, William I. "The Rise and Fall of Human Rights? Searching for a Narrative from the Cold War to the 9/11 Era." *Human Rights Quarterly* 37, no. 1 (February 2015): 80–106.

Hodgson, Jane E. *Abortion and Sterilization: Medical and Social Aspects*. London: Academic Press Grune & Stratton, 1981.

Hofman, Ana. *Staging Socialist: Femininity, Gender Politics and Folklore Performance in Serbia*. Leiden, Netherlands: Brill Academic, 2011.

Hrešanová, Ema. "'Nobody in a Maternity Hospital Really Talks to You': Socialist Legacies and Consumerism in Czech Women's Childbirth Narratives." *Sociologický časopis* [Czech sociological review] 50, no. 6 (January 2014): 961–985.

———. "The Psychoprophylactic Method of Painless Childbirth in Socialist Czechoslovakia: From State Propaganda to Activism of Enthusiasts." *Medical History* 60, no. 4 (October 2016): 534–556.

Hristov, Petko. "Ideological Dimensions of the 'Balkan Family Pattern' in the First Half of the 20th Century." *History of the Family* 19, no. 2 (March 2014): 218–234.

Iacob et al., "State Socialist Experts in Transnational Perspective. East European Circulation of Knowledge during the Cold War (1950s–1980s): Introduction to the Thematic Issue." *East Central Europe* 45 (2018): 145–159.

Ignaciuk, Agata. "'Clueless about Contraception': The Introduction and Circulation of the Contraceptive Pill in State-Socialist Poland (1960s–1970s)." *Medicina nei secoli* 26, no. 2 (November 2014): 509–535.

———. "Innovation and Maladjustment: Contraceptive Technologies in State-Socialist Poland, 1950s–1970s." *Technology and Culture* 63, no. 1 (2022): 182–208.

Ilič, Melanie, Susan Emily Reid, and Lynne Attwood, eds. *Women in the Khrushchev Era*. New York: Palgrave Macmillan, 2004.

Irvine, Janice M., ed. *Sexual Cultures and the Construction of Adolescent Identities*. Philadelphia: Temple University Press, 1994.

———. *Talk about Sex: The Battles over Sex Education in the United States*. Berkeley: University of California, 2002.

Isić, Momčilo. *Seljanka u Srbiji u prvoj polovini 20. veka* [Peasant women in Serbia in the first half of the twentieth century]. Belgrade: Helsinški odbor za ljudska prava, 2008.

Jakovina, Tvrtko. *Američki komunistički saveznik: Hrvati, Titova Jugoslavija i SAD 1945–1955* [America's communist ally: Croats, Tito's Yugoslavia and the USA 1945–1955]. Zagreb: Profil, 2003.

Jambrešić, Renata, and Marina Blagaić. "The Ambivalence of Socialist Working Women's Heritage: A Case Study of the Jugoplastika Factory." *Narodna umjetnost* 50, no. 1 (2013): 39–73.

Jambrešić, Renata, and Reana Senjković. "Legacies of the Second World War in Croatian Cultural Memory: Women as Seen through the Media." *Aspasia* 4 (January 2010): 71–96.

Jancar-Webster, Barbara. "Neofeminism in Yugoslavia: A Closer Look." *Women and Politics* 8, no. 1 (January 1988): 1–30.

———. *Women and Revolution in Yugoslavia, 1941–1945*. Women and Modern Revolution. Los Angeles: Arden, 1990.

———. *Women under Communism*. Baltimore: Johns Hopkins University Press, 1978.

Jarska, Natalia, and Agata Ignaciuk. "Marriage, Gender and Demographic Change: Managing Fertility in State-Socialist Poland." *Slavic Review* 81, no. 1 (2022): 142–162.

Joffe, Carole E. *Doctors of Conscience: The Struggle to Provide Abortion before and after Roe v. Wade*. Boston: Beacon, 1995.

Johnson, Janet Elise. *Gender Violence in Russia: The Politics of Feminist Intervention*. Bloomington: Indiana University Press, 2009.

Johnson, Janet Elise, and Jean C. Robinson, eds. *Living Gender after Communism*. Bloomington: Indiana University Press, 2007.

Jordanova, L. J. *Sexual Visions: Images of Gender in Science and Medicine between the Eighteenth and Twentieth Centuries*. Madison: University of Wisconsin Press, 1989.

Jovanović, Miroslava. "The Heroic Circle of Serbian Sisters: A History." *Serbian Studies: Journal of the North American Society for Serbian Studies* 24, no. 1 (Winter–Summer 2012): 125–139.

Kajevska, A. Miškovska. "Taking a Stand in Times of Violent Societal Changes: Belgrade and Zagreb Feminists' Positionings on the (Post-)Yugoslav Wars and Each Other (1991–2000)." PhD diss., University of Amsterdam, 2014.

Keene, Judith. "The Filmmaker as Historian, above and below Ground: Emir Kusturica and the Narratives of Yugoslav History." *Rethinking History* 5, no. 2 (July 2001): 233–253.

Kerewsky-Halpern, Barbara. "Trust, Talk and Touch in Balkan Folk Healing." *Social Science and Medicine* 21, no. 3 (January 1985): 319–325.

Kirschenbaum, Lisa A. "'Our City, Our Hearths, Our Families': Local Loyalties and Private Life in Soviet World War II Propaganda." *Slavic Review* 59, no. 4 (Winter 2000): 825–847.

Kligman, Gail. "Abortion and International Adoption in Post-Ceausescu Romania." *Feminist Studies* 18, no. 2 (Summer 1992): 405–419.

———. *The Politics of Duplicity: Controlling Reproduction in Ceausescu's Romania*. Berkeley: University of California Press, 1998.

Kline, Wendy. *Bodies of Knowledge: Sexuality, Reproduction, and Women's Health in the Second Wave*. Chicago: University of Chicago Press, 2010.

Kokanović, Renata, Paula A. Michaels, and Kate Johnston-Ataata, eds. *Paths to Parenthood: Emotions on the Journey through Pregnancy, Childhood and Early Parenting*. London: Palgrave MacMillan, 2018.

Koonz, Claudia. *Mothers in the Fatherland: Women, the Family and Nazi Politics*. London: Routledge, 2013.

Koraljka, Vlajo. "Designing a Socialist Man." *AM Journal* 19 (2019): 15–27.

Kralj-Brassard, Rina, and Kristina Puljizević. "Clandestine Birth: Care of Unwed Pregnant Women and Parturients within the Dubrovnik Foundling Hospital in the Second Half of the Eighteenth Century." *Dubrovnik Annals* 16 (2012): 37–67.

Krementsov, Nikolai. "From 'Beastly Philosophy' to Medical Genetics: Eugenics in Russia and the Soviet Union." *Annals of Science* 68, no. 1 (January 2011): 61–92.

Kuhar, Martin. "'From an Impure Source, All Is Impure': The Rise and Fall of Andrija Štampar's Public Health Eugenics in Yugoslavia." *Social History of Medicine* 30, no. 1 (February 2017): 92–113.

Kuhar, Roman, and Alenka Švab. "The Only Gay in the Village? Everyday Life of Gays and Lesbians in Rural Slovenia." *Journal of Homosexuality* 61, no. 8 (June 2014): 1091–1116.

Lampe, John R. *Yugoslavia as History: Twice There Was a Country*. Cambridge: Cambridge University Press, 1996.

Lauren, Paul G. *The Evolution of International Human Rights: Visions Seen.* Philadelphia: University of Pennsylvania Press, 2011.

Leavitt, Judith Walzer. *Brought to Bed: Childbearing in America, 1750 to 1950.* Oxford: Oxford University Press, 1986.

———. "'Science' Enters the Birthing Room: Obstetrics in America since the Eighteenth Century." *Journal of American History* 70 no. 2 (September 1983): 281–304.

———. *Women and Health in America: Historical Readings.* 2nd ed. Madison: University of Wisconsin Press, 1999.

———. "A Worrying Profession—the Domestic Environment of Medical-Practice in Mid-Nineteenth-Century America." *Bulletin of the History of Medicine* 69, no. 1 (Spring 1995): 1–29.

Leavitt, Judith Walzer, and Ronald L. Numbers, eds. *Sickness and Health in America: Readings in the History of Medicine and Public Health.* 3rd ed. Madison: University of Wisconsin Press, 1997.

Lees, Lorraine M. *Keeping Tito Afloat: The United States, Yugoslavia, and the Cold War.* Philadelphia: Pennsylvania State University Press, 1997.

Leffler, Melvyn P., and Odd Arne Westad, eds. *The Cambridge History of the Cold War.* Cambridge: Cambridge University Press, 2010.

Levine, Phillip B., and Douglas Staiger. "Abortion Policy and Fertility Outcomes: The Eastern European Experience." *Journal of Law and Economics* 47, no. 1 (April 2004): 223–243.

Lilly, Carol S. *Power and Persuasion: Ideology and Rhetoric in Communist Yugoslavia, 1944–1953.* New York: Routledge, 2001.

———. "Problems of Persuasion: Communist Agitation and Propaganda in Post-War Yugoslavia, 1944–1948." *Slavic Review* 53, no. 2 (Summer 1994): 395–413.

Lilly, Carol S., and J. A. Irvine. "Negotiating Interests: Women and Nationalism in Serbia and Croatia, 1990–1997." *East European Politics and Societies* 16, no. 1 (February 2002): 109–144.

Lišková, Kateřina. *Sexual Liberation, Socialist Style: Communist Czechoslovakia and the Science of Desire, 1945–1989.* Cambridge: Cambridge University Press, 2018.

Lord, Alexandra M. *Condom Nation: The U.S. Government's Sex Education Campaign from World War I to the Internet.* Baltimore: Johns Hopkins University Press, 2010.

Löwy, Ilana. "'Sexual Chemistry' before the Pill: Science, Industry and Chemical Contraceptives, 1920–1960." *British Journal for the History of Science* 44, no. 2 (June 2011): 245–274.

Lukić, Jasmina, Joanna Regulska, and Darja Zaviršek, eds. *Women and Citizenship in Central and Eastern Europe.* Aldershot, UK: Ashgate, 2006.

Luthar, B., and M. Pušnik, eds. *Remembering Utopia: The Culture of Everyday Life in Socialist Yugoslavia.* Washington, DC: New Academia, 2010.

Macura, Miloš. "Population Policies in Socialist Countries of Europe." *Population Studies* 28, no. 3 (1974): 369–379.

Macura, Miloš, ed. *Problemi politike obnavljanja stanovništva u Srbiji*. Beograd: SANU, 1989.
Maguire, Sarah. "Researching 'a Family Affair': Domestic Violence in Former Yugoslavia and Albania." *Gender and Development* 6, no. 3 (November 1998): 60–66.
Majstorović, Danijela. "The Creation of the New Yugoslav Woman—The Emancipatory Elements of Media Discourse from the End of World War II." In *The Lost Revolution: Women's Antifascist Front between Myth and Forgetting*, edited by Chiara Bonfiglioli et al., 88–120. Sarajevo: CRVENA, 2018.
Maksimović, Maja. "Unattainable Past, Unsatisfying Present—Yugonostalgia: An Omen of a Better Future?" *Nationalities Papers* 45, no. 6 (November 2017): 1066–1081.
Martin, Terry. *The Affirmative Action Empire: Nations and Nationalism in the Soviet Union, 1923–1939*. Ithaca, NY: Cornell University Press, 2001.
Massino, Jill. "Something Old, Something New: Marital Roles and Relations in State Socialist Romania." *Journal of Women's History* 22, no. 1 (Spring 2010): 34–60.
Massino, Jill, and Shana Penn, eds. *Gender Politics and Everyday Life in State Socialist East and Central Europe Magazines*. New York: Palgrave Macmillan, 2009.
May, Elaine Tyler. *America and the Pill: A History of Promise, Peril, and Liberation*. New York: Basic Books, 2010.
———. *Barren in the Promised Land: Childless Americans and the Pursuit of Happiness*. New York: Basic Books, 1995.
———. *Homeward Bound: American Families in the Cold War Era*. New York: Basic Books, 1988.
Mazower, Mark. *No Enchanted Palace: The End of Empire and the Ideological Origins of the United Nations*. Princeton, NJ: Princeton University Press, 2010.
McIntosh, Tania. *A Social History of Maternity and Childbirth: Key Themes in Maternity Care*. New York: Routledge, 2012.
McLellan, Josie. *Love in the Time of Communism: Intimacy and Sexuality in the GDR*. Cambridge: Cambridge University Press, 2011.
McMillen, Christian, and Niels Brimnes. "Medical Modernization and Medical Nationalism: Resistance to Mass Tuberculosis Vaccination in Postcolonial India, 1948–1955." *Comparative Studies in Society and History* 52, no. 1 (2010): 180–209.
Meyerowitz, Joanne. "Transnational Sex and U.S. History." *American Historical Review* 114, no. 5 (December 2009): 1273–1286.
Michaels, Paula A. "Comrades in the Labor Room: The Lamaze Method of Childbirth Preparation and France's Cold War Home Front, 1951–1957." *American Historical Review* 115, no. 4 (October 2010): 1031–1060.
———. *Curative Powers: Medicine and Empire in Stalin's Central Asia*. Pittsburgh, PA: University of Pittsburgh Press, 2003.

———. *Lamaze: An International History*. Oxford: Oxford University Press, 2014.
———. "Motherhood, Patriotism, and Ethnicity: Soviet Kazakhstan and the 1936 Abortion Ban." *Feminist Studies* 27, no. 2 (July 2001): 307–333.
Mihelj, Sabina. "Koka-kola socijalizam: Amerikanizacija Jugoslovenske popularne kulture Šezdesetih godina 20 veka" [Coca-cola socialism: Americanization of Yugoslav popular culture in the 1960s]. *European Journal of Communication* 28, no. 6 (December 2013): 720–722.
———. "Persistence of the Past: Memory, Generational Cohorts and the 'Iron Curtain.'" *Contemporary European History* 23, no. 3 (August 2014): 447–468.
Milanović, Jasmina. "Materinsko udruženje – humani i socijalni aspekti delovanja 1904–1941" [Mother's society: Human and social activities 1904–1941]. *Istorija 20. veka* [History of the 20th century] 36, no. 2 (August 2018): 37–54.
Milić, Andjelka. "The Women's Movement in Serbia and Montenegro at the Turn of the Millennium: A Sociological Study of Women's Groups." *Feminist Review* 76, no. 1 (March 2004): 65–82.
Milićević, Nataša, and Predrag Marković. "Srpska istoriografija u vreme tranzicije: Borba za legitimitet" [Serbian historiography in the time of transition: The battle for legitimacy]. *Istorija 20. veka* [History of the 20th century] 1 (2007): 145–167.
Miljan, Zrinka. "Seksualna revolucija u Hrvatskoj 1960-ih i 1970-ih godina" [Sexual revolution in Croatia in the 1960s and 1970s]. PhD diss., University of Zagreb, 2018.
Miroiu, Mihaela. "Communism Was a State Patriarchy, Not State Feminism." *Aspasia* 1 (January 2007): 197–201.
———. "'Not the Right Moment!' Women and the Politics of Endless Delay in Romania." *Women's History Review* 19, no. 4 (September 2010): 575–593.
Mišković, Nataša, Harald Fischer-Tiné, and Nada Boškovska, eds. *The Non-Aligned Movement and the Cold War: Delhi–Bandung–Belgrade*. London: Routledge, 2014.
Mitterauer, Michael. "Family Contexts: The Balkans in European Comparison." *History of the Family* 1, no. 4 (January 1996): 387–406.
Mladjenović, Lepa, Vera Litricin, and Tanya Renne. "Belgrade Feminists 1992: Separation, Guilt and Identity Crisis." *Feminist Review* 45 (Fall 1993): 113–119.
Moeller, Robert G. *Protecting Motherhood: Women and the Family in the Politics of Postwar West Germany*. Berkeley: University of California Press, 1993.
Moran, Jeffrey P. *Teaching Sex: The Shaping of Adolescence in the 20th Century*. Cambridge, MA: Harvard University Press, 2000.
Morgen, Sandra. *Into Our Own Hands: The Women's Health Movement in the United States, 1969–1990*. New Brunswick, NJ: Rutgers University Press, 2002.
Morokvasić, Mirjana. "Sexuality and Control of Procreation." In *Of Marriage and the Market: Women's Subordination Internationally and Its Lessons*, edited by Kate Young, Carol Wolkowitz, and Roslyn McCullagh, 193–209. London: Routledge, 1981.

Mukherjee, Sujata. *Gender, Medicine, and Society in Colonial India: Women's Health Care in Nineteenth- and Early Twentieth-Century Bengal.* Delhi: Oxford University Press, 2017.

Novakov, Anna. "Ksenija Atanasijević and the Emergence of the Feminist Movement in Interwar Serbia." *Serbian Studies: Journal of the North American Society for Serbian Studies* 25, no. 1 (Winter–Spring 2011): 107–118.

Nakachi, Mie. "N. S. Khrushchev and the 1944 Soviet Family Law: Politics, Reproduction, and Language." *East European Politics and Societies* 20, no. 1 (February 2006): 40–68.

Neofotistos, Vasiliki P. "Cultural Intimacy and Subversive Disorder: The Politics of Romance in the Republic of Macedonia." *Anthropological Quarterly* 83, no. 2 (Spring 2010): 279–316.

———. "Postsocialism, Social Value, and Identity Politics among Albanians in Macedonia." *Slavic Review* 69, no. 4 (December 2010): 884–891.

Ochberg, Richard. "Introduction: Life Stories, Cultural Politics, and Self-Understanding." In *Storied Lives: The Cultural Politics of Self-Understanding*, edited by George C. Rosenwald and Richard L. Ochberg, 1–18. New Haven, CT: Yale University Press, 1992.

Ognjenović, Gorana, and Jasna Jozelić, eds. *Revolutionary Totalitarianism, Pragmatic Socialism, Transition.* London: Springer Nature, 2016.

———, eds. *Titoism, Self-Determination, Nationalism, Cultural Memory.* Vol. 2, *Tito's Yugoslavia, Stories Untold.* London: Springer Nature, 2016.

Olcott, Jocelynn. *International Women's Year: The Greatest Consciousness-Raising Event in History.* Oxford: Oxford University Press, 2017.

Olszynko-Gryn, Jesse. "Contraceptive Technology." In *Twentieth Century Population Thinking: A Critical Reader of Primary Sources*, edited by Population Knowledge Network, 172–209. London: Routledge, 2016.

Pavičević, Aleksandra. *Na udaru ideologija: Brak, porodica i polni moral u Srbiji u drugoj polovini 20 veka* [On the impact of ideology: Marriage, family and sexual morality in Serbia during the second half of the twentieth century]. Belgrade: Ethnographic Institute SANU, 2006.

Pence, Katherine, and Paul Betts. *Socialist Modern: East German Everyday Culture and Politics.* Ann Arbor: University of Michigan Press, 2008.

Perišić, Miroslav. "Yugoslavia: The 1950 Cultural and Ideological Revolution." In *The Balkans in the Cold War: Security, Conflict and Cooperation in the Contemporary World*, edited by Svetozar Rajak, K. E. Botsiou, Eirini Karamouzi, and E. Hatzivassiliou, 285–305. London: Palgrave Macmillan, 2017.

Perks, Robert, and Alistair Thompson, eds. *Oral History Reader.* London: Taylor & Francis, 2015.

Perović, Jeronim. "The Tito-Stalin Split: A Reassessment in Light of New Evidence." *Journal of Cold War Studies* 9, no. 2 (Spring 2007): 32–63.

Peto, Andrea, ed. *To Look at Life through Women's Eyes: Women's Oral Histories from the Former Soviet Union*. New York: Open Society Institute, 2002.

———. "Writing Women's History in Eastern Europe: Toward a 'Terra Cognita'?" *Journal of Women's History* 16 no. 4 (Winter 2004): 173–181.

Petrović, Tanja. "'When We Were Europe': Socialist Workers in Serbia and Their Nostalgic Narratives, the Case of the Cable Factory Workers in Jagodina." In *Remembering Communism: Genres of Representation*, edited by Maria Todorova, 127–153. New York: Social Science Research Council, 2010.

Petrović-Todosijević, Sanja. "Towards an Affective History of Yugoslavia." *Filozofija i društvo* [Philosophy and society] 28, no. 3 (January 2016): 504–520.

———. "Zdravstveno prosvećivanje naroda kao deo borbe za smanjenje smrtnosti dece u FNRJ" [People's health education as part of the fight to reduce child mortality in the Socialist Federal Republic of Yugoslavia]. *Istorija 20. veka* [History of the 20th century] 23, no. 2 (2005): 101–112.

Petschesky, Rosalind. "From Population Control to Reproductive Rights: Feminist Fault Lines." *Reproductive Health Matters* 6 (January 1995): 152–161.

Plant, Rebecca Jo. *Mom: The Transformation of Motherhood in Modern America*. Chicago: University of Chicago Press, 2010.

Population Council. "World Leaders Declaration on Population." *Studies in Family Planning* 9, no. 7 (July 1978): 180–181.

Port, Andrew I. "Love, Lust, and Lies under Communism: Family Values and Adulterous Liaisons in Early East Germany." *Central European History* 44 no. 3 (September 2011): 478–505.

Port, Andrew I., and Mary Fulbrook, eds. *Becoming East German: Structures and Sensibilities after Hitler*. New York: Berghahn Books, 2013.

Porter, Roy, and Lesley Hall. *The Facts of Life: The Creation of Sexual Knowledge in Britain, 1650–1950*. New Haven, CT: Yale University Press, 1995.

Posadskaya-Vanderbeck, Anastasia, ed. *Women in Russia: A New Era in Russian Feminism*. London: Verso, 1994.

Promitzer, Christian, Sevasti Troumpeta, and Marius Turda. *Health, Hygiene, and Eugenics in Southeastern Europe to 1945*. Budapest: Central European University Press, 2011.

Puljizević, Kristina. *U ženskim rukama. Primalje i porođaj u Dubrovniku (1815–1918)* [Childbirth in Dubrovnik (1815–1918)]. Dubrovnik: Hrvatska akademija znanosti i umjetnosti, 2016.

Puur, Allan, Kalev Katus and Luule Sakkeus. "Family Formation in the Baltic Countries: A Transformation in the Legacy of State Socialism." *Journal of Baltic Studies* 39, no. 2 (June 2008): 123–156.

Rajak, Svetozar. "No Bargaining Chips, No Spheres of Interest: The Yugoslav Origins of Cold War Non-Alignment." *Journal of Cold War Studies* 16 no. 1 (Winter 2014): 146–179.

Rajak, Svetozar, K. E. Botsiou, Eirini Karamouzi, and E. Hatzivassiliou, eds. *The Balkans in the Cold War: Security, Conflict and Cooperation in the Contemporary World*. London: Palgrave Macmillan, 2017.

Raleigh, Donald J. *Soviet Baby Boomers: An Oral History of Russia's Cold War Generation*. Oxford: Oxford University Press, 2012.

Ramet, Sabrina Petra, ed. *Gender Politics in the Western Balkans: Women and Society in Yugoslavia and the Yugoslav Successor States*. University Park: Pennsylvania State University Press, 1999.

———. "Memory and Identity in the Yugoslav Successor States." *Nationalities Papers* 41, no. 6 (November 2013): 871–881.

———. *The Three Yugoslavias: State-Building and Legitimation, 1918—2005*. Bloomington: Indiana University Press. 2006.

Ramet, Sabrina Petra, and Ljubiša S. Adamović, eds. *Beyond Yugoslavia: Politics, Economics, and Culture in a Shattered Community*. Boulder, CO: Westview, 1995.

Randall, Amy E. "'Abortion Will Deprive You of Happiness!': Soviet Reproductive Politics in the Post-Stalin Era." *Journal of Women's History* 23, no. 3 (Fall 2011): 13–38.

Rast, Brittany. "What's a Girl to Do? Repatriarchalization and Croatian Women's Reproductive Freedom." Master's thesis, Agnes Scott College, 2007.

Rašević, Mirjana. "The Abortion Issue in Serbia." *European Journal of Contraception and Reproductive Healthcare* 14 no. 6 (December 2009): 385–390.

———. "The Question of Abortion in Serbia." *Espace populations sociétés* 3 (September 2009): 681–693.

Reagan, Leslie J. *Dangerous Pregnancies: Mothers, Disabilities, and Abortion in Modern America*. Berkeley: University of California Press, 2010.

———, ed. *Medicine's Moving Pictures: Medicine, Health, and Bodies in American Film and Television*. Rochester, NY: University of Rochester Press, 2007.

———. *When Abortion Was a Crime: Women, Medicine, and Law in the United States, 1867–1973*. Berkeley: University of California Press, 1997.

Renne, Tanya, ed. *Ana's Land: Sisterhood in Eastern Europe*. Boulder, CO: Westview, 1997.

Rivkin-Fish, Michele. "'Change Yourself and the Whole World Will Become Kinder': Russian Activists for Reproductive Health and the Limits of Claims Making for Women." *Medical Anthropology Quarterly* 18, no. 3 (September 2004): 281–304.

———. "Conceptualizing Feminist Strategies for Russian Reproductive Politics: Abortion, Surrogate Motherhood, and Family Support after Socialism." *Signs* 38, no. 3 (Spring 2013): 569–593.

———. "Pronatalism, Gender Politics and the Renewal of Family Support in Russia: Toward a Feminist Anthropology of 'Maternity Capital.'" *Slavic Review* 69, no. 3 (October 2010): 701–724.

———. *Women's Health in Post-Soviet Russia: The Politics of Intervention*. Bloomington: Indiana University Press, 2005.

Roman, Denise. "Gendering Eastern Europe: Pre-Feminism, Prejudice, and East-West Dialogues in Post-Communist Romania." *Women's Studies International Forum* 24, no. 1 (January–February 2001): 53–66.

Rowbotham, Sheila. *Beyond the Fragments: Feminism and the Making of Socialism.* London: Merlin, 1980.

Rubinstein, Alvin Z. *Yugoslavia and the Nonaligned World.* Princeton, NJ: Princeton University Press, 1970.

Sandfort, Theo, and Aleksandar Štulhofer, eds. *Sexuality and Gender in Postcommunist Eastern Europe and Russia.* New York: Haworth, 2005.

Sauerteig, Lutz D. H., and Roger Davidson, eds. *Shaping Sexual Knowledge: A Cultural History of Sex Education in Twentieth Century Europe.* Hoboken, NJ: Taylor & Francis, 2008.

Savelli, Mat. "The Peculiar Prosperity of Psychoanalysis in Socialist Yugoslavia." *Slavonic and East European Review* 91, no. 2 (April 2013): 262–288.

Schoen, Johanna. *Abortion after Roe.* Chapel Hill: University of North Carolina Press, 2015.

Scott, Joan W. "Gender: A Useful Category of Historical Analysis." *American Historical Review* 91, no. 5 (December 1986): 1053–75.

Shiffman, Jeremy, Marina Skrabalo, and Jelena Subotić. "Reproductive Rights and the State in Serbia and Croatia." *Social Science and Medicine* 54, no. 4 (February 2002): 625–642.

Siegelbaum, Lewis H., ed. *The Socialist Car: Automobility in the Eastern Bloc.* Ithaca, NY: Cornell University Press, 2011.

Simić, Ivan. *Soviet Influences on Postwar Yugoslav Gender Policies.* Cham, Switzerland: Palgrave Macmillan, 2018.

Simić, Marina, and Ivan Simić. "'Who Should Care about Our Children?': Public Childcare Policy in Yugoslav Socialism and Its Serbian Aftermath." *Journal of Family History* 44, no. 2 (February 2019): 145–158.

Simic, Olivera. "Drinking Coffee in Bosnia: Listening to Stories of Wartime Violence and Rape." *Journal of International Women's Studies* 18, no. 4 (August 2017): 321–328.

Sklevicky, Lydia. "More Horses than Women: On the Difficulties of Founding Women's History in Yugoslavia." *Gender and History* 1, no. 1 (March 1989): 68–73.

Škrabalo, Ivo. *101 godina filma u Hrvatskoj, 1896–1997* [101 years of film in Croatia, 1896–1997]. Zagreb: Globus, 1998.

Slezkine, Yuri. *Arctic Mirrors: Russia and the Small Peoples of the North.* Ithaca, NY: Cornell University Press, 1996.

———. "The USSR as a Communal Apartment, or How a Socialist State Promoted Ethnic Particularism." *Slavic Review* 53, no. 2 (Summer 1994): 414–452.

Sluga, Glenda. "Cold War Casualties: Ethnicity, Gender, and the Writing of History." *Women's Studies International Forum* 19, no. 1 (January–April 1996): 75–85.

Sokolova, Vera. "Planned Parenthood behind the Curtain: Population Policy and Sterilization of Romani Women in Communist Czechoslovakia, 1972–1989." *Anthropology of East Europe Review* 23, no. 1 (January 2005): 79–98.

Solinger, Rickie. *Pregnancy and Power: A Short History of Reproductive Politics in America.* New York: New York University Press, 2005.

Solinger, Rickie, and Mie Nakachi. "Introduction." In *Reproductive States: Global Perspectives on the Invention and Implementation of Population Policy,* edited by Rickie Solinger and Mie Nakachi, 1–32. Oxford: Oxford University Press, 2016.

Solinger, Rickie, and Mie Nakachi, eds. *Reproductive States: Global Perspectives on the Invention and Implementation of Population Policy.* Oxford: Oxford University Press, 2016.

Spaskovska, Ljubica. "Building a Better World? Construction, Labour Mobility and the Pursuit of Collective Self-Reliance in the 'Global South,' 1950–1990." *Labor History* 59, no. 3 (February 2018): 331–351

———. *The Last Yugoslav Generation: The Rethinking of Youth Politics and Cultures in Late Socialism.* Manchester: Manchester University Press, 2017.

Spruill, Marjorie J. *Divided We Stand: The Battle over Women's Rights and Family Values that Polarized American Values.* New York: Bloomsbury, 2017.

Stone, D. *The Oxford Handbook of Postwar European History.* Oxford: Oxford University Press, 2012.

Summerfield, Penny. *Reconstructing Women's Wartime Lives: Discourse and Subjectivity in Oral Histories of the Second World War.* Manchester: Manchester University Press, 1998.

Švab, Alenka, and Živa Humer. "'I Only Have to Ask Him and He Does It . . .' Active Fatherhood and (Perceptions of) Division of Family Labour in Slovenia." *Journal of Comparative Family Studies* 44, no. 1 (January–February 2013): 57–78.

Švab, Alenka, Tanja Rener, and Metka Kuhar. "Behind and beyond Hajnal's Line: Families and Family Life in Slovenia." *Journal of Comparative Family Studies* 43, no. 3 (May–June 2012): 419–437.

Takeshita, Chikako. *The Global Biopolitics of the IUD: How Science Constructs Contraceptive Users and Women's Bodies.* Cambridge, MA: MIT Press, 2012.

Tesija, Jelena. "The End of the AFŽ—the End of Meaningful Women's Activism? Rethinking the History of Women's Organizations in Croatia, 1953–1961." Master's thesis, European University, 2014.

Thompson, Andrew S. "Tehran 1968 and Reform of the UN Human Rights System." *Journal of Human Rights* 14, no. 1 (January 2015): 84–100.

Todorova, Maria. "Historical Tradition and Transformation in Bulgaria: Women's Issues or Feminist Issues?" *Journal of Women's History* 5, no. 3 (Winter 1994): 129–143.

———, ed. *Remembering Communism: Genres of Representation.* New York: Social Science Research Council, 2010.

———. "The Trap of Backwardness: Modernity, Temporality, and the Study of Eastern European Nationalism." *Slavic Review* 64, no. 1 (Spring 2005): 140–164.

Todorova, Teodora. "'Giving Memory a Future': Confronting the Legacy of Mass Rape in Post-Conflict Bosnia-Herzegovina," *Journal of International Women's Studies* 12, no. 2 (March 2011): 3–26.

Tomasevich, Jozo. *War and Revolution in Yugoslavia, 1941–1945: Occupation and Collaboration.* Stanford, CA: Stanford University Press, 2002.

Tone, Andrea. *Devices and Desires: A History of Contraceptives in America.* New York: Farrar, Straus and Giroux, 2001.

True, Jacqui. *Gender, Globalization, and Postsocialism: The Czech Republic after Communism.* New York: Columbia University Press, 2003.

———. *The Political Economy of Violence against Women.* Oxford: Oxford University Press, 2012.

Tunc, Tanfer Emin. "Designs of Devices: The Vacuum Aspirator and American Abortion Technology." *Dynamis* 28 (2008): 353–376.

———. "Technologies of Choice: A History of Abortion Techniques in the United States, 1850–1980." PhD diss., Stony Brook University, 2005.

Unkovski-Korica, Vladimir. *The Economic Struggle for Power in Tito's Yugoslavia: From World War II to Non-Alignment.* London: Bloomsbury, 2016.

Usborne, Cornelie. *Cultures of Abortion in Weimar Germany (Monographs in German History).* New York: Berghahn Books, 2007.

———. *The Politics of the Body in Weimar Germany: Women's Reproductive Rights and Duties, Social History, Popular Culture, and Politics in Germany.* Ann Arbor: University of Michigan Press, 1992.

Valtchinova, Galia. "Between Ordinary Pain and Extraordinary Knowledge: The Seer Vanga in the Everyday Life of Bulgarians during Socialism (1960s–1970s)." *Aspasia* 3 (January 2009): 106–130.

Whelan, Daniel. *Indivisible Human Rights: A History.* Philadelphia: University of Pennsylvania Press, 2010.

Williams, Doone, and Greer Williams. *Every Child a Wanted Child: Clarence James Gamble, MD and His Work in the Birth Control Movement.* Edited by Emily P. Flint. Boston: Harvard University Press, 1978.

Wingfield, Nancy M., and Maria Bucur. *Gender and War in Twentieth-Century Eastern Europe.* Bloomington: Indiana University Press, 2006.

Wolf, Jacqueline. *Deliver Me from Pain: Anesthesia and Birth in America.* Baltimore: Johns Hopkins University Press, 2012.

———. "Film as the Medium: Reproduction, Sex, and Power as the Message." *Journal of Women's History* 22, no. 3 (Fall 2010): 173–184.

Yeomans, Rory. "Fighting the White Plague: Demography and Abortion in the Independent State of Croatia, 1941–1945." In *Health, Hygiene and Eugenics in South East Europe to 1945,* edited by Christian Promitzer, Sevasti Trubeta, and Marius Turda, 385–426. Budapest: Central European University Press, 2008.

Yow, Valerie. "'Do I Like Them Too Much?' Effects of the Oral History Interview on the Interviewer and Vice-Versa." *Oral History Review* 24, no. 1 (Summer 1997): 55–79.

Yurchak, Alexei. *Everything Was Forever, until It Was No More: The Last Soviet Generation*. Princeton, NJ: Princeton University Press, 2006.

Žabić, Snežana. "Neo AFŽ: Revolution without Premeditation." *Feminist Review* 99, no. 1 (November 2011): 147–154.

Žarkov, Dubravka. *The Body of War: Media, Ethnicity, and Gender in the Break-Up of Yugoslavia*. Durham, NC: Duke University Press, 2007.

———. "Pictures of the Wall of Love: Motherhood, Womanhood and Nationhood in Croatian Media." *European Journal of Women's Studies* 4, no. 3 (August 1997): 305–339.

Zimmerman, Jonathan. *Too Hot to Handle: A Global History of Sex Education*. Princeton, NJ: Princeton University Press, 2015.

Životić, Aleksandar, and Jovan Čavoški. "On the Road to Belgrade: Yugoslavia, Third World Neutrals, and the Evolution of Global Non-Alignment, 1954–1961." *Journal of Cold War Studies* 18, no. 4 (Fall 2016): 79–97.

INDEX

abortion, illegal: abortifacients, 52, 75, 108; as a social disease, 53; continued use of despite legality, 53, 59, 86, 160n23, 181–182, 184; economic costs associated with, 97–98, 160n23; prosecution of women, 56, 75; self-abortion, 53, 75, 185; state concerns regarding health and safety of women, 2, 29, 52, 53, 97–98, 115 126–127; vračare / wise women, 52–53, 75–76, 84, 86–87, 97–99, 151

abortion, legal: abortion committees, 56–57, 96, 182; abortion rates, 22, 53, 76, 118, 121–122, 136, 139–140, 147, 160n22, 78, 182; debates over abortion legislation, 53–57, 96, 145, 151, 180; economic costs associated with, 53, 115, 124, 139–140, 151, 184–185; health insurance, 184; indications for legal abortions, 54–57, 97, 153; experiences of, 56, 59, 67, 76, 87, 108, 124, 127, 151, 158, 184; laws regarding, 16, 22, 32, 54, 56, 97, 114, 126, 145, 151, 153, 183, 193; memories of, 178–185; pain relief, 3, 18, 124–126; technological advancements owing to legality, 108, 123, 123–128; underage pregnancy, 158, 176

Abortion (film), 158

advice columns, 1, 32, 87, 142–145. *See also* education

A ljudi ko ljudi (film), 158

Andolšek Jeras, Lidija, 111, 112, 114, 115, 118, 120, 128

antenatal care, 80, 94, 95, 96, 144. *See also* advice columns, education

Antifascist Women's Front (Antifašistički Front Žena [AFŽ]): debates with party doctors, 57, 69, 88, 89, 90; eradicating ethnomedical healing practices, 85–89; establishing and staffing clinics and hospitals, 77, 78, 81; gender equality, 51; health hygiene traveling teams, 92–96; health literacy, 38, 46, 58, 83; infant and maternal mortality, 57, 80; literacy courses, 45, 46, 47, 79, 83; overseas involvement, 51; role in rebuilding the nation, 81; role in uplifting peasant women; 38, 45, 77; state propaganda, 30, 33–34, 58;

Antifascist Women's Front (cont.)
state-socialist women's organization, 15, 33–34; structure and operation, 32, 35; women's press, 82; women's reproductive health, 85; *See also* Savez Ženskih Društava (Union of Women's Societies [SŽD], 1953–1961); Konferencija za Društvenu Aktivnost Žena (Conference of the Social Activity of Women [KDAŽ], 1962–1975)

Bauk (Boogeyman), 99–100
Beluhan, Aleksandra, 155, 182
Beospir, 119, *119*. *See also* contraception
Berić, Berislav: contraception and sex education materials, 142; cost and dangers of illegal abortions, 97–98; paracervical block, 126
biomedicine, 68, 69, 70, 71, 77–78, 81, 85, 86–88, 99, 101n8, 108, 121, 137, 180, 193, 195
birth control. *See* contraception
birth rates, 2, 6, 14, 21, 29–30, 58, 60, 77, 98, 112, 120, 122, 136, 138, 139, 146, 152, 155, 182
Breznik, Dušan, 79, 155

childbirth: at home, 55, 67, 84, 85, 95; birthing centers, 80–83; dangers of, 54, 67, 68, 73, 80; female-dominated support in villages, 67, 73–74; hygienic practices and, 84–85, 94; literature on, 18; in hospitals, 18, 54, 55, 67, 68, 72, 80, 90, 95, 97; pain relief in, 18; peasant, 67, 73, 84–85, 86; shame and stigma associated with, 73
childcare: advice on, 58, 86, 82, 89, 92, 94; lack of services, 49, 60, 121; professionalization of, 50; state assistance with, 18, 32, 40, 59–60, 80, 82, 92, 99; within the home, 86
child-rearing. *See* childcare
Cold War: distinctiveness of Yugoslav way in the context of, 10–11, 194; global forums regarding human rights, 149, 152; Non-Aligned Movement, 10; 17, 18, 21; perceptions of and interconnectedness within, 17, 18, 24; Yugoslavia's shifting allegiances, 10, 17
Communist Party of Yugoslavia, 7, 8, 23, 29–30, 32, 34, 33, 40, 44, 52, 194
Contraception, 57, 98, 107, 146, 174: barrier methods (including diaphragms), 108, 109, 111, 112, 115, 120, 130n25, 142, 146, 174, 176; clinics, 98, 111, 112–113, 142, 149; contraceptive foam, 111, 112, *113*, 120; health insurance, 96, 98, 117, 178, 181; international multisite studies of, 110, 115–123; IUDs, 107, 108, 109, 110, 114, 115–123, *116*, *117*, 119, 128, 146, 147, 174, 177; oral contraceptive pills, 3, 108, 111, 112, *113*, *114*, 114–115, 120–121, 146–147, 174, 176, 177, 189n42; spermicidal jellies, 112, 120, 130n25; stigma associated with, 3, 73, 114–115, 129, 174, 178; supply via international aid, 109, 118; unreliable access and poor quality of, 112, 114, 115, 129, 177–178; women's recollections and experiences using, 173–178

decolonization, in the Global South, 10, 18, 23, 51, 150. *See also* Non-Aligned Movement
Demografska Statistika (Demographic statistics), 79
demography: construction of ethnic and cultural hierarchy, 80–81, 83,

119–120, 139–140; demographic trends and change, 14, 19, 24, 30, 45, 77–80, 98, 121, 122, 139; population loss and ill-health after WWII, 7, 29, 194; use in population policy and family planning, 14–15, 30–31, 136, 138–140, 155–157. *See also* population policies, research

diaphragms. *See* contraception

education: literacy workshops, 45, 46, 79, 83, 95; medical system and health hygiene, 67, 83–86, 93; professional training, 16, 50, 56, 78, 84, 88, 93, 170, 184. *See also* sex education, advice columns

employment: access to, 8; as a factor in making health decisions, 87, 179; as women's access to the public sphere, 13; double burden with domestic duties, 4, 13, 38, 44, 50, 60, 80, 153, 166; equality between women and men in terms of, 13, 60; legislation regarding, 30, 44, 47–50, 59, 60; sick leave due to abortion, 29, 52, 110, 140; statistics regarding, 79, 119; women's rights to partake in employment outside the home, 38, 146, 153

ethnic dress, 32, 33, 44, 47, 83

ethnography, 70, 72–73, 74, 75 100n3, 180, 186n3. *See also* ethnomedical healing customs

ethnomedical healing customs, 67–69, 71, 77, 82, 85–87, 95–96; female dominated, 67, 69, 73–74, generational, 69; health campaigns targeting, 98–99. *See also vračare*

family planning: and gender equality in the private sphere, 142, 143; and sex education, 108, 136–137, 143, 193; and the 1969 Family Planning Resolution, 149–157; as a tool of population control, 19, 107, 108, 110, 136–139, 153; clinics, 111, 142, 149, 154; feminism and, 138, 139; international exchange in the area of, 110–112, 121, 129, *See also* contraception, abortion

family policies: childcare, 59; gender-specific, 40; social protection policies reinforcing gender stereotypes, 40–44, 48–49, 60

feminism: 1978 Belgrade Conference, 12, 188n27; in Yugoslavia, 188n27, 191–192, 193; family planning, 137–138, 140; feminist theory and application, 15, 146; intersubjectivity in oral history interviews, 169, 171; literature on Yugoslav feminism and socialism, 12–13, 15, 188n27

fertility rates. *See* birth rates

folk customs / practices. *See* ethnomedical healing customs, *vračare*

foreign aid in the wake of WWII, 78, 109

Gamble, Clarence, 109, 111, 112
Gates, Edith, 28n89, 111–112
gender equality: after the Tito-Stalin split, 11; differences between policy and practice, 3, 5, 8, 13, 44, 60, 115, 146, 153, 157; memories of, 3, 7, 171–172, 185–186; promises of socialist, 2, 8, 11, 14, 39, 40, 51, 59, 69, 146, 153, 157, 173; reproductive regulation as an expression of, 14, 33–40, 52, 59, 69, 135, 145–146, 156–157; Yugoslav model for nations of Global South, 10, 18, 24, 51, 71

gender policies: 11, 14, 30, 33–34, 38–39, 40–44, 48, 52

Grossman, Stefanija, 142, 144

Halpern, Joel and Barbara, 72–73
health: infant and child, 58, 77, 79–80, 84; maternal, 54, 57–58, 77, 80–81; of the general population in the wake of Second World War, 49, 77–78, 129; women's reproductive (current and future), 14, 19, 22, 49, 70, 75, 110, 146, 194. *See also* infant mortality, maternal health.
health literacy. *See* education
healthcare system, 68, 70, 81; ad-hoc establishment of clinics immediate years postwar, 77–78, 81, 88, 90, 95, 98; bureaucratized health care network plans, 87, 90, 91; health insurance, 87, 96, 98, 117, 178, 181, 184; lacking funding, resources and infrastructure, 78, 81, 99, 100; non-Yugoslav, 70, 71, 87–89; pre-socialist, 77; propaganda to encourage women into clinics in the immediate years postwar, 82, 85, 92, 95; targeted health campaigns, 80, 92–94; women not accessing services throughout the socialist period, 82, 90–91, 95, 112; *See also* travelling teams, research

infant mortality, 57, 79–80, 93, 144; rates compared between wartime and post-war, 80; rates compared to Europe and North America, 80. *See also* health
International Planned Parenthood Federation (IPPF), 98, 115, 127, 140, 155–156

Konferencija za Društvenu Aktivnost Žena (Conference of the Social Activity of Women [KDAŽ], 1962–1975), 96, 117, 118, 148, 151
Košiček, Marijan, 142, 144–145, 154

Lippes Loop, 115–117, *117*, 118. *See also* contraception

Margulies Spiral, 115–117, *116*, 118. *See also* contraception
marriage, 33, 47–48, 114, 121, 137, 141, 142, 148; advice on, 143–144; contraceptive use and knowledge within, 141, 174, 176, 182; and fecundity, 114–115
maternal health, 57, 77, 79–80, 81. *See also* health
medical experts: input into sex education material, 138, 141–142, 147–148; opinions about abortion by, 53, 89, 145, 151; regional disparities in terms of numbers of cadres, 54, 77–78, 85, 90–93, 94, 100, 184; role in modernizing the country, 71, 86; travel by, 78, 92. *See also* education
medicalization. *See* childbirth, abortion, contraception
memory and remembering: 3, 20, 165; collective memory, 167–168, 173; comparing personal experience as children and parents, 172–173; drawing on technical knowledge, 169, 174; feelings of guilt and shame, 3, 176–177, 179–182; oral history interviews methodology, 170–172; postsocialist legacy, 2, 5, 24, 159, 165–166, 167, 168, 173–174, 193; role of intersubjectivity in, 166, 168–170; socialist utopia, 2, 167, 179; Yugo-nostalgia, 167, 168, 169, 171–172, 185–186
miscarriage, 75, 97, 160n22, 165
Mitrović, Mitra, 39–40
Mojić, Angelina, 80, 84, 94
Morokvasić, Mirjana, 3, 114, 186n3

motherhood: as women's most important function within the state, 4, 34, 47, 50, 80; single motherhood, 48; women's natural disposition to, 40, 50, 54, 59, 143, 146

Naša Žena (Our woman), 32, 36, 37, 41, 42, 43
natality. *See* birth rates
New Yugoslav Woman, 3, 4, 5, 11, 32, 47, 70, 110; as a tool of state formation and modernization, 33–34, 47, 70, 83, 88, 99; as representing changing ideals of womanhood, 34–35, 38–39, 45, 47, 70, 80, 83, 128, 135; as a consumer of biomedicine, 70, 83, 99, 109, 128–129, 135, 144–145; literature on, 4, 12
Non-Aligned Movement (NAM), 10, 11, 21, 51, 112, 150
Nova Žena (New Woman), 32, 33, 38, 45
Novak, Franc, 22, 25, 49, 53, 55, 97–98; abortion and women's health, 111–112, 123–127, 139, 185; researching and gathering contraceptives, 111–112, 125, 138, 139; sex education, 138, 142
Novak-Reiss, Aleksandra, 154

oral contraceptive pills. *See* contraception

partisans, 5, 7, 22, 33, 34, 38–39; and gender, 34, 39; and reproductive practices, 39, 61n4; women's roles within, 5, 7, 38
party doctors. *See* medical experts
Pathfinder Fund, 28n89, 111, 118, 121; as part of a larger network of experts invested in family planning, 110–112, 118. *See also* Gamble, Clarence
peasants, 44, 45, 69, 72, 75, 77–83, 121, 194; patriarchal village structures,

67, 74; shame and stigma associated with reproductive matters, 73
Petrić, Nevenka, 152
Petrović, Aleksandar, 72
population policies, 14–15, 31, 86, 109, 121, 140, 152, 155
pronatalism, 7, 15, 23, 30–31, 35, 49, 52, 57, 60–61, 77, 86, 139, 143, 152, 158, 193, 194
public health: civilizing mission of, 70–72, 77, 135; interwar, 67–68, 98

regional differences within Yugoslavia: access to contraception, 112–113, 118–120; access to health services, employment, education, income, 8, 45, 55, 69; establishment of cultural hierarchy, 79, 81, 85, 93, 119–123; literacy rates, 9–10, 45, 79; women's political participation, 7, 10, 15, 34, 83. *See also* demography
reproductive policies: in Yugoslavia, 11, 14, 30, 34, 38, 39, 52, 53, 54, 97, 141, 149–153; outside of Yugoslavia; 16, 31, 58
research, 22, 88, 99, 107–110, 118; clinical testing centralized in Ljubljana, Slovenia, 22, 98–99, 100, 117, 123; contraceptive knowledge and use, 120, 122, 189n42; international exchange in, 23, 107–108, 110, 112, 117–118, 121, 123, 126; International IUD Program, 122; into sexual behavior, 182; legislation opening avenues for, 96, 127; research institutions, 90, 98, 100, 120; statistical and demographic, 77–79, 90, 98, 107, 112, 119, 122–123, 155; testing of abortion technologies, 123, 124, 127, 128; testing of contraceptives, 108, 109; testing of IUDs, 24, 108, 110,

research (*cont.*)
115, 117–118, 121–122; with the aim of population control, 122–123, 155; women participating in, 109–110, 114, 115, 122, 126, 129, 166; Yugoslavia as ideal site for, 118–122

Savez Ženskih Društava (Union of Women's Societies [SŽD], 1953–1961), 96
sex, 3, 137, 144
sex education, 135–136; across various media, 142, 174–5; and the family, 143–145; as a human right, 136–137, 153; as moral education, 136–137; domain of women, 135–136; failure to reach youth, 154–155, 174–176, 177–179, 181, 182; in adulthood, 175–176; in schools, 147–148; gender equality, 135, 139, 143, 153; medical experts and, 142–143. state demographic requirements, 138–141. *See also* family planning, contraception
Sklevicky, Lydia, 12
socialist medicine, 16–17, 53
Štampar, Andrija, 98. *See also* public health
Štampar, Dubravka, 98, 155, 182
Stanovništvo, 98
state building, 2, 3, 4 32, 72, 108
Stein Erlich, Vera, 72; *Families in Transition*, 73–75
Svijet (World), 1, 32, 144, 145, 146

Tito, Josip Broz, 7, 9, 10, 35, 40, 44, 45, 52, 77, 88, 150
Tito-Stalin split, 8, 52, 53, 68
Tomaževič, Tomaž, 123, 124, 125, 126
Tomšič, Vida, 15, 51, 89, 140–141, 153; and family planning, 153–154, 156–157; and feminism, 15; and the Yugoslav way, 50, 51; international conferences, 50, 51, 140–141
traveling healthcare teams. *See* healthcare system

underage pregnancy, 98, 155, 158, 176–177, 179, 182
urban / rural divide, 47, 69, 72, 80–81, 119–120

VE-2, 123, 127. *See also* abortion
Vitalna Statistika (Vital statistics), 79
vračare / wise women, 73–76, 84, 86–87, 97–99, 151. *See also* ethnomedical healing customs

women's press, 4, 32, 53; abortion reporting within, 57–58, 60; and the New Yugoslav Woman, 4, 72, 80; as part of state-led modernization, 34–35, 39, 44–45, 47, 72, 115; as state propaganda, 9, 30, 32, 34, 38, 39, 45, 52, 58, 60, 70, 82, 83–85; focus on health content within, 1, 32, 38, 81, 84–86, 95; geopolitical positioning, 51. *See also* specific magazine titles
women's rights. *See* gender equality
World Population Conference, 149

Yugoslav-American Medical Research Program, 128
Yugoslav socialism, 8–9, 10, 12, 51; distinctiveness of, 5, 7, 8, 10, 11, 12, 21, 24, 145, 167, 173, 186, 194; geopolitical positioning, key to, 10, 51, 151–152; reproductive regulation, key to, 11, 14, 30, 52–53; self-management, 8–9, 21, 23, 24, 144, 168, 193, 194; Yugoslav way, 10–11, 12, 30, 50–51, 88, 90, 107, 152, 194
Yugoslav Wars of the 1990s, 14–15, 24, 168, 174

Yugoslavia: and geopolitical
positioning, 5, 10–11, 51, 107, 108, 129;
ethnic tensions, 6, 14, 31; perception
of as progressive and modern,
2–3, 30, 136, 152; pre-socialist, 5–6;
religion; 5–6; WWII, 6–7, 29

Žena danas (Woman today), 9, 32,
35, 39
Žena (Woman), 32, 145, 147
Žena u borbi (Woman in battle), 32
Zora (Dawn), 32, 44, 58,
59, 83

Branka Bogdan is an Early Career Researcher based in Auckland, New Zealand.

For Indiana University Press
Sabrina Black, Editorial Assistant
Anna Garnai, Production Coordinator
Sophia Hebert, Assistant Acquisitions Editor
Katie Huggins, Production Manager
Alyssa Lucas, Marketing and Publicity Manager
Darja Malcolm-Clarke, Project Manager / Editor
Bethany Mowry, Acquisitions Editor
Dan Pyle, Online Publishing Manager
Michael Regoli, Director of Publishing Operations
Pamela Rude, Senior Artist and Book Designer

www.ingramcontent.com/pod-product-compliance
Lightning Source LLC
Chambersburg PA
CBHW021352300426
44114CB00012B/1187